On Moral Certainty, Justification and Practice

On Moral Certainty, Justification and Practice

A Wittgensteinian Perspective

Julia Hermann
Utrecht University, The Netherlands

First published 2015 by
PALGRAVE MACMILLAN

Palgrave Macmillan in the UK is an imprint of Macmillan Publishers Limited, registered in England, company number 785998, of Houndmills, Basingstoke, Hampshire RG21 6XS.

Palgrave Macmillan in the US is a division of St Martin's Press LLC, 175 Fifth Avenue, New York, NY 10010.

Palgrave Macmillan is the global academic imprint of the above companies and has companies and representatives throughout the world.

Palgrave® and Macmillan® are registered trademarks in the United States, the United Kingdom, Europe and other countries.

ISBN: 978–1–137–44717–3

A catalogue record for this book is available from the British Library.

Library of Congress Cataloging-in-Publication Data

Hermann, Julia, 1979–
   On moral certainty, justification, and practice: a Wittgensteinian perspective / Julia Hermann, Maastricht University, The Netherlands.
     pages cm
   Includes bibliographical references and index.
   ISBN 978–1–137–44717–3
     1. Wittgenstein, Ludwig, 1889–1951. 2. Ethics. I. Title.

B3376.W564H37 2015
192—dc23   2015003233

To my father and to the memory of my mother

Contents

Preface and Acknowledgements

Writing this book has been a source of great enjoyment, but there were also times when I was close to despair, trapped by philosophical confusion without seeing any way out. It was, in every sense, a roller coaster ride, thinking at one moment that I had found the answer to a particular question, only to see everything open and confused moments later. I kept struggling with certain passages from Wittgenstein, changing my interpretation of them time and again, without reaching any satisfactory result. The topic I had chosen often appeared to be a bottomless pit.

This book does not set out my final interpretation of Wittgenstein nor does it contain a fully developed view of morality. My understanding of Wittgenstein and the implications that his thoughts have for ethics are still in flux. In a way, this book raises more questions than it provides answers for. Given the subject matter, this is probably not surprising. The remarks of the later Wittgenstein are open to multiple interpretations. Morality is a complex subject which can be engaged with from several angles. My arguments draw on some of these various perspectives, although it would have been beyond this project to investigate all the different components of morality in detail. As a result, the picture I have painted is sketchy in many places. In a spirit similar to that of Wittgenstein, I hope that this book will provide some new ideas, which the reader will then be able to take up and develop further for herself.

I am grateful to have been able to share moments of both joy and despair with others. There are several people whom I want to thank for their inspiring ideas, critical comments, challenging questions, helpful suggestions and emotional support. I shall start with Dennis Patterson, to whom I owe a special debt of gratitude for having believed in this project and always given me his full support. I am also highly indebted to Nigel Pleasants for his continuous encouragement and invaluable comments on earlier versions of several chapters of this book. I would moreover like to thank Rainer Bauböck, Marcus Willaschek and Alan Thomas for their valuable suggestions. To Christine Chwaszcza, I am grateful for countless hours of conversation concerning the issues raised in this book and her valuable comments on earlier versions. I am indebted to Barry Stroud for inviting me to come to the Department of Philosophy at UC Berkeley and for our fruitful discussions. I thank the European University Institute for an inspiring work environment, and the Philosophy Department of Maastricht University and in particular Tsjalling Swierstra for his support and helpful suggestions. I am grateful to Herman Philipse for giving me the time to finish up this project, and I thank him and my colleagues Jeroen Hopster and Joeri Witteveen for their helpful feedback on two of the chapters. I am indebted to Danièle Moyal-Sharrock for her valuable comments on the manuscript. Further thanks go to Stefan Rummens for reading and commenting on earlier versions of some of the chapters.

It would be too much to mention every participant in the conferences, workshops and colloquia at which I have presented many of the ideas developed in this book, but I would like to express my gratitude for all the helpful feedback I received on those occasions. I particularly thank Eva Buddeberg, Michael Burley, Niklas Forsberg, Nora Hämäläinen, Lisa Herzog, Beate Rössler, Thomas Schramme, Achim Vesper and Christian Wendelborn for their comments and suggestions. My friend Beate Sachsenweger deserves special mention for reading the whole book several times and suggesting numerous improvements. Her support during the final stage of the writing process made it much easier to tie up loose ends. To her I am most grateful. I am indebted to Thomas Roberts, who not only refined my English but also provided helpful suggestions that went beyond mere questions of language. I thank the German Academic Exchange Service (DAAD), the European University Institute (EUI), the Kurt-Tucholsky-Stiftung and The Netherlands Organisation for Scientific Research (NWO) for their financial support.

My work on this project coincided with some important developments in my personal life. I gained deep friendships, fell in love and had my first child. But I also lost my mother and had the painful realisation that helping a person whom you love can be more difficult than any philosophical problem.

I am most grateful to my parents for encouraging and stimulating me from early childhood, for letting me go my own way and for supporting me in every possible respect. Among the friends who accompanied me on my journey, Julia Langbein and Clara Brandi deserve special mention. Without them working on this project would have been much less fun, and I would have felt lonely at many points. I thank them for the wonderful times we had, and for all their support through difficult times. Finally, I want to express my deep gratitude to my partner, Bas, who believes in me and did everything he could to enable me to find enough time to finish this book, including taking care of our wonderful little daughter Philine. To her I owe gratitude for continuously reminding me of the fact that work – even writing a philosophical monograph – is not everything, and also for providing me with some nice examples for this book.

Abbreviations of Works by Wittgenstein

BBB *The Blue and Brown Books. Preliminary Studies for the "Philosophical Investigations"*. Oxford: Basil Blackwell, 1958.

CE "Cause and Effect: Intuitive Awareness". In *Philosophical Occasions 1912–1951*, edited by James C. Klagge and Alfred Nordmann, 370–426. Indianapolis and Cambridge: Hackett Publishing Company, 1993.

LW II *Last Writings on the Philosophy of Psychology*. Translated by C. G. Luckhardt and Maximilian A. E. Aue. Edited by G. H. von Wright and Heikki Nyman. Vol. II. Oxford and Cambridge: Blackwell, 1992.

OC *On Certainty*. Translated by Denis Paul and G. E. M. Anscombe. Edited by G. E. M. Anscombe and G. H. von Wright. New York: Harper & Row, 1972.

PI *Philosophical Investigations*. Translated by G. E. M. Anscombe. Third ed. Oxford: Basil Blackwell, 1968.

RC *Remarks on Colour*. Translated by Linda L. McAlister and Margarete Schättle. Edited by G. E. M. Anscombe. Oxford: Basil Blackwell, 1978.

RFM *Remarks on the Foundations of Mathematics*. Translated by G. E. M. Anscombe. Edited by G. H. von Wright et al. Third, revised and reset ed. Oxford: Basil Blackwell, 1978.

RPP I *Remarks on the Philosophy of Psychology*. Translated by G. E. M. Anscombe. Edited by G. E. M. Anscombe and G. H. von Wright. Vol. I. Oxford: Basil Blackwell, 1980.

RPP II *Remarks on the Philosophy of Psychology*. Translated by C. G. Luckhardt and M. A. E. Aue. Edited by G. H. von Wright and Heikki Nyman. Vol. II. Oxford: Basil Blackwell, 1980.

TLP *Tractatus Logico-Philosophicus*. Translated by D. F. Pears and B. F. McGuiness. Revised ed. London and New York: Routledge & Kegan Paul, 1974.

WL *Wittgenstein's Lectures, Cambridge 1932–1935*. Edited by Alice Ambrose. Oxford: Prometheus Books, 1979.

Z *Zettel*. Translated and edited by G. E. M. Anscombe and G. H. von Wright. Second ed. Oxford: Blackwell, 1981.

1
Introduction

1.1 Moral debates

Morality seems to be a field in which disagreement is pervasive. Debates about moral issues range from disputes about euthanasia and abortion to discussions about how we ought to treat animals.[1] A controversial ethical issue arising in relation to new forms of warfare involves the use of unmanned military airplanes, so-called military drones, which facilitate targeted killing. Drones are attractive as a means of reducing the number of military personnel who lose their life in armed conflict or come back wounded or traumatised. Moreover, they are relatively cheap and achieve a degree of precision that makes it possible to attack more specific targets. However, this last characteristic carries the risk of causing harm to far more innocent victims than conventional forms of warfare, since due to their robotic precision, drones tend to be deployed far more quickly than traditional bombers, and the precisely defined targets which they are deployed to attack tend to be close to civil locations.

Moral arguments in favour of the deployment of drones stand in contrast with arguments against their deployment. People disagree about how the reasons on both sides should be weighed. Does the possibility to protect the life of one's own soldiers outweigh the presumably higher number of civilian victims? Should we abstain from using drones because once humans can kill from a distance, without putting their own life at risk, they will kill much more easily? There is also disagreement about related non-moral facts such as the likelihood of an increase in innocent victims due to the deployment of drones. These are some of the controversies. Now imagine a person participating in the debate and raising questions

---

[1] I use 'ethical' and 'moral' interchangeably.

1

such as the following: Why should an increase in civilian victims be something to worry about? Why is killing innocent civilians in the course of a military operation a bad thing? Why is killing as such morally wrong? These questions seem entirely out of place. The puzzlement they prompt points to the existence of agreement over moral matters, notwithstanding all the moral issues people disagree about. Were someone to raise such questions in the middle of a debate about the moral status of targeted killing, she would be regarded as making a joke, as lacking moral competence or as simply wanting to shock. There are no good reasons to doubt that killing innocent civilians is bad and that killing as such is wrong.

However, despite our lack of reasons for doubt in these cases, some philosophers try to come up with theories to explain or justify a moral conviction as basic as 'Killing is wrong'.[2] They mistakenly believe that a conviction as fundamental within any moral theory as this belief has to be supported by reasons which are even more certain, on the grounds that a substantive moral theory 'cannot ultimately rest on mere convictions'.[3] As I shall argue, these philosophers try 'to prove a philosophical thesis, the negation of which cannot be taken seriously'.

The claim that the inability to explain why it is wrong to kill people is 'one of the most notorious scandals of moral philosophy'[4] echoes Kant's remark that it 'remains a scandal to philosophy and to human reason in general that the existence of things outside us [...] must be accepted merely on *faith*'.[5] However, the assumption that we need to know what it is that makes wrongful acts of killing wrong in order to be able to judge cases in which the wrongness of killing is subject to doubt (for example abortion or euthanasia) is mistaken.[6] Our everyday practices

---

    [2] See Leonard Wayne Sumner, 'A Matter of Life and Death,' *Noûs* 10 (1976); Robert Young, 'What Is So Wrong With Killing People?,' *Philosophy* 54 (1979); Barbara Baum Levenbook, 'Harming Someone After His Death,' *Ethics* 94 (1984); Don Marquis, 'An Argument that Abortion is Wrong,' in *Ethics in Practice*, ed. Hugh LaFollette (Oxford: Blackwell, 1997). It was an article by Nigel Pleasants that drew my attention to these attempts. Nigel Pleasants, 'Wittgenstein, Ethics and Basic Moral Certainty,' *Inquiry* 51, no. 3 (2008).
    [3] Sumner, 'A Matter of Life and Death,' p. 145.
    [4] Fred Feldman, *Confrontations with the Reaper. A Philosophical Study of the Nature and Value of Death* (Oxford: Oxford University Press, 1992), p. 157.
    [5] Immanuel Kant, *Critique of Pure Reason*, trans. Norman Kemp Smith, second revised ed. (Basingstoke and New York: Palgrave Macmillan, 2007), preface to the second edition, B xl.
    [6] See Nigel Pleasants, 'Wittgenstein and Basic Moral Certainty,' *Philosophia* 37 (2009): p. 672.

reveal that in justifying our moral convictions we sooner or later run out of reasons. At some point we cannot do more than repeat – though this time with stronger emphasis – a moral conviction the truth of which seems to be most obvious to us. I intend to show why this is so, and that it is nothing to be worried about.

In this introductory chapter, I shall present the four main claims of this study, discuss the ethical relevance of Wittgenstein's later philosophy, present the debate about the right view of justification that lies in the background of this book and provide an outline of the chapters which follow.

1.2   The limits of justification

The limits of reasonable doubt and justification are emphasised by Wittgenstein: 'Giving grounds, however, justifying the evidence, comes to an end; – but the end is not certain propositions' striking us immediately as true, that is, it is not a kind of *seeing* on our part; it is our *acting*, which lies at the bottom of the language-game' (OC 204).[7] In this quotation from *On Certainty*, Wittgenstein notes that at some point we stop justifying our beliefs.[8] He rejects the view that the point where no further reasons are given is one where we reach propositions which we know to be true directly, without requiring any further reasons.[9] In saying that 'it is not a kind of *seeing* on our part', he uses the language of epistemological and mathematical intuitionists, who claim that there are propositions which we know to be true immediately, through

---

[7] 'Die Begründung aber, die Rechtfertigung der Evidenz kommt zu einem Ende; – das Ende aber ist nicht daß uns gewisse Sätze unmittelbar als wahr einleuchten, also eine Art *Sehen* unsrerseits, sondern unser *Handeln*, welches am Grunde des Sprachspiels liegt.'

[8] I do not strictly distinguish between belief and judgement.

[9] Philosophers use the term 'proposition' in many different ways. It is 'sometimes assimilated to the sentence itself; sometimes to the linguistic meaning of a sentence; sometimes to 'what is said'; sometimes to the contents of beliefs or other 'propositional' attitudes'. Pascal Engel, 'Propositions, Sentences and Statements,' in *Routledge Encyclopedia of Philosophy*, ed. Edward Craig (London and New York: Routledge, 1998), p. 787. I shall use the term 'proposition' mostly as a synonym for 'sentence', but sometimes also in the sense of that which is expressed by a given sentence. Wittgenstein does not distinguish between the two. By the German term 'Satz', he means both the sentence as well as its linguistic meaning. In the original remarks of *On Certainty* the word 'Proposition' does not appear, but the word 'Satz' has often been translated with 'proposition'.

intuition.[10] The propositions concerned are thought to express objective truths, that is truths which are independent of what people believe is true. The metaphor of 'seeing' that a certain proposition is true illustrates the view that the intuitive knowledge in question is as immediate as sensual experience. There is no inferential reasoning involved. Going beyond a mere rejection of the intuitionist position, Wittgenstein makes the positive claim that 'it is our *acting*, which lies at the bottom of the language-game'.

This quotation sets the stage for the reflections contained in this study.[11] Fascinated by Wittgenstein's cryptic but powerful remarks about the limits of justification and the primacy of acting, I shall explore their significance for the practice of justifying moral judgements. This exploration will be embedded in the broader enterprise of approaching morality from a Wittgensteinian understanding of language and meaning.

Many moral philosophers adhere to the mistaken assumption that the activities of justifying and evaluating actions and judgements are constitutive of all moral practices. These practices are, by contrast, some of our more sophisticated practices and as such presuppose what Meredith Williams calls 'bedrock practices'.[12] I shall argue in favour of four main claims: (1) The demand for justification of a moral judgement or norm does not always make sense. (2) Practices of moral justification are grounded in ways of acting and reacting that are themselves unjustified. (3) Moral agency is first and foremost a matter of moral competence. (4) For morally competent agents, some moral beliefs are beyond doubt and not susceptible to justification. I shall call the view developed in this book the 'practice-based view of morality'.

---

[10] For the distinction between 'epistemological intuitionism' and 'methodological intuitionism' see Alan Thomas, *Value and Context: the Nature of Moral and Political Knowledge* (Oxford: Clarendon Press, 2006), p. 199 ff. Methodological intuitionists take our shared intuitions as a starting point. Someone like John Rawls, for instance, is a methodological intuitionist, but not an epistemological intuitionist. These two forms of intuitionism tend to be confused. For such a conflation see for example Sabine Roeser, *Moral Emotions and Intuitions* (Basingstoke: Palgrave Macmillan, 2011), p. 99. Roeser's conflation of the two forms of intuitionism leads her to accuse Rawls of being an intuitionist despite claiming the opposite.

[11] The quote will be placed within the context of Wittgenstein's later philosophy and interpreted in greater detail in Chapter 3.

[12] Meredith Williams, *Wittgenstein, Mind and Meaning* (London: Routledge, 1999), p. 198.

1.3 Why Wittgenstein?

The later Wittgenstein was relatively silent on questions of morality. Wittgenstein did not address ethical issues in the writings that follow his 'Lecture on Ethics'. In *On Certainty*, he famously claims that 'justification comes to an end' (OC 192), but he is not concerned with *moral* justification. He reflects on the peculiar role of some *empirical* propositions, but not on that of some *moral* propositions. The examples he gives of language-games do not include activities of moral evaluation, morally praising and blaming, holding someone to account, and so on, but things like '[g]iving orders, and obeying them', '[d]escribing the appearance of an object, or giving its measurements', '[r]eporting an event', and '[m]aking a joke' (PI 23).

Nevertheless, Wittgenstein's later writings are of interest to moral philosophers. They teach us a way of doing philosophy that is equally suitable for reflection on moral questions. However, I disagree with those contemporary philosophers who ascribe a fundamental ethical concern to the later Wittgenstein.[13] My understanding of the relation between Wittgenstein and ethics has to be sharply distinguished from what Nigel Pleasants calls 'intrinsically-ethical readings'.[14] According to those interpretations, everything Wittgenstein wrote has an ethical point.[15]

---

[13] Alice Crary, 'Wittgenstein and Ethics: A Discussion with Reference to *On Certainty*,' in *Readings of Wittgenstein's* On Certainty, ed. Danièle Moyal-Sharrock and W. Brenner (Basingstoke: Palgrave Macmillan, 2005). Cora Diamond, 'Ethics, imagination and the method of Wittgenstein's *Tractatus*,' in *The New Wittgenstein*, ed. A. Crary and R. Read (London: Routledge, 2000). Yaniv Iczkovits, *Wittgenstein's Ethical Thought* (Basingstoke: Palgrave Macmillan, 2012). Paul Johnston, *Wittgenstein and Moral Philosophy* (London: Routledge and Kegan Paul, 1989). Stephen Mulhall, 'Ethics in the light of Wittgenstein,' *Philosophical Papers* 31, no. 3 (2002).

[14] Pleasants, 'Wittgenstein, Ethics and Basic Moral Certainty.'

[15] According to the intrinsically-ethical reading of Stephen Mulhall, for instance, 'the best way to understand why the later Wittgenstein provided us with only very scattered and unsystematic remark on ethics is [...] to consider the possibility that he took [...] every one of his philosophical remarks [...] to have an ethical point'. Like Alice Crary, Cora Diamond, Yaniv Iczkovits and Paul Johnston, Mulhall conceives of the later Wittgenstein's view of language as having 'a pervasive moral dimension – an ethical or spiritual aspect that is not retractable even in principle to certain kinds of words, or certain kinds of uses of words'. Mulhall, 'Ethics in the light of Wittgenstein,' pp. 321 and 315. Such a reading of Wittgenstein is 'closely associated' with the 'New Wittgenstein school of exegesis' whose core principle is that Wittgenstein's early and late philosophy are much closer than is usually assumed. New Wittgensteinians hold that the

On my view, by contrast, the later Wittgenstein's remarks on language, meaning, rule-following, training, justification and certainty, which I conceive of as not being ethical in nature, have implications for our thinking about ethical questions. I agree with Pleasants that there is 'no distinctively moral viewpoint [...] in Wittgenstein's later philosophy', but that this philosophy, and *On Certainty* in particular, 'can be of help in our thinking about ethics and ethical issues'.[16] Similarly, Judith Lichtenberg argues that '[a]lthough Wittgenstein never specifically discusses moral judgements, his explorations of the concepts of knowledge, certainty, belief, and justification in the context of non-moral judgements help illuminate the realm of the moral as well'.[17]

There is no good reason for restricting Wittgenstein's conception of language to its non-moral uses. If the metaphor of the language-game is illuminating at all, it has to be applicable to that dimension of human life which is characterised by 'promoting good and avoiding evil', 'encouraging virtue and discouraging vice', and 'avoiding harm to others and promoting their well-being or welfare'.[18] Wittgenstein's criticism of a particular conception of linguistic meaning and a related conception of rule-following can be applied to the moral dimension of life and language. His reflections on how justifications come to an end with regard to empirical propositions can illuminate the status of moral propositions such as 'Killing is wrong'. His insight that doubt does not always make sense has implications for the question as to whether every moral belief can be meaningfully doubted. That we do not carry on justifying indefinitely is not only true of empirical justification, but also of moral justification.

However, caution is required when attempting to apply to the moral realm Wittgenstein's claims relating to empirical propositions, empirical justification, and doubts concerning, for instance, the existence of the external world. Nothing would conflict more with Wittgenstein's understanding of philosophy than simply translating his view of empirical justification into a view of moral justification. Wittgenstein rejects

---

'Tractarian doctrine of ethical ineffability' is still present in the later writings. Pleasants, 'Wittgenstein, Ethics and Basic Moral Certainty,' pp. 243 f. In the *Tractatus*, Wittgenstein held the view that 'it is impossible for there to be propositions of ethics', and that 'ethics cannot be put into words' (TLP 6.42 f.: 'Es ist klar, daß sich die Ethik nicht aussprechen läßt.').

[16] Pleasants, 'Wittgenstein, Ethics and Basic Moral Certainty,' p. 242.

[17] Judith Lichtenberg, 'Moral Certainty,' *Philosophy* 69, no. 268 (1994): p. 184.

[18] The quotes are taken from Stephen Lukes' description of the moral domain. Steven Lukes, *Moral Relativism* (New York: Picador, 2008), p. 134.

generalisations and asks the philosopher to look at the particular practice in order to understand it. I fully agree with Cora Diamond's warning regarding an application of Wittgenstein's ideas to a different realm:

> His remarks in *On Certainty* have a particular context; they are directed to particular philosophical confusions. He wants to turn our attention to various linguistic activities of which we have (he thinks) a false and over-simple picture; we think they have to be like this or like that. *His remarks are not meant to be substitutes for such attention.* We can indeed ask whether what Wittgenstein says about the possible kinds of room for doubt in science, or the role in it of acceptance of authority, is interestingly applicable to ethics. *But Wittgenstein's method does not provide shortcuts.*[19]

There are two things that I wish to avoid in this book. First, I seek to avoid the mistake of generalising prematurely, overlooking the particularities of every practice. Second, I do not wish to ascribe to Wittgenstein a particular view of morality. Everything I shall write about moral beliefs, moral justification and moral competence is, if not indicated otherwise, my own position. I do not wish to claim that Wittgenstein would have defended such a view on these matters, had he reflected more upon them, or that it is implied by his later philosophy. Rather, I believe that it is fruitful to apply some of his views to morality, thereby expressing openness towards the particularities of our 'moral language-games'.[20]

In reading Wittgenstein's later writings, we can learn a special way of philosophising. Wittgenstein teaches his readers to look at the practice and to be open to the particularities of individual cases.[21] Resisting the strong attempt at over-generalisation is surely one of the hardest things to do in philosophy. However, every philosophical enterprise requires

[19] Cora Diamond, 'Wittgenstein, Mathematics, and Ethics: Resisting the Attractions of Realism,' in *The Cambridge Companion to Wittgenstein*, ed. Hans Sluga and David G. Stern (Cambridge and New York: Cambridge University Press, 1996), p. 239, my italics.

[20] Similarly, Nigel Pleasants takes himself to 'show how Wittgenstein's observations on the manner in which we can neither question nor affirm certain states of affairs that are fundamental to our epistemic practices can be fruitfully extended to ethics'. Pleasants, 'Wittgenstein, Ethics and Basic Moral Certainty,' p. 241.

[21] 'For if you look at them you will not see something that is common to *all*, but similarities, relationships, and a whole series of them at that. To repeat: don't think, but look!' (PI 66).

some level of generalisation. Wittgenstein also generalises. It is a difficult balancing act between looking only at individual cases and constructing a framework to fit all different kinds of practices. While I shall extend some of Wittgenstein's views to the moral realm, I shall not do so without pointing to possible differences between empirical and moral cases.

One last remark should be made before turning to the philosophical debate that gave rise to my reflections on moral justification and moral competence: the debate between foundationalists and coherence theorists of justification. Wittgenstein's later writings consist of a number of more or less loosely connected remarks, which have been interpreted in countless ways. Therefore, everything I say about his philosophical positions must be taken as my own interpretation of these remarks.[22] It is never the case that Wittgenstein can be said to have clearly meant something. As all other interpreters, I try to make sense of his writings, believing that it pays off.

1.4   The problem of the justificatory regress

1.4.1   The problem

At the heart of the philosophical debate about the right theory of justification lies an age-old philosophical problem: the problem of the justificatory regress.[23] It is this problem that inspired me to write this book. On my first acquaintance with the problem, I was unsatisfied with the main solutions suggested and thought that Wittgenstein's later philosophy provided a better answer to it. It took me some time to realise that I had been mistaken, and that instead of solving the alleged problem, Wittgenstein had dissolved it, as he did with so many traditional philosophical problems.[24] The following presentation of the apparent problem and possible solutions to it will end in its dissolution.

---

[22] My interpretation of *On Certainty* is particularly influenced by the works of Gennip, Kim van, Andreas Krebs, Danièle Moyal-Sharrock and Avrum Stroll. Gennip, Kim van, *Wittgenstein's On Certainty in the Making: Studies into Its Historical and Philosophical Background* (PhD dissertation, Rijksuniversiteit Groningen, 2008). Andreas Krebs, *Worauf man sich verlässt* (Würzburg: Königshausen & Neumann, 2007). Danièle Moyal-Sharrock, *Understanding Wittgenstein's On Certainty* (Basingstoke: Palgrave Macmillan, 2004). Avrum Stroll, *Moore and Wittgenstein on Certainty* (New York and Oxford: Oxford University Press, 1994).

[23] Aristotle addressed this problem in his *Posterior Analytics*, where he argued in favour of a foundationalist solution. Aristotle, *Posterior Analytics*, ed. J.L. Ackrill, trans. Jonathan Barnes, Clarendon Aristotle Series (Oxford: Clarendon Press, 1975).

[24] Reading Andreas Krebs' book on *On Certainty* was crucial in this regard. Krebs, *Worauf man sich verlässt*.

How is the problem traditionally thought to arise? If a belief B_1 is inferentially justified by a belief B_2, and B_2 by a further belief B_3 and so on, then the threat of an infinite justificatory regress seems to be lurking. This does not affect moral justification in particular, but justification in general, and has particularly bothered philosophers interested in the possibility of gaining empirical knowledge. How we deal with the problem depends, first of all, on whether we think that justified beliefs have to rest on beliefs for which a further justification can be given. This is a disputed question. Can beliefs that lack justification confer justification on other beliefs? While the standard view is that the answer must be negative,[25] some philosophers allow for 'unjustified justifiers'.[26]

The question is complicated by the fact that, as Alan Thomas notes, the claim that a justifying belief has to be justified is ambiguous. It can be understood in two ways: (1) 'For any belief B, if there is a context C in which that belief is justifying, then there is some context C* in which that belief is justified. [C and C* may, or may not, be identical.]' (2) 'For any belief B, if there is a context C in which that belief is justifying, then it is justified in that very same context C.'[27] While I reject the claim on both interpretations (see 1.4.3), Thomas endorses it if it is understood in the first way.

1.4.2 Foundationalism, coherentism and the 'ordinary language view'

If it is assumed that justification can only be conferred by a belief which is itself justified, there are two ways of responding to the regress problem. First, it can be claimed that the regress ends with beliefs that are somehow immediately justified. Not requiring any inferential warrant, but nevertheless being justified, these beliefs can be claimed to justify other beliefs. The different versions of this position are typically

---

[25] See Laurence BonJour, *The Structure of Empirical Knowledge* (Cambridge, Mass. and London: Harvard University Press, 1985), pp. 22 f., and Thomas, *Value and Context: the Nature of Moral and Political Knowledge*: pp. 190 f.

[26] Those who deny that a justifying belief needs to be justified include: Charles Larmore, *The Autonomy of Morality* (Cambridge and New York: Cambridge University Press, 2008); Mark Timmons, *Morality without Foundations: A Defense of Ethical Contextualism* (New York: Oxford University Press, 1999); Michael Kober, *Gewißheit als Norm. Wittgenstein's erkenntnistheoretische Untersuchungen in Über Gewißheit* (Berlin and New York: de Gruyter, 1993). I would ascribe this view also to Wittgenstein. See for instance OC 253: 'At the foundation of well-founded belief lies belief that is not founded.'

[27] Thomas, *Value and Context: the Nature of Moral and Political Knowledge*: p. 191.

classified as 'foundationalism'. Foundationalists hold that the immediately justified beliefs provide the foundation for all beliefs that are merely inferentially justified.[28] It is a theory about the structure of justified belief. *Moral* foundationalism has almost always coincided with intuitionism.[29] As Sabine Roeser points out in her analysis of traditional forms of moral intuitionism, foundationalism belongs to the 'core-theory' of intuitionism.[30]

Questions arise in relation to the foundationalist proposal as to how there can be such basic beliefs, what the plausible candidates for such beliefs are and on what basis they are justified.[31] In response to the question as to how we know the truths expressed by basic beliefs, many 18th century intuitionists refer to a 'moral faculty', which is one of the controversial concepts responsible for the widespread rejection of intuitionism.[32] Intuitionists are generally thought to assume a mysterious faculty which makes their account implausible. However, as Roeser clarifies, the term 'moral faculty', which in fact disappeared from intuitionist writings after Thomas Reid, was not meant to denote anything mysterious.[33] It simply referred to the capacity to make moral judgements. It is

---

[28] As mentioned above (note 25), Aristotle argued in favour of foundationalism. The most prominent advocate of such a position is Descartes. A distinction can be drawn between strong, modest and weak foundationalism. Strong foundationalists claim not only that foundational beliefs have to be justified, but also that they need to be infallible, incorrigible or indubitable. Modest foundationalists, by contrast, merely require that those beliefs are non-inferentially justified. Weak foundationalism accepts basic beliefs which are only minimally justified, thus being unable to support other beliefs by themselves. In explaining how it is nevertheless possible to have justified beliefs, weak foundationalists refer to relations of coherence. Weak foundationalism is thus very similar to some versions of coherentism. See BonJour, *The Structure of Empirical Knowledge*: pp. 26 ff. Examples of *moral* foundationalism are: Henry J. McCloskey, *Meta-Ethics and Normative Ethics* (The Hague: Nijhoff, 1969); G.E. Moore, *Principia Ethica* (London: Cambridge University Press, 1903); Harold Arthur Prichard, *Moral Obligation. Essays and Lectures* (Oxford: Clarendon Press, 1949); Thomas Reid, *Essays on the Active Powers of the Human Mind* (Cambridge, MA: MIT Press, 1969 [1788]); David Ross, *The Right and the Good* (Oxford: Oxford University Press, 1930); Henry Sidgwick, *The Methods of Ethics* (London and New York: Macmillan, 1901 [1874]).

[29] See David Owen Brink, *Moral Realism and the Foundations of Ethics* (New York: Cambridge University Press, 1989), p. 102. An exception is Jonathan Dancy, who is an intuitionist but not a foundationalist. See Jonathan Dancy, *Ethics without Principles* (Oxford: Oxford University Press, 2004), pp. 148 ff.

[30] Roeser, *Moral Emotions and Intuitions*, p. xiv.

[31] See BonJour, *The Structure of Empirical Knowledge*, p. 30.

[32] Roeser, *Moral Emotions and Intuitions*, p. 11.

[33] Ibid., pp. 11 and 101.

through non-mysterious cognitive capacities that we are said to discover moral truths.[34]

Secondly, it is possible to conceive of justification in a non-linear, holistic manner. When adopting such a viewpoint, the primary unit of justification is the system as a whole, so that the regress terminates in a circular way.[35] Since all beliefs are thought to support one another and to form a coherent system of beliefs, the justification for singular beliefs must be circular. Varieties of this answer are called 'coherence theories'. The view that the justification of *moral* beliefs depends on the relationships between these beliefs, as well as on the way in which they are related to non-moral convictions, is prominent today.[36] While in empirical epistemology foundationalism is dominant, in moral theory coherence views enjoy greater popularity.[37] In the absence of an immediately justified foundation, moral (and also non-moral) beliefs are thought to give one another mutual support. Within a fully coherent web of beliefs, so the story goes, all elements are justified.[38]

The coherentist approach faces the objection that there may be more than one coherent belief system, and that we lack a criterion for choosing between such systems. Moreover, it may be asked why coherence should be an indicator of truth. My main objection to coherence theorists is that

---

[34] Moral intuitionism has experienced a revival in recent years. For contemporary versions of moral intuitionism see Robert Audi, *The Good in the Right. A Theory of Intuition and Intrinsic Value* (Princeton, NJ: Princeton University Press, 2003); Dancy, *Ethics without Principles*; Michael Huemer, *Ethical Intuitionism* (Basingstoke: Palgrave Macmillan, 2005); Philip Stratton-Lake, ed. *Ethical Intuitionism: Re-evaluations* (Oxford: Clarendon Press, 2002).

[35] See BonJour, *The Structure of Empirical Knowledge*, p. 24.

[36] See Gilbert Harman, 'Three Trends in Moral and Political Philosophy,' *The Journal of Value Inquiry* 37 (2003).

[37] See ibid.

[38] Examples for moral coherentism are: John Rawls, *A Theory of Justice*, revised ed. (Cambridge, Mass.: The Belknap Press of Harvard University Press, 1999); Geoffrey Sayre-McCord, 'Coherentist Epistemology and Moral Theory,' in *Moral Knowledge? New Readings in Moral Epistemology*, ed. Walter Sinnott-Armstrong and Mark Timmons (New York and Oxford: Oxford University Press, 1996); Thomas. M. Scanlon, *What We Owe to Each Other* (Cambridge, Mass. and London: The Belknap Press of Harvard University Press, 1998); R. Jay Wallace, *Responsibility and the Moral Sentiments* (Cambridge, Mass. and London: Harvard University Press, 1994). Alan Thomas points to an ambiguity: on the one hand, moral beliefs are said to 'inherit their epistemic status from their relations to other legitimate beliefs', on the other hand they are said to inherit it 'from forming part of a total system that is maximally explanatory'. He claims that, '[i]n its pure form, coherentism ought to insist that epistemic status is always a relational property'. Thomas, *Value and Context: the Nature of Moral and Political Knowledge*: pp. 184 and 216.

they over-systematise and over-intellectualise. They demand too much of finite beings like us. If in order to have justified moral beliefs we have to engage in reflections of the sort envisaged by them, this would mean that no one could ever be said to have any justified beliefs.

When we abandon the assumption that a justifying belief has to be justified, a third possible solution to the regress problem becomes conceivable. It can then be argued that the regress terminates with beliefs which are unjustified and yet able to confer justification on other beliefs. This position has been called 'ordinary language view' and ascribed to Wittgenstein and Austin.[39] Laurence BonJour characterises it as the position that in the course of the regress we arrive at beliefs for which 'the issue of justification "does not arise" or "makes no sense"'.[40]

To these common sense approaches it can be objected that it remains unclear how we can identify the beliefs for which the demand for justification does not make sense.[41] If there is a criterion which can be justified, we arrive at a justification of these beliefs. In that case the justification was possible and the regress continues. If there is no such criterion, this is problematic, because it seems that then we can never know whether we are dealing with a belief which can serve as an unjustified justifier. On what basis could we ever claim that in the case of a particular belief the issue of justification does not arise or makes no sense?

As mentioned above, this solution to the regress problem is not correctly ascribed to Wittgenstein, who instead of providing any kind of solution to it dissolved the problem.

1.4.3   The dissolution of the regress problem

Following Andreas Krebs, I shall argue that an approach along the lines of Wittgenstein's later philosophy should not aim to provide an answer to the regress problem, but a dissolution of it.[42] The apparent problem is dissolved as follows: it is characteristic of justifying reasons that they always refer to concrete doubts.[43] As was emphasised by Wittgenstein,

---

[39] BonJour, *The Structure of Empirical Knowledge*: p. 22 and note 7. David Owen Brink calls this position 'groundless foundationalism' and considers it to be one possible reading of Wittgenstein. Brink, *Moral Realism and the Foundations of Ethics*: p. 120 and note 21.

[40] BonJour, *The Structure of Empirical Knowledge*: p. 22. See also Uwe Wiedemann, 'Auswege aus Agrippas Trilemma,' (http://www.pyrrhon.de/cohere/agrippa.htm), accessed on 29 May 2010.

[41] Widemann, 'Auswege aus Agrippas Trilemma.'

[42] Krebs, *Worauf man sich verlässt*: p. 90.

[43] See ibid., p. 91.

and pursued by contemporary moral philosophers referred to as 'epistemological contextualists' (hereafter 'contextualists'), doubt requires reasons (see for example OC 4 and 122).[44] From this it follows that the regress problem does not arise. The process of justifying an assertion comes to an end when either the person defending the assertion or the one uttering doubts run out of reasons.[45] As soon as the doubter has no reason for a further doubt, the asserter does not have to provide any more reasons for his assertion. Wittgenstein unmasks the regress problem as a pseudo problem that can only arise under the assumption that doubts do not have to be based on reasons.[46]

Accordingly, there is no such thing as a class of special beliefs for which the demand for justification does not arise. Rather, it depends on the context which doubts arise and thus for which beliefs justification is required. I take this to imply that the claim that a justifying belief has to be justified even if that claim is understood in the first of the two senses distinguished by Thomas (in the sense that it does not necessarily have to be justified in the same context as the one in which it is justifying, see 1.4.1) is invalid. Whether a belief requires justification in contexts other than those in which it has a justificatory role depends on whether it can reasonably be doubted in those contexts. There may be beliefs that are beyond doubt in any context.

1.4.4 Moral epistemological contextualism

Contextualists criticise both sides of the foundationalist/coherentist dichotomy and suggest an account of moral justification that can be

[44] Proponents of this family of views are: Charles Larmore, *The Morals of Modernity* (Cambridge and New York: Cambridge University Press, 1996); Jeffrey Stout, 'On Having a Morality in Common,' in *Prospects for a Common Morality*, ed. Gene Outka and John P. Reeder Jr. (Princeton, N.J: Princeton University Press, 1993); Timmons, *Morality without Foundations: A Defense of Ethical Contextualism*; Carl Wellman, *Challenge and Response. Justification in Ethics* (London and Amsterdam: Southern Illinois University Press, 1971); Thomas, *Value and Context: the Nature of Moral and Political Knowledge*; Marcus Willaschek, 'Moralisches Urteil und begründeter Zweifel. Eine kontextualistische Konzeption moralischer Rechtfertigung,' in *Argument und Analyse. Ausgewählte Sektionsvorträge des 4. internationalen Kongresses der Gesellschaft für analytische Philosophie*, ed. Andreas Beckermann und Christian Nimtz (http://gap-im-netz.de/gap4Konf/Proceedings4/Proc.htm, 2002). According to Thomas, Charles Larmore and Mark Timmons are the leading contextualists. Thomas, *Value and Context: the Nature of Moral and Political Knowledge*: p. 6.
[45] See Krebs, *Worauf man sich verlässt*, p. 91.
[46] See ibid., pp. 90 f. Krebs refers to OC 204, where Wittgenstein says that justifying *comes* to an end, not that it *has to come* to an end. Wittgenstein does not have to demand that the process of justifying terminate, because it simply does.

viewed as occupying an intermediate position. Their critique focuses on a view shared by most members of both camps: the view that every belief as such needs to be justified.[47] Just like Wittgenstein, contextualists regard justification as being closely related to doubt. They suggest that it be understood as a 'response to a problem', as an answer to a question or as a response to a challenge.[48] Contextualists advocate the 'double thesis' that there is 'no reasonable doubt without contextually relevant reasons, but also no justification without contextually relevant doubts'.[49] It is a disputed matter amongst them whether the beliefs we do not have to justify (or cannot even justify) possess the epistemic status of being justified and what the relevant contexts are.

Charles Larmore, one of the leading contextualists, argues that the point of justification is to remove doubts relating to the truth of a belief. He emphasises that '[o]nly what is problematic calls for justification' and claims that therefore the proper objects of justification are not beliefs as such, but 'changes in belief'. The core principle of his contextualism is that no belief as such requires justification. Questions of justification arise within a context made up of unjustified beliefs.[50]

Larmore holds that for all kinds of beliefs, the 'need for justification arises only if we have uncovered some positive reason, based on other things we believe, for thinking that the belief might be false'.[51] While I agree with him on this point, I do not think it follows that only changes in belief are the proper objects of justification, at least as far as moral justification is concerned. This, I think, would only be the case if moral justification were not directed at others. As a social, communicative practice, moral justification involves more than one person. If, for instance, I have reasons to object to your view that we have no moral obligations towards animals, I may require a justification from you for that view. In such a case it is not a change in beliefs that needs to be justified, but a belief itself. Yet the belief in question

---

[47] This is with the exception of some moral intuitionists such as Ross and Reid, who also think that 'we can hold on to our initial beliefs until we have good reason to doubt them'. Roeser, *Moral Emotions and Intuitions*: p. 73.

[48] The first of these options is defended by Larmore, the second by Stout and the third by Wellman, who argues that 'to justify an ethical statement is to meet whatever challenges have actually been made to it'. Larmore, *The Autonomy of Morality*, p. 4; Stout, 'On Having a Morality in Common', p. 223; Wellman, *Challenge and Response. Justification in Ethics*, preface.

[49] Willaschek, 'Moralisches Urteil und begründeter Zweifel. Eine kontextualistische Konzeption moralischer Rechtfertigung,' p. 634, my translation.

[50] Larmore, *The Autonomy of Morality*, pp. 4 and 11.

[51] Larmore, *The Morals of Modernity* p. 11.

is not *as such* in need of justification, but only because I have reasons to object to it.

Mark Timmons formulates his contextualist position as a response to the regress problem. He claims that 'the regress of justification ends with beliefs that, in a given context, are not in need of justification'. This means that they 'do not need the sort of epistemic status of enjoying positive evidential support (either inherently or from other beliefs and experiences) in order to play a regress-stopping role in the structure of justified belief'. The contexts in which some beliefs do not need to be justified are 'ordinary' contexts. There are other contexts in which justification for them is required, but this demand might never be met.[52] Therefore, Timmons allows for beliefs that function as 'justifiers' despite not being justified themselves. It is somehow puzzling that as a contextualist he formulates his position as an answer to the apparent regress problem. As argued above, the contextualist claim that it only makes sense to ask for a justification of a judgement if that judgement could be reasonably doubted implies the dissolution of that problem.

1.5 Preliminary remarks

Some preliminary remarks are in order regarding terminological matters. I shall distinguish between a belief being justified and someone being entitled to hold it. As I use the term, a belief is justified if it is supported by reasons that are more certain than the belief they are supposed to justify. This view of justification goes back to Aristotle, and I take Wittgenstein to hold it.[53] It is supported by the function that reasons fulfil. We need reasons in order to assure others or ourselves of an assertion, which would hardly be possible if those reasons were not more certain than the initial assertion. By reason I mean a further belief that counts in favour of the initial belief, one that makes us believe that it is true. That a belief is not justified in this sense does not imply that we

[52] Timmons, *Morality without Foundations: A Defense of Ethical Contextualism* pp. 187 and 220 f.

[53] Aristotle writes in the *Posterior Analytics* that 'it is necessary to be better convinced of the principles (either all or some of them) than of the conclusions'. Aristotle, *Posterior Analytics* p. 4 (72a37 f.). Wittgenstein writes: 'My having two hands is, in normal circumstances, as certain as anything that I could produce in evidence for it. That is why I am not in a position to take the sight of my hand as evidence for it' (OC 250; see also OC 243). See Stefan Rummens, 'On the Possibility of a Wittgensteinian Account of Moral Certainty,' *The Philosophical Forum* 44, no. 2 (2013): p. 130.

hold it illegitimately. Justification is not always needed. Sometimes it does not even make sense to ask for it. In English, the phrase 'not every belief as such has to be justified' is ambiguous. It can mean that not every belief has to possess 'the epistemic status of enjoying positive evidential support',[54] or that we do not have to provide a justification for every belief. It is clear that, in his article on moral contextualism, Marcus Willaschek denies that we have to come up with a justification for all our moral beliefs, while holding that those beliefs we do not have to justify due to a lack of contextually relevant doubts possess the epistemic status of being justified (the distinction can be clearly rendered in German, but is difficult to translate succinctly into English!).[55] But for him this does not mean that they are supported by reasons that are more certain. Timmons argues that justification is not required in either sense, but not all advocates of contextualism writing in English say explicitly what they mean when they say that not every belief needs to be justified. Like Timmons, I do not simply want to claim that we do not have to provide a justification for every moral belief, but that in addition not all the moral beliefs we hold have to possess the epistemic status of being justified. My disagreement with Willaschek in this respect appears to be merely terminological.

In my attempt to call into question some fundamental assumptions made by moral philosophers belonging to different camps, I shall not seek assistance from Wittgenstein alone. Other important reference points will be Aristotle, along with philosophers standing in the Aristotelian tradition, Gilbert Ryle and contextualists.

1.6 Structure of the book

Chapter 2, *Basic Concepts*, provides a short introduction to the later Wittgenstein's understanding of language and meaning. It explains the concepts that are crucial for the purposes of this study, such as 'language-game', 'rule', 'meaning', and 'grammatical proposition'. The

---

[54] Timmons, *Morality without Foundations: A Defense of Ethical Contextualism* p. 187.

[55] Willaschek, 'Moralisches Urteil und begründeter Zweifel. Eine kontextualistische Konzeption moralischer Rechtfertigung,' p. 634. In German, different formulations are used to say that it is not necessary to engage in the process of justifying every belief ('nicht jede Überzeugung muss gerechtfertigt *werden*') and that not every belief has to possess the epistemic status of being justified ('nicht jede Überzeugung muss gerechtfertigt *sein*').

concept of a rule is further elucidated by a presentation and discussion of John Searle's distinction between regulative and constitutive rules. The game-analogy is applied to moral uses of language and different levels of moral practice are distinguished.

Chapter 3, *Certainty*, considers Wittgenstein's views on knowledge, doubt and certainty, moving from a focus on propositions to an emphasis on acting. According to the interpretation suggested, propositions such as 'Here is one hand' uttered while looking at one's hand are under normal conditions beyond the realm of reasonable doubt and justification. They lack truth value and do not constitute knowledge. The chapter explores the relationship between these propositions and the actions and reactions that underlie our language-games. The epistemic language-games we participate in are underpinned by shared actions and reactions, including primitive verbal and non-verbal responses, shared ways of making judgements of sameness, common ways of following rules and so on. The chapter provides the basis for the analogy drawn in Chapter 5 between certainty regarding the empirical world and moral certainty.

Chapter 4, *Moral Justification*, considers the role of the justification of moral judgements in everyday practice. It discusses a number of examples in order to point out the conditions that obtain when the demand for justification arises in concrete practical situations. The chapter compares different practices of justification, such as the practice of justifying moral judgements and the practice of justifying empirical judgements, and highlights both their differences and their similarities. It is argued that in the light of the conditions that obtain when a demand for the justification of a moral judgement arises in everyday practice, certain philosophical justificatory demands appear to be senseless. Philosophers who attempt to justify moral judgements as basic as the judgement that killing is wrong disregard the practical role of moral justification, which determines its sense. They attempt to provide an answer where there is no question.

After this consideration of cases where justification is required, Chapter 5, *Moral Certainty*, turns to cases in which to demand justification would appear pointless. Renford Bambrough's attempt to prove that people have moral knowledge provides a starting point for the analogy between certainty regarding the empirical world and moral certainty. The alleged proof of moral knowledge is criticised in a way that mirrors Wittgenstein's critique of G. E. Moore's proof of the external world. It is argued that propositions such as 'Killing is wrong' are certain for morally competent agents and function as 'axes' within moral reasoning. The moral language-games we participate in are underpinned by primitive responses such as responses to another person's suffering, and the immediate responses of morally competent agents.

Chapter 6, *Moral Competence*, addresses the notion of moral competence, paying particular attention to the way in which it is acquired. The chapter starts by considering concrete cases in which moral competence is exercised, cases as diverse as raising a child and participating in a rule of law mission. It argues that moral agency is first and foremost a matter of having such competence, which is the result of training. The capacities involved in this complex competence include rational as well as emotional capacities.[56] Drawing on Ryle's distinction between knowledge-how and knowledge-that, moral competence is compared with certain practical skills such as playing the piano, which are acquired in ways that resemble the ways in which human beings learn to be moral. The account of moral competence and training leads to a refined understanding of the acting that underlies moral language-games. These games are grounded in action in at least three different ways: they are based on primitive reactions that are not specifically human; the acquisition of moral language requires certain natural reactions (for example a parent's expression of approval and affection in reaction to good behaviour); and sophisticated moral language-games such as justifying and evaluating actions and judgements presuppose moral action that is not accompanied by conscious thought and results from training. The chapter ends with a refutation of the attempt to justify morality as a whole from an external standpoint.

Chapter 7, *Objections*, addresses the two main possible objections to the practice-based view of morality: that it is a form of moral relativism and that it is conservative. The objection of relativism is rejected on the grounds that moral practices transcend cultural boundaries, there is intercultural moral agreement and the possible diversity of moral codes is limited by human nature, physical circumstances and the functions of morality. The related objection of conservatism is refuted by arguing that the proposed account allows for moral critique, change and progress, the

---

[56] I use the term 'rational' instead of 'cognitive' because I conceive of emotions as cognitive phenomena. Yet contrasting emotional capacities with rational capacities is problematic as well, since I do not want to claim that emotions are necessarily irrational. The contrast I wish to draw is between emotional capacity and the capacity to engage in forms of reasoning in which emotions do not feature prominently.

latter two being processes which result from a combination of factual changes in the 'surroundings' of moral practices, reasoning and genuine moral disagreement.

Chapter 8, *Conclusion*, summarises the main arguments of the book, points out the limits of these arguments and indicates potential avenues for future research.

2
Basic Concepts

2.1 Introduction

I this chapter, I shall present some of the themes from Wittgenstein's later philosophy, starting with the famous game-analogy. Since it is common to conceive of the rules of a (language-) game as constitutive rules, I shall then present and problematise Searle's distinction between constitutive and regulative rules. Returning to Wittgenstein's understanding of language, the close relationship between meaning and use will be addressed along with further discussion of the rules of language-games. I then embark upon the enterprise of approaching morality using methodological tools taken from Wittgenstein by introducing the concept of a moral language-game. I explain how the terms 'moral language-game' and 'moral practice' will be used, comment on the role of moral terms in moral language-games, address some differences between morality and games and distinguish between games played on different levels. Some of these games will be examined more closely in Chapter 4.

2.2 The game-analogy

In his later writings, and particularly in the *Philosophical Investigations*, Wittgenstein compares human language uses with games, in particular with chess. He argues that the philosopher who seeks to understand our language talks about it in the same manner as one talks about chess pieces, namely by stating the rules of the game (see PI 108). Within the chess-analogy, the meaning of a word corresponds to the role of a piece.

---

[1] See G. P. Baker and P. M. S. Hacker, *Wittgenstein: Understanding and Meaning*, 2nd extensively rev. ed., II vols., vol. I (Oxford: Blackwell, 2005), part I, § 1. See also Andreas Kemmerling, 'Bedeutung und der Zweck der Sprache,' in *Von Wittgenstein lernen*, ed. Wilhelm Vossenkuhl (Berlin: Akademie Verlag, 1992), p. 107.

Just like the role of the piece, it is determined by the rules.[1] The king in chess owes its role in the game to the rules which define what moves it is allowed to make. The question of what the king in chess is can only be answered by reference to these rules. This means that the rules are constitutive of the role of the king. They construct the identity of this piece. As Wittgenstein is reported to have said in one of his lectures:

> What idea do we have of the king of chess, and what is its relation to the rules of chess? The chess player has an idea of what the king will do. But what the king can do is laid down by the rules. Do these rules follow from the idea? Can I deduce the rules once I get hold of the idea in the chess player's mind? No. The rules are not something contained in the idea and got by analyzing it. They constitute it.
>
> *Wittgenstein's Lectures, Cambridge 1932–1935*, p. 86

A move in a language-game can be made by using a sentence. (The analogy is not precise here because the pieces correspond to words, not to sentences.) The rules of the game determine which moves are permissible. It depends on them whether, in a concrete case, a speaker can make a move in the game by uttering a particular sentence. A move in a language-game is thus the meaningful utterance of a sentence.

The game-analogy shows what, according to Wittgenstein, is the most important feature of language: speaking a language is part of an activity (see PI 23). It is, like playing, '*acting* in accordance with certain rules' (RFM V 1). In addition, the analogy highlights the multifaceted functions that language can have in our life, the 'diversity of ways we make sense'.[2] By using language, we do far more than describe the world we live in. Finally, the various uses of language resemble different games in that they reveal 'family resemblances' (PI 67, see 2.4). Apart from many more concrete instances of using language such as those mentioned in the introduction (1.3), Wittgenstein also calls the totality of language and the activities with which it is intertwined a language-game (PI 7). Within his understanding of language, linguistic and non-linguistic ways of acting are interwoven.

Patricia Hanna and Bernard Harrison refer to 'Wittgenstein's play with the notion of a language-game'.[3] His use of that term is indeed playful,

---

[2] Russell B. Goodman, 'Wittgenstein and Ethics,' *Metaphilosophy* 13, no. 2 (1982), p. 141. See also G. P. Baker and P. M. S. Hacker, *Wittgenstein: Rules, Grammar and Necessity*, 2nd, extensively rev. ed. (Chichester, U.K. and Malden, MA: Wiley-Blackwell, 2009), p. 135: 'A language is integrated in endless ways into human activities, actions and reactions.'

[3] Patricia Hanna and Bernard Harrison, *Word & World. Practice and the Foundations of Language* (Cambridge et al.: Cambridge University Press, 2004), p. 254.

and does not have sharp boundaries. According to him, we use the word 'game' 'so that the extension of the concept is *not* closed by a frontier' (PI 68). He notes that this does not disturb us when we use it. It is only when the philosopher starts reflecting on the *essence* of the word 'game' that the lack of frontiers seems to be problematic. Pleasants remarks that in *On Certainty*, Wittgenstein uses the term 'language-game' in a particularly 'loose, non specific, non-conceptual way', referring, for instance, to '[o]ur routine ways of going on in the world of familiar things and familiar practices'.[4]

The concrete instances of using language which can be conceived of as language-games can also be understood as moves in another language-game. Casting doubt on something, for instance, can be conceived of both as a move in a language-game and as a game by itself. Whether we conceive of it in one way or the other depends on what we want to highlight. The game-analogy serves as a heuristic device. I can argue, for instance, that I do not make a move in the game of writing a book in English by doubting my ability to understand the English language. By saying something like 'I am not sure whether I understand English' I do not make a move in that game. While the game allows for doubts regarding the correctness of a particular phrase, there is no room for doubting my general knowledge of English. Not every kind of doubt has a place in a particular language-game. 'The uncertainty of the doubt is only understandable against the background of the relative certainty of the reasons for doubting', as Timo-Peter Ertz argues.[5] In my example, the reasons for doubting the grammatical correctness of a particular sentence involve my knowledge of English grammar. Wittgenstein gives the following example: 'When I am trying to mate someone in chess, I cannot have doubts about the pieces perhaps changing places of themselves and my memory simultaneously playing tricks on me so that I don't notice' (OC 346). Doubts of that sort would make it impossible to play the game.

If, by contrast, I conceive of doubting as a game, I can think about its rules and ascertain that it needs reasons to get started, that it has an end, that it is the exception, and that it presupposes certainty (see OC 3, 160, 283, 458, 625; see also CE, pp. 377 ff.). For the language-game 'doubting', it is characteristic that it comes to an end at some point, the

---

[4] Nigel Pleasants, 'Wittgenstein, Ethics and Basic Moral Certainty,' *Inquiry* 51, no. 3 (2008): note 21. The second quotation refers to OC 559.

[5] Timo-Peter Ertz, *Regel und Witz. Wittgensteinsche Perspektiven auf Mathematik, Sprache und Moral* (Berlin and New York: de Gruyter, 2008), p. 166, my translation. In the original it says: 'Die Unsicherheit des Zweifels ist nur verständlich vor dem Hintergrund der relativen Sicherheit der Zweifelsgründe.'

end being either the removal of the initial doubts, or the rejection of the proposition doubted. Moreover, 'since doubt is an exception, the rule is its environment' (CE, p. 379). Only when what I am saying complies with these rules can it properly be called a doubt. Otherwise, my behaviour is merely one that resembles doubting (see OC 255).[6]

2.3 Constitutive and regulative rules

The rules of a language-game are often said to be 'constitutive rules'. Yet besides being widely used amongst philosophers, the concept of a constitutive rule is problematic. We may at this point consider Searle's famous distinction between constitutive and regulative rules. According to that distinction, regulative rules 'regulate a pre-existing activity', whereas constitutive rules 'constitute (and also regulate) an activity the existence of which is logically dependent on the rules'.[7] Constitutive rules 'create or define new forms of behaviour'.[8]

Examples of regulative rules are traffic rules and the rules of etiquette. The rules of chess, by contrast, present the paradigm case of constitutive rules.[9] They establish the possibility of playing chess. Constitutive rules can have the form 'X counts as Y' or 'X counts as Y in context C'.[10] It has been argued that it is characteristic for this type of rule that it does not make sense to ask whether it is possible to violate it.[11] Yet we can object to this that the term 'violation' is also used with regard to constitutive rules. For instance, I could be said to have violated the rule defining

---

[6] Ertz writes that although it could be conceived of as a rule that doubt requires reasons, there are ungrounded doubts, meaning doubts based on bad reasons (ibid., p. 168). I do not think the existence of ill-founded doubt conflicts with the view that in practice people utter doubts on the basis of reasons, since these reasons can be good or bad. The rule of the 'game of doubting' does not say that doubt requires good reasons, meaning that it needs to be justified, but that it presupposes some kind of reasons in order to occur in the first place. An utterance can be understandable as a doubt even if the doubt expressed turns out to be ill-founded.

[7] John R. Searle, *Speech Acts: An Essay in the Philosophy of Language* (London: Cambridge University Press, 1969), p. 34. For a criticism of the usual criteria governing the distinction between regulative and constitutive rules see Andreas Kemmerling, 'Regel und Geltung im Lichte der Analyse Wittgensteins,' *Rechtstheorie* 6 (1975), p. 129.

[8] Searle, *Speech Acts: An Essay in the Philosophy of Language*, p. 33.

[9] See A. G. Conte, 'Regel,' in *Historisches Wörterbuch der Philosophie*, ed. Joachim Ritter and Karlfried Gründer (Basel: Schwabe, 1992), p. 446.

[10] Searle, *Speech Acts: An Essay in the Philosophy of Language*, pp. 34 f.

[11] Conte, 'Regel', p. 448.

under what conditions a valid contract is made by not fulfilling these conditions. What I *cannot* be said to have done is to have made a contract under conditions that are excluded by the rule. Whatever I make under such conditions is anything but a valid contract. Because constitutive rules do not have an imperative form, a violation of them is not like the violation of a rule like 'If you reach a red traffic light, stop'. While I can violate the traffic rule by not stopping when I reach a red traffic light, I cannot violate the rule that the bishop may merely move diagonally by moving it horizontally and vertically instead. Whatever I would be doing in that case, I would not be playing chess, whereas if I did not stop in front of the traffic light, I would still be a participant in traffic.

We have to distinguish between different types of failures in relation to rules. A rule can be broken intentionally, and it can also be the case that it is not followed due to a lack of comprehension, because we unintentionally made a mistake, or because we are absent-minded. If I do not stop in front of a red traffic light, I might be breaking the respective rule intentionally, but I might also be absent-minded, or I might have mistakenly thought that I would still be able to stop at a very short distance from the traffic light. All these descriptions of my action could be correct. It is quite unlikely that the failure is due to a lack of comprehension, but the reason for this is the simplicity of the rule in question, not its function, that is the function of being regulative. We might very well fail to understand a particular rule of etiquette for instance.

The failures which can occur in connection to constitutive rules seem to be due either to a lack of comprehension or to a rejection of the practice of which the respective rules are constitutive. We might say that the person who moves the bishop horizontally and vertically has not yet mastered chess. Similarly, it could be said that a person who does not follow the rules for making a valid contract has not yet mastered the practice of making a contract. A person who does not follow the rules of the use of the word 'table' could be said to not have mastered this word. Alternatively, they could be expressing their rejection of chess, of the institution of contracts and of the way we use the term 'table'.

While the differences between the ways in which rules can be said to be violated are important to acknowledge, the constitutive/regulative dichotomy is not convincing as it stands. As Wittgenstein points out, it is not easy to draw the line between ways of acting which we would still call 'playing chess', and those which we would not. It might seem that we can 'test' whether a given rule is a constitutive rule by considering whether its elimination would result merely in the modification of a practice or in its elimination; however, this impression is misleading.

In many cases it is a system of rules that defines a practice. The chess rules are an example of this. Within such a system, there are 'degrees of centrality', and a slight change in a marginal rule does not turn the practice into a different one.[12] Consequently, a single rule can be part of a system of constitutive rules, even if its elimination does not amount to an elimination of the practice.

Moreover, it is questionable whether there would, for instance, still be a practice we could call 'traffic' if there were no traffic rules, and whether polite behaviour is really prior to the rules of etiquette. I take it that there are no straightforward answers to these questions. Given the fuzziness of the distinction between constitutive and regulative rules, I suggest replacing it by a view of rules that accounts for the variety of functions they can have (for this variety see PI 53 f.). I shall, for instance, refer to the functions of guiding action, defining meaning and determining what it makes sense to say.

2.4 Meaning and use

I shall now return to the later Wittgenstein's understanding of language, which stands in sharp contrast to the one that Wittgenstein presented in his early book, the *Tractatus logico-philosophicus*.[13] There he held that only declarative sentences are meaningful. According to the early Wittgenstein, a declarative sentence owes its meaning to its truth conditions (see TLP 4.063). There are (possible) facts corresponding to it, which must obtain if the sentence is to be true: 'If the elementary proposition is true, the atomic fact exists; if it is false the atomic fact does not exist' (TLP 4.25). Hence, a proposition like the one expressed by the sentence 'The glass is on the table' is true if and only if a certain glass is on a certain table. Within this 'picture theory' of meaning (see TLP 4.011), the relationship between an atomic sentence and the fact it alleges is one of 'simple correspondence or isomorphism'.[14] The names the sentence contains correspond to objects. Non-atomic sentences are truth functions of atomic sentences (see TLP 5). Having written the *Tractatus*, Wittgenstein believed himself 'to have found, on all essential points, the final solution of the problems' (TLP, preface).

---

[12] Searle, *Speech Acts: An Essay in the Philosophy of Language*, p. 34.

[13] According to New Wittgensteinians, there is no such contrast (see 1.3, note 17).

[14] Saul Kripke, *Wittgenstein on Rules and Private Language* (Oxford: Blackwell, 1982), p. 71. See TLP 4.21.

However, in the *Philosophical Investigations*, he rejects what he had himself once believed to be true: that truth conditions endow a sentence with meaning, and that words stand for objects. His target is the idea that '[e]very word has a meaning. This meaning is correlated with the word. It is the object for which the word stands' (PI 1; see also PI 40). Thus, he argues against 'meaning Platonism' and any form of psychologism.[15] While for Platonists such as Gottlob Frege the object that corresponds to a word is an abstract object in a 'third realm', the psychologist takes it to be a mental object like an idea or an image. Wittgenstein dismisses the Platonist conception of the problem of meaning, which is expressed in questions about the objects that our words denote. There are no such things as meaning-entities, either as Platonic forms or mental images.

Most importantly, Wittgenstein shows that, even if there were such entities, they would not do the job philosophers want them to do. First of all, it is unclear how we could grasp them. How could the human mind, which is finite, grasp an infinite entity? The meaning-entity would have to be infinite because it is thought to determine all correct applications of a word. By having grasped the meaning of a word, we are supposed to know its extension, that is all the things it applies to. The copy in the mind, however, would have to be finite. It would therefore be a bad copy which would not fulfil the function it is supposed to fulfil. Moreover, even if we had good copies of such meaning-entities in our minds, this would be problematic. In that case we could not make sense of disagreement, wrong applications, learning and teaching. All human beings would know everything already by virtue of the meanings they had grasped, so that disagreement and incorrect applications of words could not occur.

In contrast to the account of meaning given in the *Tractatus*, the later Wittgenstein does not aim to posit necessary and sufficient conditions for the truth of a sentence. Instead, he asks for the conditions under which a move can be made in a language-game, that is under what conditions we say something meaningful. That Wittgenstein's examples are predominantly declarative sentences is, I believe, partly due to the fact that he wishes to correct his own former account of these. Another reason is that '[t]he great majority of sentences that we speak, write and read, are statement sentences' (RFM, App. III 2). However, within our various language-games, assertions and denials are no more important than questions, orders, exclamations, and all other forms of linguistic expression.

---

[15] For a characterisation of psychologism see BBB, pp. 3 f.

Arguing that the search for meaning in terms of an entity is misleading, Wittgenstein asks the philosopher to direct his attention to the *use* of words. He tends to identify the concept of use with that of meaning. *The Blue Book* begins with the question: 'What is the meaning of a word?' (BBB, p. 1). Instead of giving a straight answer, Wittgenstein turns to the further question of what an explanation of the meaning of a word is. He wants to avoid us answering the first question by pointing to something in the mind like an image, an idea or a feeling. In the *Philosophical Investigations* he writes: 'For a *large* class of cases – though not for all – in which we employ the word 'meaning' it can be defined thus: the meaning of a word is its use in the language' (PI 43).

This use is rule-guided. The totality of rules which determine the use of a word is called the 'grammar' of the word. In *On Certainty*, Wittgenstein uses the terms 'logic' and 'grammar' synonymously (see OC 628). The propositions that state rules for the use of words are called 'grammatical' or 'logical propositions' (see PI 251 f.[16]). They relate to the use of signs and describe a language-game (PI 496 and OC 628). The grammatical proposition 'An order orders its own execution', for instance, means: 'If an order runs "Do such-and-such" then executing the order is called "doing such-and-such"' (PI 458).

The rules which are followed within linguistic communication are revealed through linguistic practice. Although he talks about grammatical and empirical propositions, Wittgenstein's view is better expressed by differentiating between different roles that propositions can play, depending on the respective context (see 3.2.2–3.2.4). A proposition which plays, in a given context, the role of an empirical proposition is one which expresses an alleged empirical fact and is either true or false.

The degree to which the use of a word is determined by rules varies from word to word. The boundaries of a concept can be more or less sharp. In the *Philosophical Investigations* we find a passage where Wittgenstein addresses ethical concepts:

And this is the position [confronted with a blurred picture, wanting to draw a sharp one corresponding to it; J.H.] you are in if you look for definitions corresponding to our concepts in aesthetics or ethics.

---

[16] There he gives the examples 'Every rod has a length' and 'This body has extension'.

In such a difficulty always ask yourself: How did we learn the meaning of this word ('good' for instance)? From what sort of examples? In what language-games? Then it will be easier for you to see that the word must have a family of meanings.

Philosophical Investigations, § 77

In order to be useful, a concept does not have to have sharp boundaries (see PI 68). As Wittgenstein formulates it in one of his late remarks, '[w]e are playing with elastic, indeed even flexible concepts'. He adds that this does not mean that 'they can be deformed *at will* and without offering resistance, and are therefore *unusable*' (LW II, p. 24). Our concepts can be compared to more or less 'blurred' pictures (see PI 76 f.). Ethical or aesthetic concepts are fuzzier than concepts like 'game', but this is merely a matter of degree (see PI 77). For many concepts, if we keep looking for a feature which all instances of them have in common – for something like the essence of, for example, a game – we will never be successful. The many different games we know – chess, tennis, patience, hide-and-seek, playing with dolls, and so on – are like the members of a family in their similarities and differences. They reveal 'family resemblances' (PI 67). This holds for the innumerable language-games we play as well (see PI 65).

With the concept of family resemblance Wittgenstein opposes that every concept has something like an essence or nature, something that is shared by all instances of the concept (PI 65). He illustrates the idea of family resemblances by reference to games (PI 66). Thus, – and here I take other examples than Wittgenstein does – basketball and hide-and-seek share the feature of being played by more than one player, while basketball, unlike hide-and-seek, is always played by two teams. Patience, unlike both basketball and hide-and-seek, is played by one player alone. Yet it shares with these games the fact that there is a clear goal of the game. The game played by someone bouncing a ball in a courtyard shares with basketball the fact that it is played with a ball, but it does not share the feature of having a concrete goal. On the other hand, it shares with patience the fact that it is played by one player alone. And so forth.

Notwithstanding their role of determining the correct use of a word, grammatical rules do not determine such use for all possible cases (see PI 80). Our linguistic practices are underdetermined by the rules of language. In *On Certainty*, Wittgenstein writes that '[o]ur rules leave loop-holes open, and the practice has to speak for itself' (OC 139). As pointed out by Ilham Dilman, 'practice' here refers to what we do in particular cases.[17] Moreover, rules do not constitute language-games by themselves. In his dissertation, in which he takes up a Wittgensteinian perspective on mathematics, language and morality, Ertz argues convincingly that games like chess or football do not only have rules, but also a point ('einen Witz').[18] It is further noted by Searle that 'one could be following those rules [the chess rules; J.H.] and still not be playing chess, if for example the moves were made as part of a religious ceremony, or if the moves of chess were incorporated into some larger, more complex, game'.[19] If people followed the same rules as our chess rules, though not for the sake of entertainment but as part of a religious ceremony, they would not be playing chess. While Searle draws from this the conclusion that our conception of constitutive rules has to be broad enough to include 'rules that make clear the "aim of the game"', Ertz holds that games are made up of more than just their rules.[20] Although not every game of chess is in fact entertaining, the aim of being entertaining is constitutive of chess. It determines the point of the game.[21]

Ertz also mentions that its 'surroundings' are constitutive of a game like chess or a practice such as weighing.[22] It is part of the surroundings of the practice of weighing that pieces of cheese do not suddenly grow, just as it is part of the surroundings of our practice of measuring that rulers do not shrink when we take them from one room into another.[23] I return to Ertz's plausible interpretation of the constituent elements of a practice in the discussion of particular moral practices in Chapter 4.

---

[17] Ilham Dilman, 'Universals: Bambrough on Wittgenstein,' *Proceedings of the Aristotelian Society, New Series* 79 (1978–1979), p. 45.
[18] Ertz, *Regel und Witz. Wittgensteinsche Perspektiven auf Mathematik, Sprache und Moral*, pp. 10 f.
[19] Searle, *Speech Acts: An Essay in the Philosophy of Language*, p. 34, note 1.
[20] Ibid.
[21] Ertz, *Regel und Witz. Wittgensteinsche Perspektiven auf Mathematik, Sprache und Moral*, p. 11. Here I mean 'Sinn' by 'point', and not 'Witz'. The original reads: 'Tatsächlich ist die Unterhaltung konstitutiv für das Spiel, allerdings nicht als Regel; es ist keine konstitutive Regel des Spiels, unterhaltsam zu sein (schließlich gibt es auch langweilige Spielpartien), und dennoch bestimmt die Funktion der Unterhaltung den Sinn des Spiels.'
[22] Ertz, *Regel und Witz. Wittgensteinsche Perspektiven auf Mathematik, Sprache und Moral*, p. 37, my translation. The German term he uses is 'Umgebung'.
[23] For the second example see RFM I 140.

2.5   'Moral practices' and 'moral language-games'

2.5.1   Singular and plural use

I shall now apply the game-analogy to the uses of language for 'moral purposes'. Throughout this book I use the terms 'moral practice' and 'moral language-game' interchangeably.[24] Both will mainly be used in the plural form, but sometimes also in the singular. Let me try to make it as clear as possible from the outset what I intend by the singular and the plural use of these notions.

I shall start with the plural use. By 'moral practices' or 'moral language-games' I first of all refer to uses of language for 'moral purposes', for example making moral judgements, holding people responsible, morally praising and blaming, morally justifying actions and so on. The practice of making moral judgements will receive particular attention. Moral uses of language are associated with non-verbal reactions and attitudes, for example reactions that have an emotional core such as shame or guilt, expectations regarding one's own behaviour and that of others, and so on. I conceive of moral language-games as involving feelings and automatic responses.

That I speak of moral 'language-games' should not be taken to mean that I assimilate moral rules to linguistic rules.[25] According to my broad use of the terms 'moral language-game' and 'moral practice', the rules of the respective games and practices include rules performing the function of determining the use of words and sentences, rules playing the role of determining what is right and what is wrong and rules with the function of guiding non-verbal action. These functions are interrelated. Thus, a rule such as the one expressed by the sentence 'Killing is wrong' can perform all three functions simultaneously.

Despite the fact that the use of moral predicates is widespread, it is not necessary for a moral language-game to include the application of such predicates. It is possible to make moral evaluations without using terms that count as specifically moral. I agree with Diamond, who points out that 'some talk and writing that one might very well take to be the

---

[24] Such use is not uncommon in the literature. See for instance Michael Kober, 'On Epistemic and Moral Certainty: A Wittgensteinian Approach,' *International Journal of Philosophical Studies* 5, no. 3 (1997). As was mentioned above, the later Wittgenstein conceives of verbal and non-verbal action as interwoven. He plays with the notion of a language-game, and in *On Certainty*, he uses the term in a particularly loose way (see 2.2).

[25] I am grateful to Herman Philipse for making me aware of the fact that the reader could misunderstand me in this way.

expression of moral thought involves no specifically moral words at all, or involves relatively few such words, which bear relatively little weight'.[26] Thus, novels can take a moral stance without being written in moral language.[27]

Diamond suggests that it depends on its use whether a sentence belongs to ethics, not on its 'subject matter'.[28] Thus, it depends on its use whether 'A shell exploded. Twenty or thirty men were blown up ... '[29] is merely 'a record of what happened' or expresses moral thought.[30] She argues that words, rules, stories – 'anything made of the resources of ordinary language' – may be related to our lives and actions in such a way that we might characterise the thinking involved as moral.[31]

Diamond conceives of 'forms of ethical thinking' in terms of language-games and emphasises that language-games involving moral terms have no 'central place in ethics'.[32] Although I sometimes identify 'playing moral language-games' with 'thinking, acting and feeling in moral terms', this needs to be qualified. First, thinking in moral terms does not necessarily involve moral terms. We can, for instance, communicate moral praise and blame without using words that count as specifically moral. Secondly, there are certainly different ways of thinking in moral terms, such as putting oneself in the shoes of others, taking up an impartial standpoint, consequentialist reasoning, deontological reasoning, and so on.

Let me elaborate a bit more on my understanding of moral language-games. Playing these games requires a moral attitude. It requires us to take up a moral standpoint, that is to respond to our environment – both rationally and emotionally – from a moral point of view.[33] As participants in moral practices or players of moral language-games, we are concerned with 'promoting good and avoiding evil', 'encouraging virtue

---

[26] Cora Diamond, 'Wittgenstein, Mathematics, and Ethics: Resisting the Attractions of Realism,' in *The Cambridge Companion to Wittgenstein*, ed. Hans Sluga and David G. Stern (Cambridge and New York: Cambridge University Press, 1996), p. 243.

[27] Ibid., pp. 243 ff. As an example, Diamond discusses *The Long Winter* by Laura Ingalls Wilder.

[28] Ibid., p. 237.

[29] Virginia Woolf, *To the Lighthouse*, cited after ibid., p. 244.

[30] Diamond, 'Wittgenstein, Mathematics, and Ethics: Resisting the Attractions of Realism', p. 237.

[31] Ibid., p. 248.

[32] Ibid., p. 253.

[33] As noted above, I do not conceive of emotions as opposed to rationality (see introduction, note 58).

and discouraging vice', and 'avoiding harm to others and promoting their well-being or welfare'.[34] We are not simply concerned with our own interest, but with the interests of others or the common interest.[35] 'Moral practices' and 'moral language-games' are technical notions, used to refer to a central dimension of human life. As an integral part of the human form of life, these practices are not separate practices like for example the practice of playing tennis. The numerous moral practices are inseparably connected with other practices.

I sometimes also use 'moral practices' to refer to the moral codes of different societies. It will be clear from the respective context in which of the two ways I am using the term. I take it that Wittgenstein's playful use of the term 'language-game' licences these two plural uses.

I shall speak of a singular moral practice or language-game if I want to stress the fact that morality as a whole should be conceived of as a practice, as opposed to a mere set of rules for instance. By asking the reader to conceive of it as a practice I emphasise the fact that morality is a communicative enterprise. Communication, in turn, is itself a social, interactive practice. Within moral practice, people make claims on each other (and on themselves), evaluate each other's actions (and their own), justify their actions towards others (and towards themselves), and react with guilt or shame when they behave towards others in certain ways, and with feelings like outrage or indignation when others behave in certain ways towards them. They know that others expect certain behaviour from them, and that they, in turn, know how they are expected to behave. They help and take care of one another. Moral practice in this sense means 'thinking, feeling and acting in moral terms', where the action includes both acting with and acting without words.

2.5.2 Moral universals or family resemblances

I shall now elaborate on the second plural use ('moral practices' used as referring to different moral codes) and distinguish between two different ways of conceiving of the relationship between different moral practices. We could conceive of them as sharing certain features which are responsible for the fact that we call all these practices 'moral'. They can be thought to share (1) something very general, or (2) something more particular. If we take what they share to be something very general, such as the fact that they distinguish between right and wrong, then

---

[34] Steven Lukes, *Moral Relativism* (New York: Picador, 2008), p. 134.
[35] Ibid. Lukes talks here about the content of moral norms, not about the concerns of the agents guided by these norms.

the concrete standards for moral evaluation can vary. Our conception of morality would thus be purely formal in the sense that it would entirely avoid determinations in terms of content. A formal conception of morality is defended, for example, by Willaschek, who defines moral judgements as 'those normative judgements for which it holds (from the perspective of the judge) that the violation of the relevant rules cannot be excused by a refusal to recognise these rules'.[36] We might also conceive of what is shared as something more substantial. Thus, we might say that we would not call a practice in which torturing babies counted as good behaviour 'moral'. On the other hand, we would allow for different moral practices to have different rules regarding the treatment of women. All moral practices are thus assumed to share certain substantial moral judgements, such as the judgement that torturing babies is a morally bad thing to do. The participants in these practices are thought to agree that morality prohibits treating babies in this way. This prohibition would thus be a 'moral universal' (see 7.2.5).

Although I said that we would still regard a practice as a moral practice in which women were treated in ways which we regard as morally wrong, we certainly do not approve of this feature of that practice. Despite the fact that we do not deny that societies in which women have fewer rights than men have a morality, the vigorousness of our disapproval of the rules of that society should not be underestimated. We do not think that what those people do is acceptable because they are simply engaging in a different practice. We are convinced that they are wrong. In following this thinking, we are applying the standards of *our* moral practice. (This can be called the 'participant's standpoint' as opposed to the standpoint of the observer (see 7.2.2).[37]) Thus, the difference between the rule 'Torturing babies is morally right' and the rule 'Women are inferior to men and therefore have fewer rights' *prima facie* does not seem to be that big. The question is whether it is a difference in degree or a difference in kind. I tend to think that it is the latter, but some doubts

---

36 Marcus Willaschek, 'Moralisches Urteil und begründeter Zweifel. Eine kontextualistische Konzeption moralischer Rechtfertigung,' in *Argument und Analyse. Ausgewählte Sektionsvorträge des 4. internationalen Kongresses der Gesellschaft für analytische Philosophie*, ed. Andreas Beckermann und Christian Nimtz (http://gap-im-netz.de/gap4Konf/Proceedings4/Proc.htm, 2002), p. 630, my translation. 'Dann kann man *moralische* Urteile als diejenigen normativen Urteile definieren, für die (aus Sicht des Urteilenden) gilt, daß man die Verletzung der einschlägigen Regeln nicht damit entschuldigen kann, daß man diese Regeln nicht anerkennt.'
37 Lukes, *Moral Relativism*, p. 20.

remain. The former rule is clearly incompatible with the whole point of morality, which I would describe roughly as regulating interactions between human beings in such a way that enables them to flourish, while the latter is at least not as straightforwardly incompatible with it as the former.[38] Yet for most members of Western societies today the claim that women are inferior is simply unjustified. Moral practices have changed and continue to change. In certain parts of the world people have arrived at the view that men and women have equal rights.

It is one question whether there in fact are or have been communities in which actions like the torturing of babies are or were regarded as morally faultless, and quite another whether it makes sense to ascribe a morality to such a community. If the first question must be denied, the answer to the second can still be positive. I shall address the question as to whether we can imagine a moral code which differed in drastic ways from our own in Chapter 7.

The second way of understanding the relation between different moral codes is conceiving of them as exhibiting family resemblances. This view seems appealing, given the apparent availability of counterexamples to many candidates for something substantive shared by all moral language-games. If we propose as a candidate the already very general and abstract belief that human life is valuable, some people will object that there are and have been practices in which human life *per se* was not seen as valuable. They might refer to the traditional Eskimo society in which infanticide, 'senilicide', 'invalidicide' and suicide were common practices,[39] or to Nazi Germany. *Prima facie*, neither the Eskimos nor the Nazis seem to have valued human life *per se*.[40] If we suggest that what all moral practices share is something even more general, such as the fact that children are treated in a particular way, it might be objected that the way children have been treated has changed significantly over time and still varies between cultures.

---

[38] The reader should not give too much weight to this attempted formulation of the point of morality. I think that it is more complex than that. What I wish to make clear is that I take morality to be first and foremost about our relations with others. Rather than providing a definition of morality, I shall, throughout this book, give several examples of moral judgements, actions, feelings, capacities and debates. I hope that this will give the reader a better idea of what I take morality to be than any definition would.

[39] E. Adamson Hoebel, *The Law of Primitive Man* (New York: Harvard University Press, 1968), p. 76.

[40] It will be argued in Chapter 7 that despite appearances, the values of the Eskimos are not fundamentally different from ours, and that not even the Nazis played a radically different moral language-game.

If we understand moral practices as revealing family resemblances, we are not committed to the claim that there is any particular belief or form of reasoning which they all share. While this understanding seems to be more faithful to Wittgenstein's views, I find the position that there are moral universals more convincing (see 7.2.5). Moreover, I believe that it is compatible with my Wittgensteinian approach.

2.5.3   Differences between morality and games

Before moving on to distinguish different levels of moral language-games, it is important to address some possible concerns regarding the adequacy of the game-analogy in the case of morality. First, the comparison of morality to a game might suggest that we could simply choose to ignore moral requirements, thus refusing to play the game. However, while we can usually stop playing chess at any time, the same does not hold for moral language-games. Moreover, with regard to morality it would be inadequate to say that 'it's only a game'.

A first response to this objection points to the fact that this is a general difference between games like chess, bridge and poker and our various language-games. As Michael Kober notes, '[w]e cannot deliberately pick out the language-games in which we want to participate just as we can deliberately choose to play chess or not'.[41] Morality is not peculiar in this respect.

Moreover, morality, as well as law, has been compared to a game which we cannot easily quit. Thus, it has been compared to a game that differs from most other games in that we are more or less forced to play it. Willaschek makes this point by saying that moral judgements can be compared with 'rules of a game which are valid also for those who do not want to play the game'. On his view, moral judgements are judgements which are valid unconditionally if they are to be valid at all. We are subjected to them, whether we accept them or not.[42] The same is true of the law. Since, as Wittgenstein has pointed out, there is no essential feature of a game, why should we not be able to conceive of a game which everyone is urged to play? It is always to bear in mind what Wittgenstein's game-analogy was supposed to highlight.

A second concern might relate to the fact that what I refer to as moral language-games have no rules that are comparable to the catalogue of

---

[41] Kober, 'On Epistemic and Moral Certainty: A Wittgensteinian Approach', p. 370.
[42] Willaschek, 'Moralisches Urteil und begründeter Zweifel. Eine kontextualistische Konzeption moralischer Rechtfertigung', p. 631, my translation.

the rules of chess. However, this point holds true for all language-games. In invoking the chess analogy, Wittgenstein surely did not wish to claim that there is anything like a fixed catalogue of linguistic rules.

Third, while chess players usually do not disagree about what is of relevance to the game and what is not, there is disagreement about what is of relevance to moral language-games. Thus, some people think that having a sexual relationship with someone of the same sex is immoral, while others hold that it is morally irrelevant whether people are homo- or heterosexual. Another example is virginity. Some people still believe that it is immoral for a woman to lose her virginity before getting married, while others take the question as to whether a woman is a virgin when she marries to be morally irrelevant. Why is the issue of what is relevant for moral language-games a matter of dispute? The dispute referred to here should not be confused with a dispute over whether a particular type of action is morally right or wrong. The question at stake here is also not whether or not someone is playing a different game.

I think that the answer to this question lies in the dynamic character of moral language-games. Morality is not static, but changes over time (see 7.3.3). Properties and forms of behaviour which were once thought to be relevant for morality are at some point believed to be morally irrelevant. Certain behaviour is no longer thought to be a wrong move in these games, but something that does not matter for them at all. It is as if people came to believe that they should play chess without rooks. Such changes do not occur from one moment to the next. Language-games develop gradually. There is a period of time where the moral relevance of the respective property (for example being homosexual or a virgin) or behaviour (for example having sexual intercourse with someone of the same sex) is disputed. In these cases we can say that the players of the same moral language-games disagree about what is relevant for these games.

Despite significant differences between games and language usage, the comparison highlights certain crucial features of human speech and action (see 2.2). Insofar as it is illuminating at all to think of the use of language in terms of the game-metaphor, it also makes sense to do so with regard to the use of language in order to make moral judgements, to assert moral praise or blame or to express outrage or guilt.[43] Applied to our moral uses of language, the game-metaphor serves to show that

---

[43] See also Ertz, who notes that his comparison between chess and morality merely highlights certain structural similarities and does not imply that moral rules are arbitrary in a way similar to rules of a game. Ertz, *Regel und Witz. Wittgensteinsche Perspektiven auf Mathematik, Sprache und Moral*, p. 217, note 17.

it is not up to each individual to decide arbitrarily what is morally right or wrong. It also holds for the realm of morality that there are limits to what it makes sense to say. The judgement that a particular action is morally wrong has meaning in the context of a shared practice of making moral judgements.

Furthermore, the analogy points to a regularity which moral practices exhibit no less than others, that is to agreement regarding actions and judgements. Despite all of the disagreement about moral matters, it should not be overlooked that this disagreement presupposes agreement. In addition, talking about moral language-games highlights the fact that moral demands do not originate from something outside our human practices. In order to make sense of them, we do not need to postulate practice-independent moral truths. As regards the philosophical demand for a justification of morality as a whole, the analogy shows that it does not make sense. Moral justification performs a function within moral practice, and it cannot simply be extended to the practice as a whole (see 6.4).

2.5.4   Different levels of moral practice

Within moral practices we can distinguish different levels: (1) the level of habitual practice, (2) the level of deliberation within the scope of traditional morality, (3) the level of critical reflection upon traditional morality, and (4) the level of critical reflection upon moral reflection and deliberation itself. Our practices of praising and blaming people, taking them to account and so on become objects of critical moral reflection, and so do our ways of reflecting upon them. Although language-games of the fourth level are more complicated, the players are no less constrained by the rules governing the moral uses of language, as well as by the purposes of moral practice. As James Tully stresses, also 'our most sophisticated forms of reflection, including reflection on language-games of reflection, are practices in the sense that participation in them presupposes customary, intersubjective ways of acting with words'.[44] This implies that not everything can be called into question.

Examples of language-games that can be located at the first level are: blaming someone for having violated a moral rule, calling someone to account, demanding justification from someone who has behaved in a

---

[44] James Tully, 'Wittgenstein and Political Philosophy. Understanding Practices of Critical Reflection,' in *The Grammar of Politics. Wittgenstein and Political Philosophy*, ed. Cressida J. Heyes (Ithaca, NY: Cornell University Press, 2003), p. 26.

morally unacceptable way, or the attempts by an adult to teach a child to act morally.[45] At the second level we reflect on the applicability of a principle in a concrete case, or deliberate about what the right action is in a given situation, referring to the moral norms accepted within our community. For example, we are reflecting at that level when we ponder whether it would in a concrete situation be justified to break a promise.

Cases of reflection upon, for instance, the validity of the rule of faithfulness within a marriage, or upon the moral condemnation of a character trait like greed can be located at the third level, the level of critical reflection on traditional morality. This form of critical moral reasoning is evoked, for instance, by the perplexity in the face of a moral problem, by socio-cultural change, the confrontation with wide-reaching moral disagreement, and so on. Philosophers who engage in meta-ethics and reflect upon the right way of moral reasoning by comparing, for instance, deontological and consequentialist reasoning are playing language-games belonging to the fourth level, as am I in writing this book.

Associated with the level of habitual moral practice is a general moral sensitivity. On that level, the *general* question as to whether our moral beliefs are true (and justified) does not arise. It is only on the fourth level, in the face of apparently fundamental disagreement regarding moral issues – for instance between the members of different cultures – that the question arises as to whether moral beliefs may be classified as true or false. (On levels 2 and 3 we are concerned with the truth and justification of *particular* beliefs, which is a different issue. We presuppose that moral beliefs can in principle be true or false, and that they can be justified.)

Some philosophers reflecting on the fourth level take 'true' to mean in accordance with, or corresponding to, a reality independent of our moral practices. Moral realists and anti-realists disagree over the question as to whether moral judgements express moral facts which are independent of people's evaluative attitudes.[46] The practice-based view can be said to sidestep this debate. As will be shown in Chapter 4 (4.3), the function of the practice of justifying moral judgements is not to assure us or

---

[45] As Hanno Sauer points out, moral reasoning is 'typically performed habitually'. Hanno Sauer, 'Educated Intuitions. Automaticity and Rationality in Moral Judgement,' *Philosophical Explorations* 15, no. 3 (2012), p. 269.

[46] See for example A. J. Ayer, *Language, Truth and Logic* (Harmondsworth: Penguin, 1971 [1936]); David Owen Brink, *Moral Realism and the Foundations of Ethics* (New York: Cambridge University Press, 1989); John L. Mackie, *Ethics: Inventing Right and Wrong* (London 1977); Russ Shafer-Landau, *Moral Realism: A Defense* (Oxford: Oxford University Press, 2003).

others that our judgements accord with the facts (which is by contrast the function of the practice of justifying empirical judgements). Rather, the former practice is aimed, amongst other things, at reaching agreement on binding rules, at clear and widely shared precepts for action, and at moral progress.

2.6 Conclusion

In this chapter, I have introduced central concepts of Wittgenstein's later philosophy and indicated how the view of language expressed in the *Philosophical Investigations* differs from that presented in the *Tractatus*. I have pointed out the central features of language that the game-analogy seeks to highlight, and argued that the purpose of the analogy justifies its application to morality despite the fact that there are significant differences between morality and games. A distinction has been made between different uses of the terms 'moral language-game' and 'moral practice' as well as between different levels of moral practice. It was noted that even at the level of reflection on reflection, not everything can be called into question. The following chapter will provide an interpretation of Wittgenstein's remarks on knowledge, doubt and certainty, which forms the basis for my account of *moral* knowledge, doubt and certainty.

3
Certainty

3.1 Introduction

Having presented some central concepts of the later Wittgenstein, I shall now consider in greater detail his reflections on knowledge, doubt and certainty. This chapter will focus on the notes published as *On Certainty*[1], which I shall seek to interpret within the context of the *Philosophical Investigations* and the notes published as *Remarks on Colour, Last Writings on the Philosophy of Psychology* (hereafter '*Last Writings*'), *Cause and Effect, Remarks on the Foundations of Mathematics*, and *Zettel*. I shall follow Gennip, Kim van who, in her detailed and well-researched study into the historical and philosophical background of *On Certainty*, argues against the common view that it is a 'stand-alone work' and places it 'more firmly in the continuous development of Wittgenstein's thinking'.[2] My reflections on Wittgenstein's views on knowledge, doubt

---

[1] *On Certainty* is comprised of notes written by Wittgenstein during the last eighteen months of his life. It is taken from four different notebooks and 'a bundle of loose sheets'. Gennip, Kim van, *Wittgenstein's* On Certainty *in the Making: Studies into Its Historical and Philosophical Background* (PhD dissertation, Rijksuniversiteit Groningen, 2008), p. 52. He did not have time to revise these notes, in which he attempts to come to grips with something by turning around the same questions and examples time and again. At some points, Wittgenstein expresses his dissatisfaction with the way in which he formulated his thoughts. According to Gennip, Kim van, he was not satisfied with the first 299 paragraphs. Ibid., p. 19. She also points out that Wittgenstein did not clearly separate the sections that were later published as *On Certainty* from those that were published as *Last Writings on the Philosophy of Psychology* Vol. II and *Remarks on Colour*. Ibid., p. 53.
[2] Ibid., p. 167.

and certainty, which of course make no claim to be a comprehensive interpretation of *On Certainty*, provide the basis for my reflections on *moral* knowledge, doubt and certainty.[3] In Chapter 5, I shall present an analogy between certainty regarding the empirical world and moral certainty.

A question that divides interpreters of *On Certainty* is whether that which cannot be reasonably doubted should be conceived of as propositional.[4] While Peter Hacker, Thomas Morawetz, Michael Williams and others defend the propositional reading, Danièle Moyal-Sharrock and Avrum Stroll are the main proponents of the non-propositional reading.[5] In her book *Understanding Wittgenstein's* On Certainty, Moyal-Sharrock presents the latter interpretation in its most developed form.

In the first part of this chapter, I shall focus on the remarks by Wittgenstein in which he reflects on the role of certain propositions. The attempt to interpret those remarks will lead to the view that our language-games are grounded in action, which is spelled out in the second part of the chapter. I thus side with those interpreters who favour a non-propositional reading.

With regard to the use of the term 'proposition' in this chapter, it must be remembered that every occurrence of this term in *On Certainty* is a translation of 'Satz', by which Wittgenstein means both the sentence as well as its linguistic meaning (see introduction, note 10.) Whenever in the following I talk about 'propositions that are beyond doubt' (OC 495) and so on, I use the term 'proposition' in this loose way. I shall also use the term 'sentence', whilst where I wish to emphasise that we are not dealing with propositional contents that can be true or false, I shall use the term 'strings of words'.

---

[3] Since this is not in the first instance a book about *On Certainty*, I have to leave aside a number of interesting exegetical questions.

[4] In German, Wittgenstein's use of the term 'Satz' does not commit him to a propositional account of certainty.

[5] P. M. S. Hacker, *Insight and Illusion: Themes in the Philosophy of Wittgenstein*, rev. ed. (Oxford: Clarendon Press, 1986). Thomas Morawetz, *Wittgenstein & Knowledge: The Importance of* On Certainty (Hassocks, Sussex: Harvester Press, 1980). Michael Williams, 'Wittgenstein, Truth and Certainty,' in *Wittgenstein's Lasting Significance*, ed. Max Kölbel and Bernhard Weiss (London and New York: Routledge, 2004). Danièle Moyal-Sharrock, *Understanding Wittgenstein's* On Certainty (Basingstoke: Palgrave Macmillan, 2004). Avrum Stroll, *Moore and Wittgenstein on Certainty* (New York and Oxford: Oxford University Press, 1994).

3.2   Propositions that are beyond doubt

3.2.1   Examples of cases in which doubt is impossible

In *On Certainty*, Wittgenstein refers to G. E. Moore's claim to know a number of things with certainty.[6] What Moore claims to know seems to be known by everyone, because we do not know what it would mean to doubt these things. We have no idea 'what consequences doubt would have, how it could be removed, and, therefore, what meaning it has' (LW II, p. 46). The examples Wittgenstein considers are numerous, and one of his last remarks echoes his anti-essentialism: 'I can enumerate various typical cases, but not give any common characteristic' (OC 674). However, Wittgenstein does point out some common characteristics of what are often called 'Moorean propositions', a term never used by Wittgenstein himself. Yet, as Andreas Krebs notes, these features – for example being beyond doubt and justification – do not only apply to 'Moorean propositions', but also, for example, to grammatical propositions.[7] It is a problem of many interpretations of *On Certainty* that they over-systematise, thereby overlooking the particularities of the different examples.[8]

These examples are not restricted to the knowledge claims made by Moore. Wittgenstein variegates these claims and adds others, including some that do not seem to be known by everyone, but merely by particular people, or even only by the speaker. The examples include 'I know that

---

[6] G.E. Moore, 'A Defence of Common Sense,' 'Proof of an External World,' and 'Certainty,' in *Philosophical Papers*, ed. G.E. Moore (London and New York: Allen and Unwin, 1959).

[7] Andreas Krebs, *Worauf man sich verlässt* (Würzburg: Königshausen & Neumann, 2007), p. 44. Strictly speaking, these features apply to that which someone like Moore tries to express with those sentences.

[8] This tendency can be found, for instance, in the interpretation of Stefan Rummens and, to a weaker extent, in that of Danièle Moyal-Sharrock. Stefan Rummens, 'On the Possibility of a Wittgensteinian Account of Moral Certainty,' *The Philosophical Forum* 44, no. 2 (2013). Rummens' reconstruction of Wittgenstein's notes results in a systematic account of certainties that does not differentiate sufficiently between the different kinds of examples. For instance, doubting a certainty is not always 'a form of insanity'. It can also be a sign of incompetence, for example linguistic incompetence. While Moyal-Sharrock accounts for some of the differences by dividing Wittgenstein's examples into four groups, she over-generalises by claiming that all certainties are expressions of grammatical rules. This view will be criticised below (3.2.5). Examples of interpreters who are particularly sensitive to the differences between the examples are Yaniv Iczkovits and Andreas Krebs.

here is my hand', 'I know that that's a tree', 'I know that my name is L.W.', 'I know that the earth existed long before my birth', 'I know that I was never on the moon', 'I know that I am a human being', and 'I know that water boils at 100°C' (OC 4, 40, 84, 91 ff., 327, 567, 576, 585 and 667).

'I know that here is my hand' refers to Moore's 'Proof of an External World', where Moore sets out to prove the existence of the external world by way of holding up his hands, saying 'Here are two hands', and concluding that at this time two human hands exist.[9] According to Moore, it has thus *ipso facto* been proven that some external objects exist. This follows from his definition of objects which can be met in space. The proof itself which is stated in a few sentences presupposes the establishment of several things, which makes it much more complex than it first seems. For our present purposes the crucial point is that Moore claims to know the premise of his proof, that is that what he is holding up are in fact his hands. This use of 'I know' is criticised by Wittgenstein.

It is characteristic of Wittgenstein's discussion of the topic that he is concerned with certain uses of propositions and not with the propositions as such. In particular, he is concerned with the use the philosopher makes of the words 'I know' (see for example OC 347).[10] He does not criticise the many innocent uses of 'I know' occurring in everyday life: 'For each of these sentences [Moore's; J.H.] I can imagine circumstances that turn it into a move in one of our language-games, and by that it loses everything that is philosophically astonishing' (OC 622). And: 'As soon as I think of an everyday use of the sentence ['I know that that's a tree'; J.H.] instead of a philosophical one, its meaning becomes clear and ordinary' (OC 347). Yet for some of the examples (for example 'I know that I am a human being') it is much harder to imagine such circumstances than for others (see OC 622).

Although it is possible to think of circumstances in which the respective sentences have sense, such circumstances are rare. Under normal circumstances, saying 'I know that that's a tree' or 'I know that I am a human being' does not make sense. If my friend and I were sitting under a tree and in the middle of our conversation she said all of a sudden 'I know that that's a tree', I would be perplexed and not know what she

---

[9] Moore here responds to Kant's complaint mentioned in the introduction (the complaint that 'the existence of things outside of us [...] must be accepted merely on faith'). Moore, 'Proof of an External World,' p. 127.

[10] As he writes elsewhere: 'The examples which philosophers give in the first person should be investigated in the third' (LW II, p. 44).

meant. I would wonder whether she was making a joke, and if it turned out that this was not the case, I would probably question her sanity. Likewise, utterances of doubt and attempts to provide justification for what these sentences express do not make sense in ordinary circumstances. Depending on the situation, they may suggest a lack of seriousness, (linguistic) incompetence, or even madness.

Human beings normally do not doubt certain things, for example that the earth existed 150 years ago or that there are physical objects. They do not have reasons to doubt these states of affairs, and reasons are required in order for a doubt to get off the ground (OC 4 and 122).[11] Despite being 'beyond doubt' (OC 495), the examples Wittgenstein looks at are not things we can be said to know, at least not in ordinary contexts, because we are unable to provide reasons for them which are more certain than they are (OC 91).[12] Thus, being beyond doubt coincides with not being justified. Wittgenstein remarks:

> The queer thing is that even though I find it quite correct for someone to say 'Rubbish!' ('Unsinn') and so brush aside the attempt to confuse him with doubts at bedrock, – nevertheless, I hold it to be incorrect if he seeks to defend himself (using, for example, the words 'I know').
>
> *On Certainty*, § 498

If someone confuses me with doubts at bedrock, he requires a justification where none is needed or even possible. I am entitled to brush his attempt aside, because by virtue of being beyond doubt, what makes up the bedrock is beyond justification. It is wrong to respond with a knowledge claim to the doubts, since what I would claim to know would not be justified.[13]

---

[11] As demonstrated by Gennip, Kim van, cases in which doubt makes no sense already occupied Wittgenstein in his lectures on private experience (1934–1936). Although concerned with knowledge and certainty of private experiences, not of physical objects, there is a striking similarity between several thoughts of *On Certainty* and those expressed in the lectures. Gennip, Kim van, *Wittgenstein's On Certainty in the Making: Studies into Its Historical and Philosophical Background*, pp. 158 ff.

[12] He states in relation to the belief that the earth existed before our birth that 'we are not at all capable of giving reasons for this because seemingly there are too many' (LW II, p. 53).

[13] Wittgenstein subscribes to the classical definition of knowledge as justified, true belief.

According to Wittgenstein, in cases where it would not make sense to say 'I don't know x', it does not make sense to say 'I know x' either (OC 58). He distinguishes between certainty and knowledge (OC 58, 151 and 194).[14] Cases where someone has knowledge of something are cases in which it can be said how he knows what he claims to know.[15] One says '"I know" when one is ready to give compelling grounds. "I know" relates to a possibility of demonstrating the truth' (OC 243).[16] Cases in which we know something are cases in which doubts are conceivable and it is possible to be mistaken. Knowledge and doubt are 'two sides of the same coin'.[17] I use the verb 'to know' wrongly if I apply it to cases where 'I rightly say that I cannot be making a mistake' (OC 674). A mistake is like a false move in a game. It presupposes that we are still thinking and speaking in accordance with the rules. We could say that it is part of the grammar of the language-game 'making a knowledge claim' that a mistake regarding the content of that claim is possible.

Following Moyal-Sharrock, I will refer to the certainty Wittgenstein deals with as 'objective'.[18] I take this to be an adequate term because Wittgenstein targets cases in which doubt and mistake are 'logically impossible' (OC 194 and 454), that is are excluded by the rules of the language-game. He emphasises that he is not interested in subjective certainty, or in other words a *feeling* of certainty (OC 194 and 415). For the sake of simplicity I shall refer below to 'certainties' and 'propositions that are beyond doubt', although features such as being beyond doubt and justification apply to that which someone in a particular case seeks to express with a 'Moorean proposition'.

---

[14] Like many of the thoughts expressed in *On Certainty*, this distinction has 'a long history'. It dates back to the late 1930s. Gennip, Kim van, Wittgenstein's *On Certainty* in the Making: Studies into Its Historical and Philosophical Background,p. 30, note 49, and p. 124.

[15] 'If someone believes something, we needn't always be able to answer the question "why he believes it"; but if he knows something, then the question "how does he know?" must be capable of being answered' (OC 550). 'How is it shown that someone knows something? For only if that is clear is the concept of knowing clear' (LW II, p. 58).

[16] See also: 'How does the language-game work then – when do we say we "know"? [...] Isn't it when we have evidence of a certain sort? – And then it's a matter of the evidence, without which it isn't knowing' (CE, p. 391).

[17] Gennip, Kim van, Wittgenstein's *On Certainty* in the Making: Studies into Its Historical and Philosophical Background, p. 20. See LW II, p. 92.

[18] Moyal-Sharrock, *Understanding Wittgenstein's* On Certainty: p. 25.

3.2.2 The peculiar logical role of some 'empirical' propositions

In one of the earlier paragraphs of *On Certainty*, Wittgenstein states that '[w]hen Moore says he *knows* such and such, he is really enumerating a lot of empirical propositions which we affirm without special testing; propositions, that is, which have a peculiar logical role in the system of our empirical propositions' (OC 136). However, as later passages show, that the respective propositions are empirical is ultimately not Wittgenstein's position (see for example OC 308 and 401).[19] The role that these sentences play in the context of Moore's use of them can be illuminated by comparing it to the role of mathematical and grammatical propositions.[20]

---

[19] Of course this too is disputed amongst interpreters. My impression is that Wittgenstein attempts to improve his understanding of the cases in which we have no reasons to doubt and cannot be mistaken, thereby correcting himself from time to time. As mentioned above (note 1), he apparently was not content with paragraphs 1–299 of *On Certainty*. Dissatisfaction with certain formulations is also expressed at later stages, for example: 'Here I am inclined to fight windmills, because I cannot yet say the thing I really want to say' (OC 400).

[20] Some interpreters have identified Moorean propositions with grammatical propositions, including for example Michael Kober, *Gewißheit als Norm. Wittgenstein's erkenntnistheoretische Untersuchungen in* Über Gewißheit (Berlin and New York: de Gruyter, 1993). Others have rejected such an identification. See Timo-Peter Ertz, *Regel und Witz. Wittgensteinsche Perspektiven auf Mathematik, Sprache und Moral* (Berlin and New York: de Gruyter, 2008); Krebs, *Worauf man sich verlässt*. Moyal-Sharrock conceives of our non-propositional certainty as grammatical. Her conception of grammar is much broader than that of for instance Krebs. According to the broad understanding of grammar that she ascribes to the 'third' Wittgenstein, grammatical propositions are 'bounds of sense'. Moyal-Sharrock, *Understanding Wittgenstein's* On Certainty, pp. 85 ff. The formulation 'the third Wittgenstein' refers to the view that we should add a third Wittgenstein to the standard distinction between the early and the later Wittgenstein. The works of that third Wittgenstein are those written after the *Philosophical Investigations*. This view is associated with the claim that *On Certainty* has long been underestimated and should be conceived of as Wittgenstein's third great work. Ibid., p. 164. This position might seem to be in conflict with Gennip, Kim van's view of *On Certainty* as containing reflections on topics that had occupied Wittgenstein for a long time already, and with her emphasis on the fact that the final form of this work is the result of some rather arbitrary editorial decisions (see note 1). However, the points emphasised by Gennip, Kim van are compatible with Moyal-Sharrock's insistence that the post-*Investigation* works go beyond Wittgenstein's previous writings and make an important contribution to philosophy. See Danièle Moyal-Sharrock, *The Third Wittgenstein: The Post-Investigation Works*, (Aldershot, UK: Ashgate, 2004) and 'Beyond Hacker's Wittgenstein: Discussion of HACKER, Peter (2012) 'Wittgenstein on Grammar, Theses and Dogmatism' *Philosophical Investigations* 35: 1, January 2012, 1–17,' *Philosophical Investigations* 36, no. 4 (2013).

In the notes published as *Remarks on the Foundations of Mathematics*, Wittgenstein expresses the thought that there are propositions which play a different role from empirical propositions:

> Let us remember that in mathematics we are convinced of *grammatical* propositions; so the expression, the result, of our being convinced is that we *accept a rule*.
>
> The proposition proved by means of the proof *serves as a rule* – and so as a paradigm. For we go by the rule.
>
> But does the proof only bring us to the point of going by this rule (accepting it), or does it also shew us how we are to go by it?
>
> For the mathematical proposition is to shew us *what it makes sense to say*.
>
> > *Remarks on the Foundations of Mathematics,*
> > part III, sections 26 and 28 (my italics)

A mathematical proposition functions as a grammatical proposition which shows us what we can meaningfully say. Within the metaphor of the language-game, serving as a rule and playing the role of a grammatical proposition are equivalent. Grammatical propositions express the rules of language-games. To the question '*What* is unshakably certain about what is proved?' Wittgenstein responds: 'To accept a proposition as unshakably certain – I want to say – means to use it as a grammatical rule: this removes uncertainty from it' (RFM III 39).

A proposition belongs to grammar by virtue of its role within a language-game, and not because of some intrinsic property.[21] It is crucial for Wittgenstein's view that the certainty attached to mathematical propositions results from our use of them.[22] They could not fulfil their role of determining sense if we did not regard them as certain. Therefore, '[t]he question here is not really one of certainty but of something stipulated by us' (RFM I 120). Elsewhere he makes this point in relation to signs and rules in general: a rule is fixed by the way we act (PI 198).[23]

---

[21] See Michael Kober, 'On Epistemic and Moral Certainty: A Wittgensteinian Approach,' *International Journal of Philosophical Studies* 5, no. 3 (1997): p. 369.

[22] See also RC I 32: '[It is; J.H.] the use, which distinguishes the logical proposition from the empirical one.'

[23] See Meredith Williams, *Wittgenstein, Mind and Meaning* (London: Routledge, 1999), p. 200: '[A] Wittgensteinian conception of practice is one in which an object becomes a standard or norm in virtue of the ways in which that object is used.'

Also the certainties that are the subject of *On Certainty* owe their status to the way we (do not) use them, that is to our treatment of them.[24] *On Certainty* contains a remark that clearly echoes the passage quoted above: '[P]erfect certainty is only a matter of their [people's; J.H.] attitude' (OC 404). The view that the certainty of a proposition results from the way in which it is used does not imply that we as individuals simply decide how to treat a particular proposition. Rather, it is assumed that we treat certain propositions as fixed as a matter of our common practice. The attitude in question is one that we share with the other participants in the respective practice(s).

Wittgenstein emphasises that a proposition like 'Here is a hand' is no less certain than a mathematical proposition (OC 651 and 653). He makes the grammatical remark that '[t]he physical game is just as certain as the arithmetical', thereby placing certain statements about objects on the same level of certainty as mathematical propositions (OC 447, see 340). Neither the proposition '12 x 12 = 144' nor 'Here is one hand' are immune from the possibility that we may be deceived by our senses (OC 446 f.): 'the mathematical proposition has been obtained by a series of actions that are in no way different from the actions of the rest of our lives, and are in the same degree liable to forgetfulness, oversight and illusion' (OC 651).

With this consideration, Wittgenstein denies mathematical 'truths' a superior position within human knowledge. On the one hand, they become as 'liable to forgetfulness, oversight and illusion' as empirical propositions. On the other hand, some statements about objects become as indubitable as mathematical propositions, because of the way we learn

---

[24] The term 'use' could be misleading in this context, since it is characteristic of certainties that they are normally not formulated propositionally. The view that Wittgenstein's remarks on mathematical propositions can illuminate his notes on propositions that are beyond doubt is supported by Gennip, Kim van's study, which demonstrates that Wittgenstein's account of knowledge and certainty is ultimately rooted in his criticism of intuitionism in mathematics. Gennip, Kim van, *Wittgenstein's* On Certainty *in the Making: Studies into Its Historical and Philosophical Background, PhD dissertation*, p. 108. Marie McGinn's discussion of the peculiarity of Moorean propositions also departs from Wittgenstein's reflections on the role of mathematical propositions. Marie McGinn, *Sense and Certainty. A Dissolution of Scepticism* (Oxford: Basil Blackwell, 1989), pp. 121 ff. Wittgenstein was critical of L. E. J. Brouwer's account of rule-following in mathematics, according to which the application of a mathematical rule requires 'a fresh intuition at every step'. Gennip, Kim van, *Wittgenstein's* On Certainty *in the Making: Studies into Its Historical and Philosophical Background, PhD dissertation*, p. 111. I will not go into the details of Wittgenstein's critique.

and use them: 'We learn with the same inexorability that this is a chair as that 2 x 2 = 4' (OC 455). Wittgenstein asks: 'If one doesn't marvel at the fact that the propositions of arithmetic (e.g. the multiplication tables) are "absolutely certain", then why should one be astonished that the proposition "This is my hand" is so equally?' (OC 448). Attributing their certainty to our attitude towards them, Wittgenstein deprives mathematical propositions of their status as indubitable truths.

The role of a mathematical proposition, which resembles that of a grammatical proposition and which is said to be fundamentally different from the role of an empirical proposition,[25] thus appears to be similar to the 'peculiar logical role' of the propositions Wittgenstein is puzzled by in *On Certainty* (OC 136). Contrary to appearance, these propositions are only *apparently* empirical: 'I am inclined to believe that not everything that has the form of an empirical proposition *is* one' (OC 308). In the *Philosophical Investigations* he talks about 'something whose form makes it look like an empirical proposition, but which is really a grammatical one' (PI 251).

In many of the cases Wittgenstein reflects upon in *On Certainty*, the role of the respective proposition resembles the role of a grammatical proposition. He writes that not only propositions of logic but also those that are statements about material objects 'form the foundation of all operating with thoughts (with language)' (OC 401). Moyal-Sharrock interprets this as the realisation that grammar is much more comprehensive than Wittgenstein used to think, and that it includes 'certainties of our world-picture'.[26] Wittgenstein remarks in relation to the propositions that describe his 'world-picture' that 'their role is like that of rules of a game' (OC 95). This world-picture itself is 'the inherited background against which I distinguish between true and false' (OC 94).

There is a striking similarity between those passages from *On Certainty* where Wittgenstein reflects on cases in which we are convinced that we cannot doubt something or cannot be making a mistake and his remarks elsewhere regarding the inconceivability of the opposite of what some propositions state (see for example OC 32, 117, 219 ff., 380, 624 ff.). He

---

[25] See RFM I 110 f., where Wittgenstein points 'to the *fundamental difference*, together with an apparent similarity, between the roles of an arithmetical proposition and an empirical proposition'.

[26] Danièle Moyal-Sharrock, 'Coming to Language: Wittgenstein's Social "Theory" of Language Acquisition,' in *Language and World: Essays on the Philosophy of Wittgenstein*, ed. V. Munz, K. Puhl, and J. Wang (Frankfurt am Main: Ontos Verlag, 2010), p. 306.

writes that by saying of a proposition that we are unable to imagine the opposite, we ascribe the role of a grammatical proposition to it, whereas 'to say of a proposition: "This could be imagined otherwise" or "We can imagine the opposite too", ascribes the role of an empirical proposition to it' (RFM IV 4). The words 'I can't imagine the opposite of this' are 'a defence against something whose form makes it look like an empirical proposition, but which is really a grammatical one' (PI 251). And: 'A proposition which it is supposed to be impossible to imagine as other than true has a different *function* from one for which this does not hold' (RFM IV 4).[27] Thus, the proposition 'Every rod has a length' differs in function from 'This table has the same length as the one over there'. With regard to the latter it is understandable what it means to have a picture of the opposite (PI 251).

3.2.3   The distinction between senseless propositions and nonsense

In *On Certainty*, Wittgenstein looks at situations where the utterance of certain propositions makes no sense. Elsewhere, he tells us why it usually does not make sense to utter grammatical propositions: these propositions *determine* sense.[28] As he writes in the *Remarks on the Foundations of Mathematics*: 'What I always do seems to be – to emphasise a distinction between the determination of a sense and the employment of a sense' (RFM III 37). That a proposition is senseless means that 'a combination of words is being excluded from the language', that it is not used (PI 500). Wittgenstein writes in *On Certainty* that '[m]uch [...] is removed from the traffic', it is 'shunted onto an unused siding' (OC 210). It is 'only in use that [a] proposition has its sense' (OC 10).

Calling a proposition 'nonsense' is not the same as to say that it is senseless. Many interpreters mistakenly use the terms 'senseless' and 'nonsense' ('sinnlos' and 'Unsinn') interchangeably. In the *Tractatus*, Wittgenstein clearly distinguishes between senseless propositions and propositions that are nonsense. The propositions of mathematics and

---

[27] In spite of appearances, he is not concerned with necessary truth. He makes observations about the different functions of sentences, and those which we cannot imagine as being anything other than true in fact lack truth value.

[28] An exception is a 'teaching-game'. In a context in which someone is being taught the meaning of certain words, propositions about the use of words can be meaningfully uttered. Yet the propositions themselves remain senseless even in that context, given that they are not open to doubt. The teaching could not be successful if either the teacher or the pupil questioned the things taught (OC 160 and 283).

logic are senseless, whilst philosophical propositions turn out to be nonsense (TLP 4.461, 4.4611, and 6.54). Although the distinction is still present in Wittgenstein's later philosophy, his use of the two terms does not reveal a clear picture of their meaning.[29] The idea seems to be that a senseless proposition becomes nonsense if it is conceived of as one that has sense, that is, a use. For example a proposition playing the role of a grammatical proposition becomes nonsense when it is conceived of as playing the role of an empirical proposition. Wittgenstein asks why we have the tendency to affirm the proposition 'This body has extension' instead of calling it nonsense (PI 252). The answer is that it strikes us as expressing something natural or obvious. As I understand Wittgenstein, the proposition 'This body has extension' is nonsense, if it is understood as performing the role of an empirical proposition. It is merely senseless, that is it lacks use, if it is understood to perform the role of a grammatical proposition, that is, as saying that the term 'body' is correctly applied to extended things. Also regarding Moore's use of 'This is one hand' we have the tendency to affirm it rather than calling it nonsense. The proposition would merely be senseless (and not nonsense) if it were treated as expressing something that is objectively certain.

Wittgenstein also characterises 'talking nonsense' as the use of 'a mode of speaking that is valid in *one* language-game in another one where it doesn't belong' (LW II, p. 48). We can apply this to Moore, saying that his use of 'I know' does not belong to his language-game. He borrows it from ordinary contexts in which people are able to provide reasons for what they claim to know. In such contexts it is valid, that is it is possible to make a move in the language-game by saying 'I know'.[30]

3.2.4   Change of status of a proposition

As I understand Wittgenstein, a string of words can play different roles in different contexts and at different times. The metaphor of the river-bed can be interpreted as depicting how a role changes over time:

It might be imagined that some propositions, of the form of empirical propositions, were hardened and functioned as channels for such

---

[29] See Stroll, *Moore and Wittgenstein on Certainty*: p. 115.

[30] In the words of Stanley Cavell: 'What is left out of an expression when it is used 'outside its ordinary language-game' is not necessarily what the words mean [...], but what we mean in using them when and where we do. The point of saying them is lost.' Stanley Cavell, *The Claim of Reason: Wittgenstein, Skepticism, Morality and Tragedy* (Oxford: Oxford University Press, 1979), p. 207.

empirical propositions as were not hardened but fluid; and that this relation altered with time, in that fluid propositions hardened, and hard ones became fluid.

The mythology may change back into a state of flux, the river-bed of thoughts may shift. But I distinguish between the movements of the waters on the river-bed and the shift of the bed itself; though there is not a sharp division of the one from the other.

But if someone were to say 'So logic too is an empirical science' he would be wrong. Yet this is right: the same proposition may get treated at one time as something to test by experience, at another as a rule of testing.

And the bank of that river consists partly of hard rock, subject to no alteration or only to an imperceptible one, partly of sand, which now in one place now in another gets washed away, or deposited.

On Certainty, §§ 96–99[31]

Wittgenstein claims that there is no sharp distinction between the movement of water over the river-bed of thoughts (strings of words playing the role of an empirical proposition) and the alteration of the river-bed itself (strings of words playing the role of a grammatical proposition or a similar role). His remark that propositions of the form of empirical propositions can be hardened, while hard propositions can become fluid again, can be understood as saying that propositions can change their roles. In a paragraph preceding the metaphor of the river-bed, Wittgenstein asks: 'Can't an assertoric sentence, which was capable of functioning as a hypothesis, also be used as a foundation for research and action?' (OC 87). He also distinguishes between different parts of the bank of the river: hard rock and sand. Here I take him to refer respectively to beliefs that are beyond doubt in every context and to beliefs that are subject to role changes. This distinction thus reflects differences between the examples Wittgenstein considers. According to Krebs, who thinks that Moorean propositions 'stand in a very peculiar way between rule and empirical proposition', 'hard rock' stands for propositions that are more like grammatical propositions, whilst 'sand' stands for those that are more like empirical propositions.[32]

'No one has ever been on the moon' is an example of a proposition that became fluid again. While for Wittgenstein it was beyond doubt,

---

See also RC I 32: 'Sentences are often used on the borderline between logic and the empirical, so that their meaning changes back and forth and they count now as expressions of norms, now as expressions of experience.'

[32] Krebs, *Worauf man sich verlässt*, pp. 76 f.

we today treat it as a false empirical proposition. The example 'This is a hand', to which Wittgenstein returns continuously, plays the role of an empirical proposition in very special contexts. If, for example, I had been waking up after an operation, finding my entire arms in bandages, not knowing whether my hands had been amputated, I could, by uttering such a proposition, express my conviction that at least one of my hands was still there. In this case, it would be possible that I was mistaken.

3.2.5 The heterogeneity of the examples of objective certainty

The view that the sentences considered by Wittgenstein are grammatical propositions ascribes a homogeneity to Wittgenstein's examples that they in fact lack. In a number of places in *On Certainty*, Wittgenstein refers to grammar or logic and considers the possibility that certain propositions belong to it. However, he does not go so far as to account for these sentences as grammatical propositions. In this section, I will point out some differences between the examples and mention a further problem for the view that the propositions that are beyond doubt have grammatical status.

Wittgenstein does not claim that all of Moore's propositions play the *same* role, but that their 'role in the system of our empirical judgements' is *similar* (OC 137). That not all of the propositions considered by Wittgenstein have the same role is emphasised by Iczkovits, who points to the fact that not all of them are such that, were they to turn out to be false, this would drag our conceptual system into chaos.[33] Wittgenstein writes in connection with *some* of his examples that 'a doubt would drag everything with it and plunge it into chaos', and that 'the foundation of all judging would be taken away from me' (OC 613 f., see also OC 494). In other cases, it would be possible to abandon the respective conviction without thereby losing one's standards for judging. Were scientists for instance to falsify the proposition that water boils at 100°C, this would not amount to the 'annihilation of all yardsticks' (OC 492).

There is one example to which Wittgenstein explicitly denies logical status: 'My name is L.W.' He says that this proposition does not belong to logic, because 'the language-game that operates with people's names' does not depend on the fact that he is not mistaken about his name (OC 628). As noted above, it is crucial for the examples taken from Moore's 'Defence of Common Sense' that we all seem to know them with certainty. Unlike

---

[33] Iczkovits, *Wittgenstein's Ethical Thought*, p. 133.

them, the certainty regarding one's name is restricted to the speaker. While 'the language-game that operates with people's names' does not depend on the fact that I am not mistaken about my name, the language-game that operates with historical data does depend on the fact that I am not mistaken in my belief that the earth existed long before my birth.[34] Here it is not important that *I* am mistaken about the long age of the earth, but that the practice would not be the same if it turned out that the earth had only come into existence shortly before I was born. This does not mean that my belief grounds the practice of history (see 3.2.6).

It is moreover far from clear whether Moorean propositions or propositions about such propositions are supposed to be grammatical. Thus, Wittgenstein says of the proposition 'I cannot doubt this proposition without giving up all judgement' that it has 'the character of a rule' (OC 494). In *Cause and Effect* he writes: 'A philosopher who protests [against a sceptic], 'We KNOW there's a chair over there!' is simply describing a game' (CE, p. 381). Thus it seems that it is not propositions such as 'This is a chair' that have the status of a rule, but propositions such as 'I know that this is a chair' or 'I cannot doubt this proposition without giving up all judgment' (OC 494), that is propositions forming part of the description of language-games that include propositions such as 'This is a chair'.

If an understanding of some moral propositions as grammatical can be reconciled with the differences between the examples at all, it requires a broad conception of grammar such as that suggested by Moyal-Sharrock. Since it would take up too much space to delve deeper into the question over whether we should conceive of objective certainty as being grammatical in Moyal-Sharrock's sense, I shall leave this as an open question and turn to Wittgenstein's use of foundationalist and coherentist metaphors.[35]

3.2.6   Wittgenstein's foundationalist and coherentist metaphors

Wittgenstein's position in *On Certainty*, in its incomplete form, points to an alternative to the foundationalist and coherentist views of justification

---

[34] The first game does 'presuppose that it is nonsensical to say that the majority of people are mistaken about their names' (OC 628). What depends on me not being mistaken about my name is my ability to trust my own judgements.

[35] For most of the time that I have been writing this book I subscribed to the view that we should conceive of the strings of words that express certainties as playing the role of a grammatical proposition. I now tend to think that this view is mistaken, but since not too much hangs on it with regard to my endeavour in this book, I will leave it open for the time being. It is one of Wittgenstein's intellectual virtues that he does not generalise prematurely, and I wish to follow his example as well as I can.

mentioned in the introduction (1.4.2). It was argued there that, unlike foundationalists and coherentists, Wittgenstein does not aim to provide a solution to the regress problem. Nevertheless, *On Certainty* contains a number of both foundationalist and coherentist metaphors which make his position look at times foundationalist and at times coherentist. As I shall argue in this section, coherence has a different role in his account than it has in coherence theories of justification and, despite his use of foundationalist metaphors and terminology, he should not be regarded as a foundationalist.

Wittgenstein seems to assume, like an empirical foundationalist, some sort of basic beliefs.[36] He uses the terms 'bedrock', 'rock bottom of my convictions', and 'foundation of all judging', and speaks about propositions that 'underlie all questions and all thinking' (OC 498, 248, 614 and 415). However, in contrast to the basic beliefs postulated by foundationalists, the ones he takes from Moore, and those he adds, lack both truth value and justification. They are thus not items of knowledge. Despite these differences between Wittgenstein's idea of basic beliefs and that of foundationalists, Wittgenstein's position has been interpreted as a (special) form of foundationalism.[37]

The fact that Wittgenstein sometimes speaks about their truth has led some interpreters to believe that these propositions can be true or false, whereas Wittgenstein explicitly writes that they can be regarded as true only in a special sense: they are true only inasmuch as they are 'an unmoving foundation of [our] language-games' (OC 403).[38] Instead of saying that they are true, we should say that they 'stand fast' for us (OC 152).[39] Justification and truth are only applicable to propositions that operate as an empirical proposition.

In discussing cases where doubt is impossible, Wittgenstein also makes use of coherentist metaphors. He writes that what 'stands fast [...] is

[36] I refer to these basic beliefs also as convictions and as judgements.

[37] See for example G.D. Conway, *Wittgenstein on Foundations* (Humanity Books, 1989); R. Shiner, 'Foundationalism, Coherentism and Activism,' *Philosophical Investigations* 3 (1980); Nigel Pleasants, 'Wittgenstein, Ethics and Basic Moral Certainty,' *Inquiry* 51, no. 3 (2008); Stroll, *Moore and Wittgenstein on Certainty*.

[38] One of the interpreters who take almost all of Wittgenstein's examples to be 'straightforwardly true' is Williams, 'Wittgenstein, Truth and Certainty.' Pleasants claims that the beliefs in question are true, though neither analytically nor necessarily true. Pleasants, 'Wittgenstein, Ethics and Basic Moral Certainty,' p. 250, note 5.

[39] That truth is not what is at stake here is emphasised for instance by Moyal-Sharrock, *Understanding Wittgenstein's* On Certainty, p. 86, note 23.

[...] held fast by what lies around it' (OC 144),[40] that 'the movement around [the axis; J.H.] determines its immobility', that the propositions concerned are like hinges on which our questions and doubts turn, and that the 'foundation-walls are carried by the whole house' (OC 152, 341 and 248).[41] It therefore comes as no surprise that his account has been interpreted as a form of coherentism as well.[42]

As has been pointed out by Peter Winch and subsequently stressed by Iczkovits, the hinge-metaphor differs from the metaphor of the axis. Although interpreters have tended to focus on the former, using terms such as 'hinge propositions', 'hinge beliefs' or 'hinges', the latter seems to be more suitable for expressing Wittgenstein's view of that which is certain.[43] While hinges are stuck to something, fixed independently of the motion of the door, the immobility of the axis is determined by the movement around it (OC 152). The existence and meaning of the axis depend on that movement.[44] This metaphor encapsulates the idea that that which stands fast has not explicitly been determined by anyone, but is fixed by our practice of judging.[45] Changes within our empirical judgements occur around those points of rest.[46]

That which is beyond doubt is therefore not isolated from the realm of knowledge, justification and doubt. If we were for example asked whether the earth really existed before we were born, we could not 'answer the questioner by way of *one* particular piece of instruction, but only by gradually imparting to him a picture of our world' (LW II, p. 53). Some of Wittgenstein's remarks in *On Certainty* suggest a picture of beliefs that

---

[40] 'What stands fast does so, not because it is intrinsically obvious or convincing; it is rather held fast by what lies around it.' Since the formulations 'stand fast' and 'held fast' are common in the literature on *On Certainty*, I also use them, along with 'are fixed', 'are certain' and 'are beyond doubt' as synonyms for 'stand fast'.

[41] See also LW II, p. 53: 'The one seems to be supported by the other, but neither obviously serves as the basis for the other.'

[42] See for example Yong Huang, 'Religious Beliefs after Foundationalism: Wittgenstein between Nielsen and Phillips,' *Religious Studies: An International Journal for the Philosophy of Religion* 31, no. 2 (1995).

[43] Iczkovits, *Wittgenstein's Ethical Thought*: p. 134. The view that not all of the metaphors used by Wittgenstein are equally suitable for his purposes fits in well with Moyal-Sharrock's interpretation of *On Certainty* as a 'nonlinear and nonprogressive struggle [...] to understand the nature of our foundational beliefs'. Moyal-Sharrock, *Understanding Wittgenstein's* On Certainty: p. 89.

[44] Peter Winch, 'Judgment: Propositions and Practices,' *Philosophical Investigations* 21 (1998): p. 198.

[45] Krebs, *Worauf man sich verlässt*, p. 75.

[46] Ibid.

cannot reasonably be doubted as being fixed by our empirical beliefs and *vice versa*. The fundamental role of certain beliefs is thus explained by coherence,[47] that is not by an intrinsic property but by their relations with other beliefs and by their position within our 'web of beliefs', to use a term coined by Quine. Instead of 'web of beliefs' we could also say 'practices'.

These relations between beliefs must not be confused with relations of justification, which range from what is less certain to what is more certain. Krebs stresses that Wittgenstein rejects a coherentist view of justification and that here we are dealing with two independent structures. While the relationship between a justifying belief and the belief it justifies is asymmetric, the relationship of coherence is symmetric. These two relationships constitute 'independent and complementary structures of rationality'.[48]

To assert that the 'foundation-walls are carried by the whole house' means to state that what belongs to the foundation owes its role to the practice of making judgements. It is that practice which turns something into a foundation.[49] Iczkovits has a similar view, but he refers to several practices which relate to a certainty in this way. The conviction that the earth has existed for many years past, for instance, acquired the status of a certainty through the practices that revolve around it such as history and geology. However, the relationship is not only one-way: 'There is a constant *interpenetration* between our thoughts and modes of thoughts, between facts and our frame of reference.'[50] We end up taking for granted that the Earth has existed for a long time by virtue of our participation in certain practices, and those practices are in turn influenced by that certainty. Krebs makes the point by using one of Wittgenstein's metaphors: the foundation-walls 'sustain our reasons and are at the same time sustained by the coherence of the whole'.[51]

As mentioned above, it is the *fundamental role* of some beliefs which considerations of coherence can explain. As far as justification is concerned, Wittgenstein's view is closer to foundationalism than to coherentism, and we might want to ascribe a form of weak foundationalism to him.[52] However, the problem with ascribing any type of foundationalism to him is that it is usually conceived of as providing

---

[47] Krebs, *Worauf man sich verlässt*, p. 104.
[48] Ibid., p. 108, my translation.
[49] Ibid.
[50] Iczkovits, *Wittgenstein's Ethical Thought*, p. 134.
[51] Krebs, *Worauf man sich verlässt*, p. 108, my translation.
[52] For an explanation of weak foundationalism see introduction, note 30.

a solution to the regress problem, while for Wittgenstein that problem does not arise in the first place (see 1.5). Therefore, I will refrain from classifying Wittgenstein's stance in this way, and simply state that he makes use of foundationalist terminology in order to express the fact that human beings rely on objective certainties in all of their activities, and that doubt has no reference point.

3.3   The acting underlying the language-game

3.3.1   The apparent tension

I have so far focused on those remarks made in *On Certainty* in which Wittgenstein considers Moore's propositions and other propositions. These remarks suggest that any justification has to stop where we reach propositions for which mistakes and doubt are impossible. However, this interpretation seems to conflict with passages such as the following: 'As if giving grounds did not come to an end sometime. But the end is not an ungrounded presupposition: it is an ungrounded way of acting' (OC 110). Wittgenstein claims that it is 'our *acting*, which lies at the bottom of the language-game' (OC 204). This conviction is frequently expressed by variations of the phrase 'This is simply how we act' (see for example PI 211 and 217).[53] He contrasts the acting in question with 'a kind of *seeing* on our part' (OC 204).

As will be argued in this section, the apparent tension between Wittgenstein's remarks about propositions that are beyond doubt and the passages in which he stresses that justification does not terminate with ungrounded propositions can be resolved.[54] I shall try to throw some light on his remarks about human action, relating them to other passages and presenting plausible interpretations proposed by others. We shall see that Wittgenstein might be referring to different things, including shared natural reactions, unreflective uses of language, unreflective non-linguistic actions, and the regularity with which we act. All of these are related to propositions that are beyond doubt.

3.3.2   Animal certainty

Clues for what Wittgenstein has in mind when he is referring to 'our acting' can be found in passages in which he compares objective

---

[53] 'If I have exhausted the justifications I have reached bedrock, and my spade is turned. Then I am inclined to say: 'This is simply what I do.' (PI 217).

[54] The view that justification terminates with ungrounded propositions has been referred to as the 'ordinary language view' or 'groundless foundationalism' (see 1.4.2).

certainty with the certainty of an animal or an infant, as well as in remarks about the primitive form of a language-game. Let us first look at the former:

> Now I would like to regard this certainty, not as something akin to hastiness or superficiality, but as a form of life. (That is very badly expressed and probably badly thought as well.)
>
> But that means I want to conceive it as something that lies beyond being justified or unjustified; as it were, as something animal.
>
> Does a child believe that milk exists? Or does it know that milk exists? Does a cat know that a mouse exists?
>
> On Certainty, §§ 358–359 and 478

We sometimes say that a baby or child knows something 'instinctively', for example that it can find milk in its mother's breasts. What we mean by that is something very different from proper knowledge. While we would not ascribe knowledge to an infant, the infant's behaviour shows that it takes the existence of milk for granted. It communicates that it wants milk, it drinks milk, and sometimes it refuses it. Similarly, that a cat has no doubt whatsoever regarding the existence of mice is shown through its behaviour. It chases mice, plays with them and brings them home. It is characteristic of these examples that while we would not take them to be instances of (proper) knowledge, behaviour reveals certainty.

Some interpreters have called the certainty Wittgenstein is concerned with 'animal certainty'.[55] According to Moyal-Sharrock, it resembles a reflex or an automatic action and manifests itself only in the form of a 'know-how' which 'does not involve any degree of attention'.[56] Thus, the certainty regarding one's body is manifested in the way living beings act. Similarly, the certainty that *this* is a table is manifested in a way of handling the table that shows expertise and lacks thought.[57] Objective certainty is '*enacted*': it is 'not thought out but acted out'.[58]

---

[55] For example Ertz, *Regel und Witz. Wittgensteinsche Perspektiven auf Mathematik, Sprache und Moral;* Moyal-Sharrock, *Understanding Wittgenstein's* On Certainty. Ertz compares only the certainty that *some* Moorean propositions try to state with the certainty of an animal.

[56] Moyal-Sharrock, *Understanding Wittgenstein's* On Certainty, p. 64 and 68.

[57] Ibid., p. 64.

[58] Ibid., p. 98.

3.3.3 Primitive reactions

I shall now turn to the remarks about primitive language-games. In *Cause and Effect*, Wittgenstein distinguishes between the 'primitive form of a language-game' and 'more complicated forms'. The latter develop from the former, which is 'a reaction' (CE, p. 395). Wittgenstein states that '[t]he basic form of the game must be one in which we act' (CE, p. 397). It is characterised as 'certainty, not uncertainty', because 'uncertainty could never lead to action' (CE, p. 397).

According to Gennip, Kim van, Wittgenstein criticises Moore for not realising that 'at the level of our reactions, there is no room for doubt'.[59] As she argues convincingly, this critique of Moore should be viewed in conjunction with Wittgenstein's criticism of Bertrand Russell, who aims to ground our knowledge on something empirical and propositional to which he ascribes indubitably.[60] What Russell takes to be knowledge immediately derived from the senses is, according to Wittgenstein, not a form of knowledge at all.[61] As Gennip, Kim van's study reveals, what primarily motivated Wittgenstein to write about doubt and certainty was not his encounter with Moore's texts, but Russell's view of causation, according to which we can perceive 'causal or quasi-causal relations'.[62] His criticism of this view, which is for instance expressed in paragraph 204 quoted above, is in turn rooted in his critique of intuitionism in mathematics.[63]

Wittgenstein objects to Russell that the expression 'being immediately aware of ... ' is misleading because it leads us to believe that we are dealing with a case where we are, and can be shown to be, right about something, whereas in fact 'there is no *right* (or wrong) about it' (CE, Appendix A, p. 407). What Russell takes to be immediate awareness or knowledge is actually an immediate reaction, a 'reaction against a cause' (ibid., p. 409). Wittgenstein provides the following examples of such a reaction: 'You threaten me with a dagger and I make a gesture' (ibid., p. 408). 'Someone throws a stone, I feel it and see him in a particular position, I throw back' (ibid., p. 410).

---

[59] Gennip, Kim van, *Wittgenstein's* On Certainty *in the Making: Studies into Its Historical and Philosophical Background*, p. 105.

[60] Ibid.

[61] Bertrand Russell, 'The Limits of Empiricism,' *Proceedings of the Aristotelian Society* 36 (1937): p. 132.

[62] Gennip, Kim van, *Wittgenstein's* On Certainty *in the Making: Studies into Its Historical and Philosophical Background*, p. 91. Russell expressed this position in Russell, 'The Limits of Empiricism.'

[63] Gennip, Kim van, *Wittgenstein's* On Certainty *in the Making: Studies into Its Historical and Philosophical Background*, p. 108.

In the notes published as *Zettel*, he characterises a primitive reaction as the pre-linguistic behaviour on which a language-game is based. Such behaviour is 'the prototype of a way of thinking and not the result of thought' (Z 541). The example he gives is 'to tend, to treat, the part that hurts when someone else is in pain; and not merely when oneself is – and so to pay attention to other people's pain behaviour' (Z 540). (It should be noted that, while of course this is not central for him here, the example he gives is one of behaviour that arguably underlies moral language-games. As Goodman already argued in 1982, 'some moral activity, and the associated moral judgments are, on this view, as much a prototype of our way of thinking as is the belief that the world has existed for more than the last five minutes'.[64] I will return to this in Chapter 5.) There is a continuous development from the primitive forms of behaviour at the beginning of language acquisition, which are closely related to our instinctive endowment, to the complex forms of behaviour that characterise our linguistic practice.[65] On the level of reactions, doubts do not arise, and it is therefore incorrect to talk about knowledge. On Wittgenstein's view, the basis of our knowledge can be found in our actions and reactions, and not in principles or propositions.[66]

That the reactions that ground our language-games are primitive and animal-like does not imply that they cannot involve the use of language.[67] These adjectives refer to the absence of conscious thought, not of language. As Moyal-Sharrock convincingly argues, '*some* of what we say can be a primitive reaction – part of our nonreflective, animal behaviour'. If we say something spontaneously, our words are equivalent to a spontaneous deed.[68] As Wittgenstein remarks: 'The primitive reaction may have been a glance or a gesture, but it may also have been a word' (PI II, p. 218). Thus, in the example of the dagger we could replace the gesture with a spontaneous utterance such as 'No!' or 'Help!' Although such a primitive verbal reaction is not available to animals

[64] Russell B. Goodman, 'Wittgenstein and Ethics,' *Metaphilosophy* 13, no. 2 (1982): p. 145.
[65] Krebs, *Worauf man sich verlässt*: p. 114.
[66] Gennip, Kim van, Wittgenstein's *On Certainty* in the Making: Studies into Its Historical and Philosophical Background, p. 105.
[67] The sharp distinction between language and action is also criticised by Iczkovits. Iczkovits, *Wittgenstein's Ethical Thought*, p. 20.
[68] Danièle Moyal-Sharrock, 'Words as Deeds: Wittgenstein's "Spontaneous Utterances" and the Dissolution of the Explanatory Gap,' *Philosophical Psychology* 13, no. 3 (2000): pp. 364 and 369.

and infants, it is animal in the sense of being instinctive and not involving any kind of reasoning.[69] As Moyal-Sharrock points out, the boundaries between word and deed, between language and the world are porous. There are even points where they 'dissolve; where behaviour and language melt into one another, become indistinguishable; where the word *is* behaviour, a reflex action'.[70]

3.3.4 Agreement in action

In *Remarks on the Foundations of Mathematics* Wittgenstein writes in relation to the practice of giving descriptions that rule-following is 'FUNDAMENTAL to our language-game' (RFM VI 28). The concept 'rule' is associated with the concept 'regularity', and regularity is, in turn, agreement in the way we act. Language-games are grounded in regularity: 'the phenomenon of language is based on regularity, on agreement in action' (RFM VI 39). Wittgenstein does not claim that all acting is an instance of rule-following in the strict sense. Rather, the fundamental acting he refers to is essentially one that reveals regularity.[71] Human language develops out of '*shared* natural reactions'.[72]

In addition to 'agreement in action', Wittgenstein also uses the terms 'agreement in judgements' and 'agreement in form of life'. In the *Philosophical Investigations* he states: 'If language is to be a means of communication there must be an agreement not only in definitions but also (queer as this may sound) in judgments. This seems to abolish logic but does not do so' (PI 242). In the previous paragraph he lets his interlocutor ask: 'So you are saying that human agreement decides what is true and what is false?' And he responds: 'It is what human beings *say* that is true and false; and they agree in the *language* they use. That is not agreement in opinions but in form of life.' The 'agreement in form of life' includes, amongst other things, agreement in how human beings react to pointing, how they make judgements of sameness, and how they react to pain.[73]

---

[69] Ibid., p. 362.

[70] Ibid., pp. 361 f.

[71] See G.P. Baker and P.M.S. Hacker, *Wittgenstein: Rules, Grammar and Necessity*, 2nd, extensively rev. ed. (Chichester, U.K. and Malden, MA: Wiley-Blackwell, 2009), p. 155: 'It is *acting* according to a rule, a *practice* of normative behaviour, regularities *perceived as uniformities* that lie at the bottom of our language-games.'

[72] Moyal-Sharrock, 'Coming to Language: Wittgenstein's Social "Theory" of Language Acquisition,' p. 293.

[73] See Williams, *Wittgenstein, Mind and Meaning*: pp. 201 f.

This agreement does not decide what is true and what is false. It must be possible for people to agree on something that is false. Agreement does not function as justification either: it has an enabling role. We can only speak meaningfully with one another if we use at least a large number of words in roughly the same way, if we agree in most cases on what counts as doing the same as before and so on. Krebs emphasises the fact that 'in the absence of such fundamental agreement there would be no linguistic rule-following at all'.[74]

Going beyond an interpretation of *On Certainty*, Krebs argues that Moorean propositions can be understood as articulating core parts of the agreement over judgements. They express facts which are presupposed by a concrete practice of judging.[75] By setting limits on what can be regarded as confirming an assertion, or as rebutting it, they make the justification of other propositions possible, 'defining so to speak the space in which operating with reasons is possible in the first place'.[76] What Moore claims to know are 'matters of course, which are deeply anchored in the human form of life'.[77] They are presupposed by every confirmation or rebuttal of a knowledge claim and by every instance of doubt.[78] Thus, they are like the axes around which our confirmations, rebuttals and doubts turn. Krebs' suggestion, which is overall very plausible, should be slightly modified by saying that not Moorean propositions but the certainties they articulate have this function.

Wittgenstein indirectly refers to agreement over judgements when he remarks that in order for it to be possible for a person to be mistaken, one has to already judge in conformity with humankind (OC 156). A mistake is the exception and needs correct moves as its 'surrounding'. If Moore asserted that he did *not* have a body, that the earth had *not* existed long before he was born and so on we would not say that he was mistaken but think of him as demented (OC 155), because these assertions are too much at odds with those of our linguistic community.

---

[74] Krebs, *Worauf man sich verlässt*: p. 82, my translation. The original reads: 'Ohne eine solche grundsätzliche Übereinstimmung *könnte* es ein Befolgen unserer sprachlichen Regeln tatsächlich nicht geben [...].' That without an agreement in judgements 'there would be no understanding of any rules at all' is also pointed out by Barry Stroud. Barry Stroud, 'Wittgenstein and Logical Necessity,' *The Philosophical Review* 74, no. 4 (1965): p. 515.
[75] Krebs, *Worauf man sich verlässt*: p. 82. See OC 308.
[76] Ibid., p. 34, my translation.
[77] Ibid., p. 41, my translation. In the original it says: '[...] Selbstverständlichkeiten [...], die tief in menschlichen Lebensvollzügen verankert sind.'
[78] Ibid., p. 84.

The link between certainty and the fundamental agreement Wittgenstein is referring to has also been noted by Williams, who argues that our language-games of justification and knowledge presuppose 'conformity within bedrock practices'. These bedrock practices are constituted by 'the harmonious "blind" agreement in words and deeds of a group of people over a period of time', where 'blind' means that it does not result from the self-conscious and explicit application of rules.[79] In the absence of such an agreement, there is 'logically no space for justification, doubt, challenge, or dispute'. Williams puts the connection between the notions of agreement and objective certainty in a nutshell by saying that '[c]onformity and agreement in our bedrock judgments [...] constitutes the bedrock certainty that is logically required for any normative action', that is actions that can be evaluated as correct or incorrect.[80]

As Krebs points out, 'in the case of Moorean propositions the indissoluble *connection* between language and acting becomes particularly evident'.[81] There is no contradiction between the passages in *On Certainty* in which ways of acting are said to form the basis for our judging and the remarks in which Moorean propositions seem to play this role.[82] The fact that no one doubts the things that Moore claims to know reflects the certainty with which we act. In Krebs' words: The 'naturalness of Moorean propositions' is the '*expression* of the naturalness of our acting'.[83] It should be added that those propositions are natural only in the sense that they express something that normal people cannot imagine doubting, not in the sense of us being familiar with their use in ordinary discourse. It is characteristic of these propositions that they are not usually used.

The propositions in question reflect the unreflective and unhesitating ways of dealing with our own body and the world around us, both with and without language. To take some of the examples Wittgenstein looks at: that we have absolutely no doubts regarding the existence of our hands and the existence of trees is revealed by the way in which we deal with our body and the environment around us day in, day out, and by the way

---

[79] Williams, *Wittgenstein, Mind and Meaning*: p. 198.
[80] Ibid., pp. 7 f.
[81] Krebs, *Worauf man sich verlässt*: p. 114, my translation.
[82] Ibid., p. 113. Such a contradiction is seen for instance by Stroll, *Moore and Wittgenstein on Certainty*: p. 157.
[83] Krebs, *Worauf man sich verlässt*: p. 112, my translations. The German original reads as follows: 'Vielmehr ist die Selbstverständlichkeit Moore'scher Sätze *Ausdruck* der Selbstverständlichkeit unseres Handelns.'

we refer to them verbally. In contexts in which they express something that is objectively certain, propositions such as 'I know that that's a tree' refer to our entirely confident ways of interacting with the world. If we did not in general recognise the objects around us, we could not play the language-games we in fact play. I use my hands and refer to them verbally without any hesitation, but at the same time without justification. 'I know that my name is J.H.' reflects the certainty with which I present myself to people, answer to the question 'What's your name?', sign documents and so on. 'I know that the earth existed long before my birth' reflects the certainty that is shown, for instance, in my ways of talking about events that took place long before I was born. 'I know that I have never been on the moon' reflects the certainty with which Wittgenstein was ready to answer questions such as 'Have you ever been on the moon?', 'Has anyone ever been on the moon?', or 'Is it possible for human beings to go to the moon?' 'I know that I am a human being' reflects a certainty that is shown, for instance, in my expectations of how I want to be treated by others, and in my relations with non-human animals. Pleasants notes that '[w]hat underlies our epistemic practices and capacities is not itself an epistemic practice or capacity, but *our fundamental ways of being and acting in the world*'.[84]

In *Last Writings*, Wittgenstein stresses that '[t]he important thing about certainty is the way one behaves' and that 'the most important expression of conviction is [...] the way one behaves'. 'Ask not "What goes on in us when we are certain ... ?", but "How does it show?"' (LW II, p. 21). Reflecting the certainty with which we act, the propositions concerned turn out to be 'artificial formulations of certainties whose only occurrence *qua certainty* is *in action*'.[85] It should be added that those certainties also occur – presumably even more often – in inaction.[86]

Certainties are formulated for heuristic and philosophical purposes. We as philosophers have to put them into propositional form in order to be able to reflect on them and to consider them as certainties. The fact that someone like Moore put them into propositional form made Wittgenstein and others aware of the fact that some things stand fast for us. While an agent who is not engaged in philosophical activity usually has no use for such propositions, the philosopher does.[87] However, the

---

[84] Nigel Pleasants, 'Wittgenstein and Basic Moral Certainty,' *Philosophia* 37 (2009): p. 670, my italics.
[85] Moyal-Sharrock, *Understanding Wittgenstein's* On Certainty: p. 8.
[86] I thank Nigel Pleasants for pointing this out.
[87] This is another point I owe to Pleasants.

formulations used by the philosopher do not encapsulate the respective certainty in all of its complexity (see 5.6)

3.4   Conclusion

In this chapter, I have considered Wittgenstein's views on knowledge, doubt and certainty, moving from a focus on propositions to an emphasis on acting. In the cases Wittgenstein considers, the propositions he is concerned with are meant to express something that is beyond doubt – for the speaker, for a group of people, or for all reasonable persons. What they are supposed to express is akin to an axis around which our justifications and doubts turn. Wittgenstein's examples are not homogeneous. In many of the cases he considers, there is a similarity between the role of the respective proposition and the role of a grammatical proposition.

A link between Wittgenstein's remarks on propositions and his emphasis on practice can be established by considering certainty in relation to the agreement that is a precondition for communication and normative action. 'Moorean propositions' manifest an attempt to articulate the certainty with which we act. The acting that grounds our language-games can be understood as shared actions and reactions, including primitive verbal and non-verbal reactions, shared ways of making judgements of sameness, shared ways of following rules and so on. All of these actions and reactions form part of the agreement in action, which includes agreement over judgements, and which makes sophisticated practices such as justifying, doubting and evaluating possible.

The interpretation provided in this chapter lays the basis for Chapter 5, where an analogy will be drawn between certainty regarding the empirical world and moral certainty. However, before moving on to explore the limits of reasonable doubt in the moral realm, it is necessary to take a closer look at the situations in everyday life in which we ask for moral reasons or feel the need to provide a justification for our moral views. The next chapter will scrutinise different practices of justification, focusing on the conditions under which the demand for justification usually arises. In order to understand why certain justificatory demands and claims do not make sense, it is necessary to establish a clearer picture of the role of (moral) justification in the context of our daily lives.

4
Moral Justification

4.1 Introduction

I shall start my discussion of moral justification by looking at the practices of morally justifying actions as well as particular and general moral judgements. As Wittgenstein rightly says, asking for reasons loses its sense at some point (see for example PI 211 and 217). In order to reach a better understanding of cases where the demand for justification makes no sense, I shall take a look at cases in which justification is required, asking what its role is and when it is accepted. Why do we ask for moral reasons, and why do we in certain situations feel the need to provide them? Tully argues that 'our reflection on the role of giving reasons' can, in a given context, be 'our reason for *not* raising further doubts'.[1] By way of examples, I shall present the conditions under which we usually require justifications for actions and moral judgements, thereby highlighting the contrast between normal situations in which the issue of justification arises and certain philosophical demands.

In order to sharpen our understanding of the practice of justifying moral judgements, I shall compare it with the practice of justifying empirical judgements. In particular, I shall compare the aims of these practices, the kinds of reasons for doubt involved, the forms of evidence available, and the ways in which we justify. Having pointed out differences as well as similarities between the two practices, I shall discuss the

---

[1] James Tully, 'Wittgenstein and Political Philosophy. Understanding Practices of Critical Reflection', in *The Grammar of Politics. Wittgenstein and Political Philosophy*, ed. Cressida J. Heyes (Ithaca, NY: Cornell University Press, 2003), p. 25. See also Yaniv Iczkovits, *Wittgenstein's Ethical Thought* (Basingstoke: Palgrave Macmillan, 2012), p. 166: 'But sometimes not giving any reasons is the highest mode of rationality (and morality).'

alleged distinction between epistemically and morally justifying moral beliefs, and reject it.

4.2   Justification of actions

Since in practice the primary subject of moral justification seems to be an objectionable action, I shall address the practice of justifying actions first. A look at this practice should help answer the following question: 'Under what conditions does the issue of justification usually arise?'

In everyday life, moral justification functions mainly as the means for defending one's actions against criticism, or for seeking approval of them (either by others or by oneself). Approval of the actions partly gains significance from being associated with the approval of oneself as a person. Others make inferences from our acting to our character. And so do we. Whether we are regarded as virtuous or vicious depends to a significant extent on how we act. As Ertz emphasises, in the case of a moral judgement, we do not merely evaluate actions, but also the person who is acting.[2] Approval of our action is tied to the acceptance as a competent participant in moral practices. Moral justification is required for actions that are or appear to be morally objectionable.

As Ertz points out, the aims of a practice fall under its constituents.[3] Thus, it is constitutive for the practice of morally justifying actions that it aims to defend an action against criticism, seek approval, and be regarded as morally competent. It is a peculiarity of moral practice that someone who acts in a bad way is a bad person, while someone who calculates badly is merely a bad calculator, and someone who plays badly a bad player.[4] It is thus also an aim of the practice of justifying actions that the agent is considered to be a good person.

The classical case of an action which requires moral justification is one that constitutes the violation of a moral rule, for example the rule 'Keep your promises' or the rule 'Do not lie'. A person who breaks a promise can justify her violation of the general precept by showing that some of the generally accepted justifying conditions apply.[5] As shall be argued below, anyone who understands the point of promising accepts that under certain conditions it is justifiable to break a promise (5.6).

---

[2] Timo-Peter Ertz, *Regel und Witz. Wittgensteinsche Perspektiven auf Mathematik, Sprache und Moral* (Berlin and New York: de Gruyter, 2008), p. 218.

[3] Ibid., p. 11.

[4] Ibid., p. 223.

[5] See Thomas. M. Scanlon, *What We Owe to Each Other* (Cambridge, Mass. and London: The Belknap Press of Harvard University Press, 1998), p. 200.

Let me give an example from everyday life of a situation in which the issue of justification arises. Sarah requires a justification from her friend Susan for having disclosed a secret with which Sarah had trusted her. By requiring a justification from Susan for her action, Sarah not only expresses her belief that Susan's action was wrong, but also the belief that it would in principle be possible for Susan to give reasons for her action which Sarah could accept. If Sarah did not hold the second belief, she would simply condemn Susan, not allowing for the possibility of her action being justified. Thus, the requirement for justification implies the belief in its possibility, that is, the belief that Susan might convince Sarah that some of the accepted justifying conditions obtained. Whilst Susan might be unable to give reasons which Sarah accepts, from Sarah's point of view it is not ruled out from the start that Susan might come up with reasons that bar Sarah from condemning her. In addition, Sarah must think of her and Susan as sharing a number of moral beliefs. Susan, in turn, will only make an attempt to justify the way she acted if she takes them to have such a 'common ground' of shared moral beliefs. If Susan succeeds in justifying the retelling of Sarah's secret, this can have important consequences for both. Possible consequences in this case include the reestablishment of mutual trust, the continuity of their friendship, and a belief on the part of Sarah that Susan is responsive to moral concerns.

Similarly, if the citizens of a state demand moral justification from their government for an instance of corruption, the acceptance or rejection of the justification provided will have important consequences. If the government's justificatory attempt succeeds, it will regain the confidence of the citizens. If it fails, the government will lose support, and possibly the next elections. Those objecting to the corruption do so on moral grounds. In demanding justification from their government instead of simply trying to bring it down, the citizens give them the chance to provide reasons in defence of their behaviour. Thereby, they give them the possibility to reestablish their moral integrity. Here again it is presupposed that there is a basis of shared moral beliefs.

I intend by these examples to illustrate the following characteristics of our practice of justifying actions: (1) what raises the demand for justification is a morally objectionable action, (2) success in providing a justification for the respective action is not ruled out from the start, (3) each party believes that a number of moral beliefs are shared with the other (that is an agreement over judgements is assumed), and (4) the success or failure of the justificatory attempt has important consequences for the persons involved. These four statements so to speak describe the grammar of the game of morally justifying actions.

4.3   Justification of moral judgements

While the justification of an action could be seen as the paradigm case of moral justification, we also morally justify attitudes, forms of reasoning and judgements. It makes sense, for instance, to ask somebody how she can justify her conviction that blacks are inferior to whites. The kind of justification required here is a moral justification, in the sense of a justification referring to moral standards. By moral justification I do not mean justification relating to a goal such as loyalty.[6] Since it is the justification of all kinds of moral judgements in which moral epistemologists are interested, I shall focus on these practices, distinguishing between the justification of particular and of general moral judgements. I shall concentrate on general moral judgements, since those will be the focus of the following chapter. Again the guiding question is 'Under what conditions does the issue of justification usually arise?'

4.3.1   General moral judgements

As regards the practice of justifying general moral judgements, let us consider the example of Bill and Simon, who disagree about the legitimacy of abortion. Bill holds that the unborn life may under no circumstances be sacrificed. Simon disagrees with that and tries to convince him that the life of the embryo has to be weighed against the life of its mother. He defends the view that if the mother's life is in danger or if her having the child would result in psychological disturbance, then having an abortion is justified. Simon provides reasons for his view, which would be pointless if there were no alternative to it.

It is characteristic of such a debate that reasons can be given to support the respective standpoints. Whether Simon succeeds in convincing Bill depends on whether the reasons he provides involve more basic moral beliefs, whether they are non-rejectable for Bill, and whether or not Bill can accept them and at the same time reject Simon's judgement about abortion.[7] Justification goes from what is less certain to what is more certain. Simon will come up with reasons which are less disputed and ideally with reasons which are generally accepted. Other beliefs that Bill holds play a role, since he can only assess Simon's reasons on the basis of his other beliefs. Those beliefs may in principle be altered by

---

[6] See Mark Timmons, *Morality without Foundations: A Defense of Ethical Contextualism* (New York: Oxford University Press, 1999), p. 191. Different conceptions of moral justification will be discussed below (4.5.1).

[7] Of course, Bill might irrationally accept the validity of Simon's reasons and still reject the view that follows from them.

Simon's arguments. Yet some of them will be beyond doubt for Bill (and presumably also for Simon, given their participation in the same moral practices). There has to be a certain agreement over moral judgements. The beliefs which are beyond doubt for Bill can also be said to form the background against which Simon's reasons are assessed.

In parallel with the case of justifying an action, if Bill requires a justification from Simon, he thinks that it is at least not impossible for Simon to come up with reasons in favour of his standpoint (see (2) above). Despite thinking of Simon's view as objectionable, Bill expects Simon to be able to provide reasons which he might accept. The issue of justification would not arise if Bill did not have an idea of what a justification might look like in this case. From his perspective, the success of the justificatory attempt cannot be ruled out from the start.

Moreover, Simon's justificatory attempt would not have even the slightest chance of being successful if Simon and Bill did not agree on many views, including many moral considerations (see (3) above). Without such common ground, all of the reasons Simon could possibly give would be ineffective. However, in order for the issue of justification to arise it suffices that Bill *thinks* that justification is possible, leaving open the possibility that he may later discover that they in fact lack a common ground, with the result that justification in fact is not possible.[8]

The agreement which is presupposed by practices of justification is depicted by Tully as a 'tacit agreement':

> [any] critical and reflective argumentation [which] involves the giving of reasons in the search for mutual understanding and/or agreements [...] is based in a more fundamental form of speech activity in which we are always already in tacit agreement and understand one another in our thoughtful, confident, rational, yet unreflective uses of words that *eo ipso* act as grounds in these circumstances.[9]

Here Tully seems to spell out what Wittgenstein means when he says that human beings 'agree in the *language* they use' and that this is 'not an agreement in opinions but in form of life' (PI 241). The members of a language community use at least a large number of words in roughly the

---

[8] The question with whom we can be said to share such a common ground will be discussed in Chapter 7.

[9] Tully, 'Wittgenstein and Political Philosophy. Understanding Practices of Critical Reflection,' p. 26.

same way. These 'customary, intersubjective ways of acting with words' provide the common ground on which justification is possible.[10]

The example of Bill and Simon suggests that the grammar of the game of justifying general moral judgements is similar to that of the game of morally justifying actions. It can be described by the following statements: (a) what raises the demand for justification is a morally objectionable view, that is it is assumed that there are moral reasons that count against adopting the position concerned,[11] (b) it is supposed that there are reasons in favour of it, that is the success of the justificatory attempt is not thought to be ruled out from the start, (c) it is assumed that there are shared moral beliefs which serve as common ground (agreement in judgements), and (d) the success of the justificatory attempt has important consequences.

The first rule is crucial for my critique of those philosophers who claim that beliefs *as such* require justification. If a proposed view were such that no one could have any reason to reject it, the issue of justification would not arise. If we can at least imagine reasons to reject the view, these reasons support alternative standpoints. Therefore, the goal of justification is to show that the standpoint concerned is more convincing than its alternatives. Along with the aim of reaching an agreement, this goal is constitutive of the practice of justifying (general) moral judgements.

It is important to point out that (b) does not apply to all cases. It does not for instance correctly describe a case in which we require justification for a person's conviction that blacks are inferior to whites. Here, we exclude the possibility that he may come up with sufficient reasons in support of his belief. In this case, the demand for a justification has the function of forcing someone to reflect on his prejudices. The best possible outcome from the perspective of the critic is that the person in question comes to see the falsity of his belief, and abandons it. However, although in this case the success of the justificatory attempt is, from the standpoint of the critic, ruled out from the start, she has an idea of what a justification could look like. She can imagine that the opponent could

---

[10] Ibid.

[11] For the view that, in practice, we usually attempt to justify a moral attitude if it has been criticised by reference to good reasons see Marcus Willaschek, 'Moralisches Urteil und begründeter Zweifel. Eine kontextualistische Konzeption moralischer Rechtfertigung,' in *Argument und Analyse. Ausgewählte Sektionsvorträge des 4. internationalen Kongresses der Gesellschaft für analytische Philosophie*, ed. Andreas Beckermann und Christian Nimtz (http://gap-im-netz.de/gap4Konf/Proceedings4/Proc.htm, 2002), p. 635.

argue that, for instance, due to a lack of certain capacities which whites have, blacks do not have the same moral status as whites. The difference between this case and the discussion of Bill and Simon reminds us of the importance of being cautious about the particularities of each language-game.

In practice we only ask for a justification if we have at least an idea of what a justification of the respective judgement would look like. Some philosophers fail to see that, in the case of a general moral judgement like 'It is wrong to break a promise', we do in fact not know what a justification would look like. A person who demands justification for it seems to lack understanding.

In the example of the person who believes in the inferiority of blacks, the aim of bringing that person to abandon his belief by forcing him to reflect upon it only seems to be achievable if there is common ground. If the critic does not expect her interlocutor to share many moral and non-moral beliefs with her, and thus also to use moral terms in roughly the same way, she cannot hope that the interlocutor will be able to see the wrongness of his belief. A shared ethical language must be presupposed.

Let me add a further remark about the grammar of the game discussed in this section. The demand for justification of moral judgements is closely connected to disagreement about moral matters. Since the moral status of the practice of abortion is contested, both the belief in the legitimacy of abortion and the belief in its illegitimacy require justification. The same holds for the moral status of humanitarian interventions, homosexuality, cloning, euthanasia, vivisection, the use and killing of animals, duties to distant people in need, and many other issues. These are the 'proper objects of practical ethical enquiry'.[12]

It must be noted however that it is not correct to assert categorically that certain issues are such that a moral judgement about them requires justification. Whether a moral judgement, whatever its subject, needs to be supported by reasons depends on the context in which it is made. In a context in which there are no reasons to object to homosexuality – for instance, in ancient Greece – the judgement that having a sexual relationship with someone of the same sex is morally permissible does not require justification. And with regard to a practice like cloning, it is imaginable that it becomes commonly accepted at some point, so that justification is no longer required. At that point we would accept

---

[12] Nigel Pleasants, 'Wittgenstein, Ethics and Basic Moral Certainty,' *Inquiry* 51, no. 3 (2008): p. 264.

cloning as morally desirable and this acceptance would be reflected at the level of habitual moral practice. Critical moral reflection about the moral status of cloning can lead, in the long run, to the unquestioned acceptance of that practice. Such reflection can also, together with other factors, lead to the condemnation of a practice that was previously accepted, for instance slavery (see 7.3.3).

Among philosophers, classical problems of moral justification are political sovereignty, coercion, the restriction of individual liberty, discrimination, and the relationship between freedom and equality. Political sovereignty is regarded, particularly by the liberal tradition, as being in need of moral justification, because it presupposes that individuals relinquish certain rights. The idea that some people govern over others conflicts, prima facie, with the belief in individual freedom and self-determination. Moral justification is required in cases where an institution or a practice is in tension with moral values or principles. What moral justification can achieve in these cases is the legitimisation, and thereby the (public) acceptance, of the respective institution or practice. Thus, moral justification is able to legitimise power.

4.3.2   Particular moral judgements

As in the case of general moral judgements such as 'Having an abortion is under all circumstances morally impermissible', situations in which a demand for a particular moral judgement to be justified arises usually display characteristics (a) to (d). The distinctive feature of the grammar of the game of justifying particular moral judgements is that morally relevant features of a particular situation play a role. Particular moral judgements may be doubted and justified by reference to such features. Disagreement as to how a particular action should be judged can result from different interpretations of the respective situation. The giving of different weight to different features of a given situation may lead to conflicting moral judgements.

In the case of particular moral judgements of the form 'A acted wrongly in situation S' or 'B's decision D in situation S was wrong', a demand for justification can be motivated in different ways. We might object to John's judgement 'Maria acted rightly when she punished her son for coming home too late', because we think that he failed to take certain morally relevant aspects of the situation into account, for example the fact that it was not the son's fault that he was not on time. In this case, we accuse John of ignorance. This is a case of disagreement about which information is morally relevant. Alternatively, our objection could be grounded on the impression that John lacked relevant information about the case. Thus, it might seem that he did not know anything about the reasons for the delay by Maria's son. While in the first case we take John to have disregarded a relevant fact when forming his judgement, in the second case we take him to lack situational information necessary in order to make a justified judgement.

Although it is a lack of factual information that grounds our objection in the second case, that objection is prompted by our belief that Maria acted wrongly. In the case of moral judgements, whether general or particular, we do not demand justification merely because we have reasons to believe that the respective judge did not have access to all the relevant information relating to the situation. What prompts our demand is that we judge the matter differently, by virtue of the moral views we hold. The issue of justification would not arise if we did not disagree with the judgement concerned.

4.4 Comparison with the justification of empirical judgements

With the aim of sharpening our understanding of the practices of justifying general and particular moral judgements, I shall compare them with the practice of justifying empirical judgements. For the purpose of simplicity, and since the differences are not relevant within the present context, I will refer to the practices of justifying moral and empirical judgements, and will thus not explicitly distinguish between particular and general judgements. These practices certainly have a lot in common. For instance, in both cases the issue of justification arises only if there are reasons to doubt the respective judgement.

The two practices may differ as regards their function, the kind of reasons for doubt we have, the way we justify, and the evidence available. I shall start the comparison by looking at the functions of these practices. In the case of empirical judgements, justification has the function of assuring us or others that our judgements accord with the facts. As the discussion of the previous section has shown, this is not the function of the practice of justifying moral judgements. That practice is aimed, amongst other things, at reaching agreement on binding rules, at clear and widely shared precepts for action, and at moral progress.

Are the reasons on which doubts are based similar in the two practices? In the case of empirical judgements, the demand for justification arises, for instance, when confronted with a judgement which seems to be based on information originating from a dubious source. This could be a badly informed person (or one who is not trustworthy) or, for instance, a newspaper controlled by a government. Yet another reason for doubt is the existence of evidence to the contrary.

John Pollock distinguishes between 'defeaters' which *undercut*, and defeaters which *rebut* the original evidence for a belief: 'Intuitively, where E is evidence for H, an undercutting defeater is evidence which undermines the evidential connection between E and H.'[13] Let me give an example. Tom tells me that all his colleagues are against him. What would normally give me good reason to believe that what he says is true, namely his testimony, is undercut by the testimony from his doctor that he suffers from a persecution complex. As opposed to that, 'a rebutting defeater is evidence which prevents E from justifying belief in H by supporting not-H in a more direct way'.[14] Thus, it could be the case that the behaviour of Tom's colleagues which I have witnessed supports the view that they are not against him, thereby rebutting the evidence that Tom's testimony initially provides. Evidence that information comes from an unreliable source is an *undercutting* defeater, while direct evidence to the contrary of what is claimed is a *rebutting* defeater.

Can we apply the distinction between the two kinds of defeaters to moral beliefs? The answer seems to be yes. An example of a defeater which undermines the evidential connection between a moral belief and the evidence for it is a manifestation of moral incompetence. I would not trust the moral judgement of a psychopath, for instance. Also, in view of recent findings regarding the role of emotions in moral judgement, I would doubt the moral judgements of a person where I am certain that her emotional capacities have been impaired.[15] Moral competence seems to be for moral judgements what credibility is for empirical judgements. Compare the following two cases:

(1) You are listening to a talk about a historical figure you do not know anything about. In this case, if you are convinced that the speaker knows what he is talking about, and that he speaks truthfully, you will not have any reasons to doubt what he says. If, however, you have reason to doubt the speaker's credibility, this gives you a direct reason to doubt the things he says about the historical person concerned (undercutting defeater). (2) You are listening to someone arguing in favour of the view that the legalisation of euthanasia is morally required. In this case, even if you know that the speaker knows all of the facts about the practice

---

[13] Thomas Kelly, 'Evidence,' in *Stanford Encyclopedia of Philosophy* (2006). Kelly refers to John Pollock, *Contemporary Theories of Knowledge* (Towota, NJ: Rowman and Littlefield Publishers, 1986).

[14] Kelly, 'Evidence.'

[15] Such impairment is characteristic of psychopaths (see Chapter 6), but of course not every person whose emotional capacities are impaired in some way qualifies as a psychopath.

of euthanasia, presumably much more than you know, you will have doubts about the view she defends, if it conflicts with your moral views connected to the issue. In addition, the role played by credibility in (1) seems to be played by moral competence here. Reasons for doubting the moral competence of a person are reasons for doubting her moral judgements. At the same time, whether we regard someone as a morally competent judge depends on the moral judgements she makes. There is no indicator for a person's moral competence that is independent of her judgements (and her acting). Also a lack of such competence can only be manifested through judgement and acting.

For an example of a rebutting defeater, let us return to the case of John who holds that Maria acted rightly when she punished her son for coming home too late. Let the belief that the punishment will teach the son to come home on time be the original 'evidence' for John's belief. The information that it was not the son's fault that he was not on time would then function as a rebutting defeater.

Although we can distinguish between undercutting and rebutting defeaters in the case of moral beliefs, the differences between reasons for doubting an empirical and reasons for doubting a moral judgement have to be pointed out. Thus, regarding moral judgements we rarely question the reliability of the source of information it is based on. When I object to a general moral judgement such as the judgement 'It is morally right to help someone who asserts a desire to die to fulfil that desire', I ask for justification because the judgement clashes with many of my moral and non-moral views. For instance, I might believe that helping someone to commit suicide is a form of killing, that the desire to die is never a genuine desire, or that committing suicide is wrong. There are also reasons for doubt which are specific to the practice of justifying moral judgements, such as the fact that one has gained more experience. Having lived in a foreign country for a number of years can for instance give me reasons to doubt some of the moral views I used to hold about certain practices prevalent in that country. A reason for doubting traditional moral views is socio-cultural change.

As far as the way we justify is concerned, it can be said of the practice of justifying empirical judgements that we justify an assertion or a knowledge claim by 'stating either how we arrived at the belief in question, or how it would be possible to assure oneself (in accordance with certain rules) of the matter'.[16] This is clearly not how we justify a moral

---

[16] Andreas Krebs, *Worauf man sich verlässt* (Würzburg: Königshausen & Neumann, 2007), p. 90, my translation.

judgement. Yet it seems that we can cite similar forms of evidence in both practices.

I can justify my empirical judgement that a storm has destroyed the roof of my house by providing evidence in the form, for instance, of a newspaper article about a very strong storm in my neighbourhood shortly before I noticed the damage. I could support my judgement 'Maria should not have punished her son for coming home too late' by pointing out to her that her son was not able to come home earlier due to a bus strike. If, alternatively, I criticised Maria on the basis that I reject the practice of punishing children in general, I could refer to empirical studies about the effectiveness of punishment, or about the negative consequences of it for the child. In this case I justify my particular moral judgement by reference to a general moral judgement, which I then justify by reference to certain empirical studies.

On the basis of a conception of moral knowledge as primarily propositional, it might seem plausible to presume that we wish our moral beliefs to be true as well as justified according to epistemic standards, such as being sufficiently supported by evidence, or where all relevant 'counter-possibilities' have been checked, and so on.[17] Nonetheless, as convincing as these demands may be in the case of many empirical beliefs, such as the belief that a storm has destroyed the roof of my house, it is far from clear what they mean when applied to moral beliefs.

Timmons formulates an epistemic norm for what he calls 'epistemic responsibility'.[18] His notion of epistemic responsibility seems to be slightly weaker than the notion of epistemic justification. According to him, it is possible to be epistemically responsible in holding an unjustified belief (given that in that context the belief is not in need of justification).[19] Timmons, as mentioned above, holds that some very basic moral beliefs are not in need of justification in ordinary contexts (1.4.3). The epistemic norm says that '[n]ormally, a person S is epistemically responsible in believing some proposition p at time t only if S checks all of those obvious counter-possibilities whose seriousness is indicated by an adequate set of background beliefs at t'.[20]

---

[17] See Timmons, *Morality without Foundations: A Defense of Ethical Contextualism*, p. 200. See also Alan Thomas, *Value and Context: the Nature of Moral and Political Knowledge* (Oxford: Clarendon Press, 2006), p. 183. Such a conception of moral knowledge will be challenged in Chapter 6.

[18] Timmons, *Morality without Foundations: A Defense of Ethical Contextualism*, p. 195.

[19] Ibid., p. 205.

[20] Timmons, *Morality without Foundations: A Defense of Ethical Contextualism*, p. 200.

Timmons applies this norm to moral propositions, which seems problematic. What am I supposed to do when told to check the relevant counter-possibilities for the belief that having an abortion is morally impermissible? How can I check whether facts obtain that make having an abortion morally permissible? What would make having an abortion morally permissible? The answer to the last question could be that having an abortion can contribute to greater happiness, reduce suffering, or that the possibility to have an abortion enhances the independence of women or even reduces the rate of crime. But it is by no means clear what has to be ruled out, and how it could be ruled out. There is nothing comparable to the possibility that there was no storm or that a burglar destroyed the roof. While there is no question of what would make the belief that a storm has destroyed the roof false, there is a big question as to what would falsify the belief that having an abortion is morally impermissible. If one of the possibilities mentioned above did obtain, the initial belief would not necessarily be false.

What does it mean to rule out a possibility such as the one that having an abortion reduces suffering? Do we have to investigate the matter empirically? Is it possible to investigate it in that way? In the case of the destroyed roof, I can easily ask my neighbours whether there was a storm, or consult the newspapers. What should also be taken into consideration is the role of religion. If someone opposes abortion for religious reasons, his background beliefs will probably not indicate the seriousness of any counter-possibilities. My suspicion is that in the case of our moral beliefs we do not require from ourselves or others that we or they check counter-possibilities. Timmons' epistemic norm seems not to apply to moral beliefs. And although we can cite evidence similar to that supporting empirical beliefs, the main question regarding our moral beliefs is not whether they are sufficiently supported by evidence.

However, empirical and moral judgements share the feature that they ultimately rest on things that are certain and are thus not amenable to justification. Even in the case of empirical beliefs, a point can always be reached where the call to check countering possibilities is pointless. While it makes sense to check whether a storm may have been the cause of my destroyed roof, under normal circumstances it does not make sense to require, for instance, that one check whether the object supposed to have been destroyed was really a roof, whether the roof already existed a few days ago, whether storms can destroy roofs at all and so on.[21]

---

[21] I am grateful to Danièle Moyal-Sharrock for emphasising this similarity between empirical and moral beliefs.

Irrespective of whether moral or empirical judgements are at issue, the kind of justification that is required depends on the kinds of doubts that have been raised. The concrete doubts in a particular case indicate the direction in which the justification ought to go.[22] When we have doubts regarding the way in which a person has come to believe something, we expect him, for instance, to demonstrate that his judgement has been inferred by a valid rule of inference from true premises, or to show that it is based on a reliable source of information. If we doubt that someone is a competent judge, we expect him to demonstrate that he has the required capacities and possesses the information necessary to make a correct judgement. If more experience makes us doubt a moral view, a justification of the doubted view has to show that the perspective in question is not actually challenged by the additional experience. As a response to a doubt referring to socio-cultural change, a justification has to allude to the irrelevance of the respective changes for the validity of the moral position concerned.

As this discussion has shown, we can talk about evidence both in relation to the practice of justifying empirical judgements as well as the practice of justifying moral judgements, although evidence plays a different role in each case. The two practices differ with regard to their aims and the nature of the reasons for doubt. The ways in which we justify in each practice reveal differences as well as similarities. Consequently, whilst it would not be correct to state that moral judgements are doubted and justified in the same manner as empirical judgements, it would also not be correct to assert that the two practices are entirely different. The picture is more complex.

4.5   Epistemic versus moral justification of moral beliefs

4.5.1   The distinction

When dealing with the justification of moral beliefs, we need to clarify whether a distinction should be drawn between moral and epistemic justification. Whether a moral belief is epistemically justified, and whether it is morally justified, are usually conceived of as two different questions. The answer to the first question is thought to depend on epistemic standards, while the response to the second question is assumed to depend on moral standards. Philosophers concerned with the epistemic justification of moral beliefs try to respond to questions like: Do our moral beliefs amount to knowledge (understood as propositional

---

[22] I am indebted to Marcus Willaschek for stressing this point.

knowledge)? Are our moral beliefs sufficiently supported by evidence? Are our moral beliefs likely to be true? I shall briefly present three views of the different kinds of justification.

Timmons notes that beliefs can be justified in relation to different goals.[23] Epistemic justification is connected to epistemic goals such as the goal of having true beliefs and of having knowledge (of course understood as propositional knowledge), whereas non-epistemic justification is connected to non-epistemic goals, for example pragmatic goals like survival.[24] On this view, moral justification is understood as justification relating to a moral goal such as loyalty. This conception of moral justification differs from mine. When I speak about the moral justification of beliefs or judgements, I mean a practice of giving reasons which refer to shared moral standards. The 'moral' in 'moral justification' refers in the first instance to those standards. The practice of justifying moral judgements is, as we have seen, also constituted by certain goals, but loyalty is not amongst them (see 4.3).[25]

BonJour gives an example for a non-moral belief which we can be said to be morally justified in holding:[26]

> [S]uppose that I have a dear friend who has stood by me and supported me through many trials and crises, often at considerable cost to himself. Now this friend stands accused of a horrible crime, everyone else believes him to be guilty, and there is substantial evidence for this conclusion. Suppose too that I have no independent evidence concerning the matter and also that my friend knows me well enough that an insincere claim to believe in his innocence will surely be detected. If in these difficult circumstances I can bring myself to believe in his innocence, it is surely plausible to say that there is a sense in which I am justified in so believing; indeed such a belief might well be regarded as obligatory. But the justification in question is simply not epistemic justification, but rather a kind of *moral* justification: even if my friend is in fact innocent, I obviously do not *know* on this basis that he is innocent, no matter how compelling a reason of *this sort* I may have for my belief.[27]

---

[23] Timmons, *Morality without Foundations: A Defense of Ethical Contextualism*, p. 191.

[24] Ibid.

[25] 'Moral' refers also to those goals.

[26] BonJour does not claim that the belief is itself morally justified.

[27] Laurence BonJour, *The Structure of Empirical Knowledge* (Cambridge, Mass. and London: Harvard University Press, 1985), p. 6.

Here, BonJour gives the example of a person who is, despite evidence to the contrary, morally justified in believing that a friend to whom he feels obliged is innocent of a crime. He even has a moral obligation to believe that. The kind of moral justification BonJour describes is not related to knowledge. The close connection with knowledge is distinctive of epistemic justification. That holding the respective belief is supported by moral reasons of a certain kind does not entail that he (BonJour) can be said to know the content of his belief.

In this example, it is not the respective belief itself, but BonJour's holding the belief that is supported by moral reasons. This belief, the possession of which is thus supported and at the same time not epistemically justified (since the belief is not supported by evidence), is not a moral belief. In fact, I do not think that it makes sense to say that someone is morally justified (in BonJour's sense of morally justified) in holding a false moral belief. While we can be morally justified in this sense in not condemning a friend who acted immorally, because we have the duty to stick by our friends, we would not be justified in believing that what he did was morally right.

The question of interest in the context of this study is whether the distinction between moral and epistemic justification is applicable to *moral* beliefs. Can a moral belief be morally, though not epistemically, justified and vice versa? Let us consider yet another way of distinguishing between different kinds of justification. Geoffrey Sayre-McCord mentions three different standards in relation to which a person can be justified in holding a belief: moral, pragmatic and epistemic standards.[28] Regarding moral standards, he writes that whether a person is *morally* justified in holding a belief can be said to depend on 'whether she is within her rights to believe it, or [...] whether her believing it is (or is expected to be) conducive to the greatest happiness, or [...] whether her believing it is compatible with her other obligations'.[29] The beliefs in question are not necessarily moral beliefs. The moral standards Sayre-McCord mentions differ radically from those to which I refer, and they are clearly standards in order for one to be justified in holding a belief, not for the respective belief itself to be justified.

---

[28] Geoffrey Sayre-McCord, 'Coherentist Epistemology and Moral Theory,' in *Moral Knowledge? New Readings in Moral Epistemology*, ed. Walter Sinnott-Armstrong and Mark Timmons (New York and Oxford: Oxford University Press, 1996), p. 145. He does not claim that these are the only possible standards. I shall only discuss moral and epistemic standards.
[29] Ibid.

Whether a person is *epistemically* justified in holding a belief can be said to depend on 'whether her believing it is appropriately sensitive to her evidence, or [...] whether her believing it means it is (subjectively or objectively) likely to be true, or [...] whether her believing it is the result of a reliable belief-forming process'.[30] It seems that the issues as to whether a person is epistemically, pragmatically, and morally justified in holding a belief can be detached from one another.[31]

Sayre-McCord is, like Timmons, concerned with the epistemic justification of moral beliefs, which he distinguishes from their moral justification. On his view, in the case of *moral* justification, 'we might say that a person's belief that she ought to support a local soup kitchen is morally justified and [...] mean [...] that what she believes is both true and, say, justified by the more general duty we have to help others'.[32] The belief in question is itself a moral belief.

4.5.2 Critique of the distinction

I am not convinced by the distinction between the two kinds of justification of moral beliefs. If what Sayre-McCord writes was what we mean when we state that the belief concerned is *morally* justified, what would we mean if we were to say that it was *epistemically* justified? That it is not justified by such a duty or any kind of moral principle, but by some sort of evidence (where evidence does not include compliance with moral principles)? Further reasons in support of such a belief could be that the relevant person has the means to support the local soup kitchen, that the local soup kitchen concerned is actually helping people in need, and that it would not be better to help those people in a more effective way which is incompatible with supporting the soup kitchen.

It seems to me that the question as to whether we are to say that the respective belief is justified depends on factors which we would classify as moral (such as its compliance with a more general duty) *and* on factors which we would not classify in that way, such as the effectiveness of the soup kitchen compared to other charities, the capacity of the person who holds that belief, and so on. In order to see what kind of justification we usually require for a belief like the one discussed here, we should consider what kind of doubts we might have with regard to it. In the present case, it would be possible to doubt that we are under a moral obligation to support charities, but also that the person ought to

---

[30] Ibid., p. 146.
[31] Ibid., p. 146, note 13.
[32] Ibid., p. 146.

support this particular charity and not another one, assuming that she cannot support them all. Another possibility would be to doubt that she ought to support a *local* soup kitchen, assuming that people in poorer countries than her own need her help more urgently.

What kind of justification are we asking for in raising doubts like these? Moral justification or epistemic justification? We are asking for reasons to think that the person in question really ought to support the local soup kitchen. As we saw, such reasons can be both moral and non-moral considerations. Sayre-McCord seems to think that moral duties or other moral considerations play no role in the epistemic justification of a moral belief. Yet this would mean that a moral belief can be said to be epistemically justified, even though it is in conflict with moral standards such as moral obligations. That is, my belief that a particular action is morally wrong can be epistemically justified despite the action in question complying with shared moral standards. Although I acknowledge that not only moral considerations can be invoked as reasons in support of moral beliefs, I deny that there is a justification of moral beliefs that ignores moral reasons entirely. If we appeal to beliefs about empirical facts, such as the effectiveness of the soup kitchen, this is associated with our moral belief that we ought to use our time and money to support charities that make a difference. Sayre-McCord is committed to the view that the answer to the question as to whether a moral belief is epistemically justified ought not to draw on moral standards, and that such a conception of epistemic justification of moral beliefs makes sense. I think that this position is untenable.

4.6   Conclusion

I started this chapter by looking at different practices of moral justification, asking under what conditions the issue of moral justification usually arises. Considering cases in which moral justification is required, I came to understand these practices as having a variety of functions, such as legitimising actions, attitudes, institutions, and practices, avoiding blame, demonstrating one's innocence, reaching agreement on binding rules, convincing dissenters, and achieving moral progress. I have described and compared the grammar of these practices. The following rules belong to the grammar of the game of justifying moral judgements:

a. What raises the demand for justification is a morally objectionable view, that is, it is assumed that there are moral reasons that count against adopting the relevant position.

b. It is supposed that there are reasons in favour of it, that is, the success of the justificatory attempt is not thought to be ruled out from the start.[33]

c. It is assumed that there are shared moral beliefs which serve as common ground (agreement over judgements).

d. The success or failure of the justificatory attempt has important consequences for the individuals involved.

This view conflicts with the claim that all moral beliefs are *per se* in need of justification. I compared the practice of justifying moral judgements with that of justifying empirical judgements, pointing out their differences as well as their similarities. The idea behind this comparison was that we should not simply construct an account of the justification of moral judgements that is analogous to accounts of the justification of empirical judgements, but look at the former practice in its own right. The comparison revealed that although we can, for instance, talk about evidence in both cases, the two practices differ with regard to their aims and the kinds of reasons for doubt. The way we justify in the two practices reveals differences as well as similarities. A discussion of Timmons' epistemic norm made it seem questionable that the same epistemic norms apply to both empirical and moral beliefs. My rather sketchy discussion of these practices showed their complexity. Neither the claim that moral judgements are doubted and justified in the same manner as empirical judgements, nor the claim that the two practices are entirely different, is correct.

Finally, I discussed the alleged distinction between epistemically and morally justifying a moral belief. I rejected the distinction on the grounds that in the case of moral beliefs our doubts and justifications are never based on non-moral reasons alone. It does not make sense to say that a moral belief can be epistemically justified despite not being morally justified.

---

[33] Here I noted that in some cases it is ruled out, but the person demanding a justification has at least an idea of what it could look like.

5
Moral Certainty

5.1 Introduction

By focusing on the practices of morally justifying actions and moral judgements, it has been possible to support the view that justification is required only for that which seems to be morally problematic. I shall now return to those judgements which seem to be anything but problematic, the justification of which however has worried moral philosophers. I shall start by presenting Bambrough's proof of moral knowledge, which he intends to construct in an analogous manner to Moore's proof of the external world. Bambrough's defence of common sense in the moral realm raises the question as to whether we can respond to it along the same lines as Wittgenstein responded to Moore. It seems to me that we can. Thus, Bambrough's proof provides a good starting point for this study's attempt to draw an analogy between certainty regarding the empirical world and (objective) moral certainty.[1] It will be argued that we encounter cases with some or all of the following features also in the moral domain:[2]

1. Reasonable doubt is impossible.
2. Everyone seems to know the issue in question.

---

[1] Just like certainty regarding the empirical world, I take this certainty to be objective in the sense explained in Chapter 3, as opposed to a (subjective) feeling of certainty. For the sake of simplicity I shall refer below to this certainty simply as 'moral certainty'. Unlike Pleasants and others, I do not add the adjective 'basic' because being objectively certain implies having a fundamental role.

[2] Like the examples Wittgenstein ponders, cases of moral certainty reveal family resemblances.

3. Attempts to doubt or justify suggest a lack of seriousness, competence or even sanity.
4. Mistake is impossible.
5. There are no supporting reasons that are more certain.
6. That which is certain cannot be meaningfully uttered in ordinary contexts.

When exploring cases of moral certainty, I shall refer to other versions of the analogy and point out differences between certainty regarding the empirical world and moral certainty. My reflections in this chapter build on a number of insights gained in Chapter 3:

a. It is illuminating to compare the role of the sentences in the examples Wittgenstein considers with the role of grammatical propositions.
b. Objective certainty is manifested in the way we act.
c. Moorean propositions manifest attempts to articulate this 'enacted' certainty.
d. Doubts do not arise on the level of reactions, and it is therefore not correct to talk about knowledge.
e. The basis for our knowledge can be found in our actions and reactions, not in principles or propositions.
f. Action presupposes certainty (uncertainty could never lead to action).[3]
g. There is continuous development from the primitive forms of behaviour at the start of language acquisition, which are closely related to our instinctive endowment, to the complex forms of behaviour that characterise our linguistic practice.

The moral implications of these insights will be explained below, starting with a discussion of Bambrough's proof.

5.2 Bambrough's proof of moral knowledge

Bambrough claims that '[i]f we can show by Moore's argument that there is an external world, then we can show *by parity of reasoning*, by an exactly analogous argument, that we have moral knowledge, that there are some propositions of morals which are *certainly* true, and which we *know* to be true'. Bambrough describes Moore's proof as 'consist[ing]

---

[3] Also in cases where we have to act under uncertainty, some things are certain.

essentially in holding up his hands and saying, "Here are two hands; therefore there are at least two material objects"'. He describes his analogous proof of moral knowledge as 'consist[ing] essentially in saying, "We know that this child, who is about to undergo what would otherwise be painful surgery, should be given an anaesthetic before the operation. Therefore we know at least one moral proposition to be true"'.[4]

Although as he formulates it, Bambrough's proof is not exactly analogous to Moore's, it seems that, like Moore, he claims to know something he could neither doubt nor justify. This stance may thus be vulnerable to Wittgenstein's critique. Before presenting this criticism, it is important to address briefly the differences between the two proofs. In order for Bambrough's proof to be exactly analogous, what is to be proven would have to be the reality of morality ('that at least *some* things are bad and *some* acts morally wrong'[5]), not our knowledge of it. While knowledge does not figure explicitly in the conclusion of Moore's proof, knowledge of the existence of his hands is taken as a premise. His claim to know that there was a hand was Wittgenstein's target, and Bambrough in fact makes an (almost) analogous claim: the claim that '[we] know that this child, who is about to undergo what would otherwise be painful surgery, should be given an anaesthetic before the operation'. Bambrough's formulation of his proof incorporates Moore's claim to know the premise of his proof and Moore's claim in 'A Defence of Common Sense' that everybody knows the things that he claims to know.

Unlike Wittgenstein, Bambrough is convinced by Moore's proof, which he regards as an adequate response to the sceptic. He accuses philosophers who accept that proof while at the same time denying that we have moral knowledge of defending common sense in one field but attacking it in another.[6] I would like to follow Wittgenstein in countering Bambrough's knowledge claim regarding the child that he is right *if* he thereby wants to say that we cannot imagine doubting this, or in other words that it stands fast for us. He does indeed point to an interesting similarity between the certainty that I have two hands, which are really hands and not just a bundle of ideas à la Berkeley, and the certainty of some moral states of affairs, for instance that killing *this* child is wrong.[7]

---

[4] Renford Bambrough, *Moral Scepticism and Moral Knowledge* (London and Henley: Routledge and Kegan Paul, 1979), pp. 12 and 15.

[5] Nigel Pleasants, 'Wittgenstein, Ethics and Basic Moral Certainty,' *Inquiry* 51, no. 3 (2008): p. 262.

[6] Bambrough, *Moral Scepticism and Moral Knowledge*, pp. 15 f.

[7] Berkeley thought that only minds and ideas existed, and that what appeared to be physical objects were nothing other than bundles of ideas.

Bambrough states that according to common sense, 'we *know* that stealing is wrong, that promise-keeping is right, that unselfishness is good, that cruelty is bad'.[8] I agree with him that

[w]e speak as naturally of a child not knowing the difference between right and wrong as we do of his not knowing the difference between right and left.[9] We say that we do not know what to do as naturally as we say that we do not know what is the case. We say that a man's moral views are unreasonable as naturally as we say that his views on a matter of fact are unreasonable. In moral contexts, just as naturally as in non-moral contexts, we speak of thinking, wondering, asking; of beliefs, opinions, convictions, solutions; of perplexity, confusion, consistency and inconsistency, of errors and mistakes, of teaching, learning, training, showing, proving, finding out, understanding, realising, recognising and coming to see.[10]

It is not merely with regard to the realm of empirical facts, but also in connection with questions of right and wrong, good and bad, permissible and impermissible, that we ask for reasons, justify beliefs, and say that we do or do not know something. Words such as 'knowing', 'thinking', 'believing' and so on play a vital role in our moral language-games. It would be unconvincing to deny that it ever makes sense to say that one knows what the right thing to do is or that a particular moral judgement is wrong. The grammar of the word 'know' seems to be the same whether we use it in relation to empirical facts or to moral issues. Also within moral language-games, 'I know' is used in cases in which the speaker thinks that there is no reason for doubt, while such reasons are at the same time not excluded. It is moreover characteristic of uses of 'I know' that what is claimed to be known can be justified, mistake is not ruled out, and it makes sense to say 'I do not know'. These are the characteristics emphasised by Wittgenstein in his critique of Moore.

[8] Bambrough, *Moral Scepticism and Moral Knowledge*: p. 16.

[9] As will be argued in Chapter 6, what we refer to when we say of a child that it does not yet know the difference between right and wrong is first and foremost a complex competence, not propositional knowledge. Likewise, knowing the difference between right and left is a matter of competence. Hanna and Harrison give a detailed account of what knowing that difference amounts to. Patricia Hanna and Bernard Harrison, *Word & World. Practice and the Foundations of Language* (Cambridge et al.: Cambridge University Press, 2004), pp. 169 ff.

[10] Bambrough, *Moral Scepticism and Moral Knowledge*, p. 16.

There are certainly many instances of the use of the word 'to know' within moral language-games that are entirely innocent and unobjectionable. For instance, someone might say that he knows that he should have helped his friend, but that he was too lazy. How would he answer the question of how he knew that? Wittgenstein writes that the expression 'I know' often refers to the reasons on which a knowledge claim is based:

> 'I know' often means: I have the proper grounds for my statement. So if the other person is acquainted with the language-game, he would admit that I know. The other, if he is acquainted with the language-game, must be able to imagine *how* one may know something of the kind.
>
> *On Certainty*, § 18

Being acquainted with our moral language-games, we have no problems imagining how someone may know that he should have acted differently in a particular situation. This can be known by being aware of one's obligations in concrete cases. In the example in question, the person knows that laziness is not a valid excuse for not honouring the obligation to help a friend. In addition, he knows that in the relevant situation he could have helped his friend, and that the costs of helping him would not have been so high as to release him from the obligation. He can refer to all this in responding to the question of how he knows what he claims to know.

5.3　Moral knowledge versus moral certainty

This use of the term 'know' differs from Bambrough's use of it. It is clear from the context that by saying that '[w]e know that this child, who is about to undergo what would otherwise be painful surgery, should be given an anaesthetic before the operation', he implies that what we thus know is as obvious as the existence of our hands when we refer to them and gesture with them. It seems that we can respond in the spirit of *On Certainty* that he is right in noting that for any morally competent agent who lives in a society where anaesthetics exist and is familiar with their effects, there would, in the situation envisaged by Bambrough, be no question as to whether the child about to undergo the operation should be given an anaesthetic.[11] But this fact is not rightly expressed by claiming that he knows the truth of a moral proposition.

---

[11] The competence I am referring to here will be addressed in detail in Chapter 6. I take it to involve different kinds of dispositions, including emotional dispositions.

If Bambrough can rightly be said to know what he claims to know, it must be possible to raise doubts regarding the object of his knowledge claim. Yet what reasons could a morally competent agent who fulfils the criteria mentioned above have to doubt that giving the anaesthetic is what should be done in that situation? We can conceive of scenarios in which it could be doubted that this was the right course of action, for example if the child were allergic to all available anaesthetics, or if all available anaesthetics had serious adverse effects. However, Bambrough's use of the proposition in question shows that he is referring to a situation in which there are no such reasons for doubting that giving the anaesthetic is the morally right thing to do. He intends to give an example of a paradigm case in which gratuitous suffering by a person is avoided where there are the means to do so. It is stressed that 'no proposition that could plausibly be alleged as a reason in favour of doubting the truth of the proposition that the child should be given an anaesthetic can possibly be more certainly true than that proposition itself'.[12] He thus gives an example of a case where the issue of justification does not arise because the fact that, absent any countervailing reasons, the child should be given the anaesthetic is presupposed by any doubt that might arise (for example a doubt regarding the rightness of the action where there are reasons to believe that the child is allergic to the anaesthetic) and any justification that could be given (for example a justification for not giving the anaesthetic that refers to the child's allergy).

Not only are reasons for doubt absent in this case, but there are also no reasons in favour of the truth of the proposition concerned that are more certain than that proposition itself. If there were someone with us in the operating theatre who asked us why the child should be given an anaesthetic, we would not know how to respond to him. If we had the time (which is unlikely), we would perhaps try to make sure that he had understood us correctly and that he knew what an anaesthetic was.[13] Once it was clear that the person was a competent speaker and that there was no terminological disagreement, we would probably send him outside because his presence would make us feel highly uncomfortable.

The reader will notice that my description of this example includes aspects which seem to be specific to the moral case. If someone were

---

[12] Bambrough, *Moral Scepticism and Moral Knowledge*, p. 15.
[13] See Judith Lichtenberg, 'Moral Certainty,' *Philosophy* 69, no. 268 (1994): p. 193.

asking us, for instance, for our reasons for thinking that our hands existed, we would presumably be less emotional. We might ultimately shrug our shoulders and move on, whereas in the moral case we would experience feelings such as outrage or consternation and might not be able to tolerate the continued presence of the other person.[14]

In cases in which reasonable doubt is impossible, it is also impossible for us to be mistaken. In the same way as in the case of Moore's claim to know that his hands exist, it is not clear what a mistake would look like. If someone said that the child should *not* be given an anaesthetic, we would not think that he was mistaken, but rather that he was sick, either a sadist or a psychopath. It would not be an instance of mistake because that person would have ceased to judge 'in conformity with mankind' (OC 156).

Moreover, it must seem to Bambrough that if it turned out that he was mistaken, that is that we should in fact *not* give the anaesthetic (which would amount to not trying to avoid the gratuitous suffering of another person even though the means to do so are available), he would be deprived of the standards for making moral judgements. He must have the impression that if he were mistaken about *that*, he would no longer know what 'right' and 'wrong' meant.

If what Bambrough refers to as a moral proposition which he knows to be true is something about which, under normal circumstances, he cannot be mistaken, which he cannot imagine doubting and for which he cannot provide justification, then what he refers to is not properly conceived of as an object of knowledge, but rather as something that stands fast for him. That the child in question should receive the anaesthetic should then be conceived of as true only insofar as it is 'an unmoving foundation of his moral language-games' (see OC 403). Within his moral reasoning, it operates as an axis. We as morally sensitive people simply try to prevent a person from suffering gratuitously if it is in our power to do so without incurring costs that are intolerably high. Doing so does not involve any more reflection than answering the question of what '2 + 2' amounts to. We might reflect upon how we could best prevent that person from suffering, but we do not reflect on whether we should do anything to help her in the first place.

Having criticised Bambrough along these lines, it must be noted that he did not choose the best example. A better example would be one relating to a situation with which everyone may be confronted, and

---

[14] Differences between cases of non-moral and cases of moral certainty will be addressed in greater detail below (5.9).

not only surgeons and nurses. Consider the well-known pond-example used by Peter Singer in order to convince people that they have strong obligations towards the world's poor: 'If I am walking past a shallow pond and see a child drowning in it, I ought to wade in and pull the child out. This will mean getting my clothes muddy, but this is insignificant, while the death of the child would presumably be a very bad thing.'[15] No morally competent agent would deny that rescuing the child is what the situation requires. This is not up for moral debate. When Singer uses the example in his talks about poverty, no one in the audience raises a doubt regarding the obligation to pull the child out of the pond. However, his core focus is on the question as to whether citizens of affluent countries are under an obligation to give money to the distant poor instead of spending it on expensive clothes, smart phones and so on. While morally competent agents disagree about *that* question and over whether Singer's argument in favour of such an obligation is sound, they take the obligation towards the drowning child for granted. In debates about moral obligations, no one (apart from perhaps a few philosophers) would think it necessary to provide an argument in favour of the obligation to (attempt to) rescue a child in a situation such as that described by Singer. If someone in Singer's audience were to claim that a businessman wearing a tailored Armani-suit would not be obliged to wade into the pond, she would be regarded as making a joke, as wanting to be polemical for the sake of it, or as being out of her mind.

It therefore looks as if the certainty Wittgenstein was concerned with has a moral analogue. The above reflections suggest that there are things which are certain for us as participants in moral language-games, just as there are things we cannot doubt as players of epistemic language-games.[16] The objects of this certainty could be said to be the axes around which our moral doubts and justifications turn, or core parts of our agreement over (moral) judgements. If the analogy holds, the end of our justifications of moral judgements is 'an ungrounded way of acting' (OC 110), that is, the basis of our moral knowledge can be found in our actions and reactions, and not in principles or propositions. There are

---

[15] Peter Singer, 'Famine, Affluence, and Morality,' *Philosophy and Public Affairs* 1, no. 3 (1972): p. 231. Singer argues that we as citizens of affluent countries are in a parallel situation with regard to the people who are dying of starvation far away from us.

[16] I distinguish here between epistemic and moral language-games although the moral language-games I am concerned with involve epistemic practices such as doubting and justifying. By 'epistemic language-games' I mean language-games in which we apply epistemic predicates to (alleged) empirical facts.

propositions that only look like moral claims that are open to doubt and justification, but are in fact attempts to put into propositional form something that manifests itself only in action.

Wittgenstein's claim that 'uncertainty could never lead to action' (CE, p. 397) seems to be particularly relevant for ethics, where action is of utmost importance. In order for moral action to be possible, there has to be some certainty over moral matters. It is obvious that were someone to doubt whether the concepts 'good', 'bad', 'right', 'wrong' and so on were applicable to anything at all, that person would be unable to act on the basis of a moral conviction. Moreover, he or she would be unable to make a moral judgement about any particular case. The statement that uncertainty would not lead to action also implies that participation in moral language-games presupposes some agreement on the meaning of moral terms. Agreement – and thus certainty – is an enabling condition for moral discourse. Were there no consistency at all in our applications of words such as 'right', 'wrong', 'honest' or 'generous', these words could not serve as tools of communication.[17] I thus disagree with Stefan Rummens, who acknowledges that moral disagreement presupposes a 'background agreement', but denies that this needs to be an agreement concerning moral matters.[18]

5.4   Further examples of moral certainty

5.4.1   'It is wrong to kill this child'

Now that I have sketched out the analogy that I have in mind, we should explore its plausibility further by considering other possible cases of moral certainty. Staying close to Moore's claim to know that his hands exist, let us start by considering the case in which a person points to a particular child on the street and says 'It is wrong to kill this child'.

To begin with, such an act would strike us as highly bizarre. Were we to witness such a scene, we would wonder about the speaker's intentions. Does he want to achieve a particular effect on his audience? By contrast, to say within a political discussion that 'It is wrong to kill children in the course of bombing military targets' makes perfect sense. What is it therefore that makes the first scenario so peculiar?

---

[17] See Oswald Hanfling, 'Learning about Right and Wrong: Ethics and Language,' *Philosophy* 78, no. 303 (2003): pp. 27 f.

[18] Stefan Rummens, 'On the Possibility of a Wittgensteinian Account of Moral Certainty,' *The Philosophical Forum* 44, no. 2 (2013): p. 145. The issue of moral agreement will be addressed in greater detail in Chapter 7.

5.4.1.1 *Reasonable doubt is impossible*

We would be puzzled by the utterance, first, because we do not understand why anyone would say this and what he could mean by it. Second, we would not know how anyone could doubt the wrongness of such an act. What reasons could there be for thinking that killing the child would not be wrong? That the speaker makes the respective utterance suggests that he thinks that others might have reasons to doubt the wrongness of the action. However, I cannot conceive of any reason that would still be within our moral framework. Someone who had doubts in this case would have to be someone who did not value life, but by not valuing life he would already be 'beyond good and evil' or 'beyond the moral pale'. He would be regarded as abnormal just like someone who under normal circumstances doubted the existence of his hands. While we would think of the former as mad, we would conceive of the latter as suffering from sociopathy. Neither could be trusted.[19]

The point that doubting the wrongness of the action seems impossible can also be expressed by saying that 'It is wrong to kill this child' is something that everyone seems to know, 'without being able to say how' (OC 84). If the person uttering the sentence can be said to know it, everybody can (see ibid.). Yet as Wittgenstein shows in relation to Moore's knowledge claims, we are dealing here not with an item of knowledge but with something that stands fast for us.

Killing the child would be one of the paradigm cases of killing towards which we have the attitude of 'basic certainty', as Pleasants puts it.[20] Not only the wrongness of killing this particular child is beyond doubt, but also the wrongness of killing in general. People disagree about whether or not particular cases of killing might be justified, for example the killing of a dictator; however, they do so on the basis of their agreement regarding the moral wrongness of killing as such. That wrongness is simply taken for granted.[21] I can no more doubt that it is morally wrong to kill someone than I can doubt that what I am now using to type these words are my hands. The wrongness of (paradigmatic cases of) killing

---

[19] Of course I do not deny the existence of immoral behaviour and practices. However, as will be argued below, the fact that human beings do not always act morally and do not oppose all immoral practices does not undermine the claim that there are moral certainties (5.9 and 7.2.5).

[20] Nigel Pleasants, 'Wittgenstein and Basic Moral Certainty,' *Philosophia* 37 (2009): p. 678.

[21] See ibid., p. 671.

'is just as certain as any logical or analytic truth, or any object of basic empirical certainty'.[22]

5.4.1.2   *Mistake seems impossible*

If the person in our example said that it was right to kill that child, we would not think of him as being mistaken, since it would seem that he was not judging in conformity with the moral community. It would almost seem as if he used the terms 'right' and 'kill' with a different meaning. By contrast, in a situation in which a number of people could be saved by killing one particular child – or in a philosophical discussion about such a situation – anyone who thought that it would be wrong to kill the child would think that someone claiming the opposite was mistaken. Here there would be 'a place [...] in the game' for such a mistake (OC 647). Both sides would agree that killing (a child) is ordinarily wrong, whilst disagreeing over whether special circumstances obtained in the case at hand that warranted the killing of this particular child. The possibility of mistake rests on a conformity in judgements.

As regards the original scenario, we would not think that the speaker was mistaken, but that he lacked moral competence or simply wanted to shock. We could compare him to someone who pointed to a fresh blood stain and said sincerely, in good lighting conditions, that it was green. The latter person would either be joking or lack the capacity to distinguish between red and green, being red-green colour blind. Similarly, the former person could be said to be morally blind. By contrast, we would not regard a person as colour blind if she identified as turquoise something which we had identified as green. Similarly, we would not regard someone who disagreed with us on the moral status of the practice of paying bonuses to managers as morally blind. There is, however, no sharp boundary between cases involving blindness and cases involving a different moral view of an equally morally competent agent.[23] As there are different degrees of visual limitation, moral blindness comes in degrees. Some people are only slightly less morally sensitive than agents who are fully morally competent: for instance, some people act selfishly only in very few cases, while others lack moral sensitivity to a greater

---

[22] Pleasants, 'Wittgenstein, Ethics and Basic Moral Certainty,' p. 263. Pleasants refers to the certainty Wittgenstein is concerned with in *On Certainty* as 'empirical'. I have decided to refrain from using this term in order to avoid giving the impression that the certainty concerned is derived from experience.

[23] Some people might consider those who defend the practice of paying bonuses to managers to be morally blind.

extent. Examples of the latter kind are people who ignore the needs and interests of others in most cases or who often use others as mere instruments in order to achieve their own goals.

5.4.1.3 Doubt as a sign of moral incompetence

If someone were to raise doubts regarding the wrongness of killing the child, this would also provide us with a reason to call into question the moral competence of the speaker. As we saw in Chapter 3, not doubting certain things is a sign of competence. This holds for moral agency as well. If we had no reason to assume that the speaker was making a joke, wanted to shock or lacked linguistic competence, we would call into question her moral competence. It goes without saying that this is not our normal reaction to people who disagree with us on moral issues. In moral controversies, we usually consider our interlocutor to be a morally competent agent. We assume that, despite disagreeing with us on a certain moral issue, the person debating with us is like us in being generally morally competent, that is capable of adopting a moral standpoint and trading moral reasons. This implies the assumption that he shares a range of moral beliefs with us, including first and foremost beliefs concerning paradigm cases of right and wrong action. This was the third characteristic mentioned in Chapter 4 (4.2). It is thus assumed that he already judges in conformity with the moral community.

5.4.1.4 Non-availability of reasons more certain than what they are invoked to support

Could the person in our example support his claim with reasons that are more certain than the wrongness of killing the child? Are there such reasons? I do not think that any such reasons are available. Pleasants' discussion of philosophical attempts to explain or justify the assertion that killing is wrong and that death is bad nicely illustrates this point. These attempts fail in a similar way to Moore's proof, namely 'in a manner that discloses the phenomenon of basic (moral) certainty'.[24]

Pleasants criticises what he calls 'deprivation explanations' for the fact that killing is wrong and that death is bad.[25] According to explanations of this kind, the wrongness of killing lies in the loss or deprivation imposed on the victim. Such explanations imply that the killing of an old person is less wrong than the killing of a child or middle aged person, since the latter may be deprived of more possibilities and a

---

[24] Pleasants, 'Wittgenstein and Basic Moral Certainty,' p. 669.
[25] Ibid., p. 674.

future of greater value. Thus, we can imagine the person in our scenario saying that killing the child would be wrong because it would deprive it of a future of great value, greater than that of an adult. How does that sound as a reason?

As pointed out by Pleasants, the biggest deficiency of these theories is that they fall short of explaining why death is bad and killing is wrong. I fully agree with him that they do not illuminate the ways we ordinarily talk about death as being bad and killing as being wrong. Instead they 'rephrase in grandiloquent philosophical language what everyone already knows just in virtue of being able to use the concepts "death", "killing" and "murder" appropriately'.[26]

5.4.1.5   *The utterance does not make sense in ordinary contexts*

Is the assertion 'It is wrong to kill this child' an example of a meaningful utterance? Does the speaker make a move in a moral language-game by uttering this sentence? I already noted that the utterance would strike us as highly bizarre and that we would wonder about the speaker's intentions. Without an appropriate 'surrounding' (OC 350), the utterance lacks sense. It is unintelligible to us. Although its literal meaning is clear, we do not know what the speaker is saying. This suggests that what the speaker is trying to say is something that, just like the states of affairs invoked by Moore's assertions, 'no-one (apart from a philosopher trying to prove a philosophical thesis the negation of which cannot be taken seriously) would ever think of putting into propositional form'.[27] However, we can imagine circumstances in which the utterance would be meaningful. In the above mentioned situation in which a number of people could be saved by killing one particular child, the sentence 'It is wrong to kill this child' makes sense. In this context the wrongness of the action can be doubted and reasons can be cited in support of it.

It also holds for the general principle 'It is wrong to kill innocent and non-threatening people' that we usually do not make a move in a moral language-game by uttering it. This is stressed by Pleasants:

---

[26] Pleasants, 'Wittgenstein and Basic Moral Certainty,' p. 676. A philosophical attempt to doubt or justify a moral certainty such as the fact that killing is wrong is just as pointless as such an attempt by a non-philosopher. I disagree with Timmons, who argues that basic moral beliefs that do not require justification in ordinary contexts require justification in philosophical contexts. Mark Timmons, *Morality without Foundations: A Defense of Ethical Contextualism* (New York: Oxford University Press, 1999), pp. 210 ff.

[27] Pleasants, 'Wittgenstein, Ethics and Basic Moral Certainty,' p. 250.

So we might say that it was wrong of Smith to kill Jones because his victim was an innocent and non-threatening person; but then to add 'and it is wrong to kill innocent and non-threatening people' would not merely be redundant, it would betray a lack of moral sensibility.[28]

The justification of the judgement that it was wrong for Smith to kill Jones stops with the information that Jones was an innocent and non-threatening person. At this point the position is clear, and asking for further reasons would only make one look morally incompetent. No morally competent agent will ask for further reasons in this case, or try to provide any. The assertion 'It is wrong to kill innocent and non-threatening people' would only be a move in a moral language-game if it were taken to be an emphatic utterance (as opposed to an informative utterance).[29]

The attempt to provide a justification can thus also reveal incompetence. What if the person saying 'It is wrong to kill this child' were to add 'because it is "an irrevocable, maximally unjust prevention of the realisation of the [child's] life purposes"'?[30] I agree with Pleasants that the effect would be 'a mixture of absurdity, mirth, incongruity, bemusement and offensiveness'.[31] Iczkovits notes that 'sometimes giving reasons and justification are a proof of cruelty'.[32] That providing a reason like the one mentioned above would have this kind of effect suggests that the original utterance ('It is wrong to kill this child') constitutes an attempt to articulate something that is certain and therefore does not admit of justification.

5.4.2 'Promises have to be kept'

A further example of moral certainty is the wrongness of breaking a promise. Doubting the general obligation to keep one's promises is not a possible move in our moral language-games. Anyone who voiced this doubt would appear to lack moral competence. Unless we assumed that she were joking, we would properly conclude that she had not understood what a promise is. Promises have to be kept by virtue of what promises are. While it can be meaningfully asked whether in a concrete

---

[28] Pleasants, 'Wittgenstein and Basic Moral Certainty,' p. 677.
[29] I thank Danièle Moyal-Sharrock for pointing this out.
[30] Pleasants, 'Wittgenstein and Basic Moral Certainty,' p. 676.
[31] Ibid., p. 675.
[32] Yaniv Iczkovits, *Wittgenstein's Ethical Thought* (Basingstoke: Palgrave Macmillan, 2012), p. 166.

situation a particular promise has to be kept, the question as to whether promises have to be kept in general does not make sense. In a particular case, grounds for justification might obtain that, all things considered, meant that it was right to break the promise. If there were no general obligation to keep one's promises, the institution of promising would not exist. As Thomas Scanlon points out, promises would be rendered meaningless if we were allowed to break them for any reason whatsoever.[33] This does not mean that we would no longer know what the word 'promise' meant (we would still have knowledge of past instances of promising), but that the institution of promising could not fulfil its function any longer. The utterance 'I promise...' would have ceased to be a possible move in a moral language-game.

Can we imagine any circumstances in which the question 'Why is it not generally permitted to break one's promises?' is fully intelligible? A possible context in which we would take that question seriously is an educational context in which we try to explain to a child what we mean by saying that we promised something to someone or that someone had promised something to us.

What would convince someone of the truth of the judgement 'It is wrong to break a promise'? It is incomprehensible how a competent participant in the practice of promising could question it. The only way to convince a person who lacks an understanding of that practice seems to be to teach it to her, thereby also explaining to her the meaning of the word 'promise'. However, this would not be called 'providing a justification for that judgement', but rather 'explaining the meaning of that judgement'. We would be teaching her to participate in the practice of promising. Once the relevant person has understood the practice, she will no longer require any justification for the judgement that it is wrong to break a promise.

5.4.3 'Slavery is wrong'

Another example is the moral wrongness of slavery, which today has 'the status of an established fact'.[34] Just as the fact that it is impossible for human beings to go to the moon, which was referred to by Wittgenstein, this proposition is an example of something that changed its status. For Wittgenstein it was beyond doubt that no one could ever

---

[33] Thomas. M. Scanlon, *What We Owe to Each Other* (Cambridge, Mass. and London: The Belknap Press of Harvard University Press, 1998), p. 200.

[34] Nigel Pleasants, 'Moral Argument Is Not Enough: The Persistence of Slavery and the Emergence of Abolition,' *Philosophical Topics* 38, no. 1 (2011): p. 152.

have been to the moon. Today, we read his reflections on this example with bemusement.[35]

'Slavery is wrong' is an example of a proposition the status of which has changed from that of a moral claim that was not taken seriously to that of a certainty. The socioeconomic practice of slavery was taken for granted and regarded as a natural feature of the social world for centuries, though was subsequently turned into a 'paradigm of a morally wrong institutionalized practice'.[36] Despite the existence of new forms of slavery,[37] the wrongness of the old forms is now taken for granted by all morally competent agents.[38] Pleasants refers to Abraham Lincoln's famous statement that 'if slavery is not wrong, then nothing is wrong'[39], which echoes Wittgenstein's insight that in some cases, if it turned out that we were mistaken 'the foundation of all judging would be taken away from [us]' (OC 614). I shall return to this example in Chapter 7, where I address the possibility of moral criticism and moral change. The case of slavery can be regarded as 'the paradigmatic case of radical moral criticism, which was successful to such an extent that not only were attitudes changed fundamentally, but the object of criticism [was] itself abolished'.[40]

5.4.4 'People are free to do otherwise'

A slightly different example of something that is beyond doubt in our moral language-games is the freedom to do otherwise, which itself is said to be the *conditio sine qua non* of moral responsibility. In everyday life, we praise and blame people for their actions, presuming that they could have done otherwise. Here I am referring to the ability to do

---

[35] However, although it was unimaginable for Wittgenstein that human beings could go to the moon, this was no longer excluded by the physical knowledge of his time. See Avishai Margalit, 'Was Wittgenstein Moon-Blind?,' in *Wittgenstein. Eine Neubewertung/Towards a Re-Evaluation* [Akten des 14. Internationalen Wittgenstein-Symposiums 1989] (Wien: Hölder-Pilcher-Tempsky, 1990), p. 209 f. I shall return to this example in my discussion of moral change in Chapter 7.

[36] Pleasants, 'Moral Argument Is Not Enough: The Persistence of Slavery and the Emergence of Abolition,' p. 139.

[37] See Kevin Bales, *Disposable People: New Slavery in the Global Economy*, 2nd ed. (Berkeley: University of California Press, 2012).

[38] New forms of slavery constitute an example of an institutionalised practice the harmful character of which is acknowledged, whilst its existence is not opposed. See Pleasants, 'Moral Argument Is Not Enough: The Persistence of Slavery and the Emergence of Abolition,' pp. 146 ff.

[39] Ibid., p. 140.

[40] Ibid., p. 141.

otherwise in the 'libertarian' sense, and not in the 'compatibilist' sense. Compatibilists take people to have the ability to act otherwise counterfactually, that is they argue that people are able to do otherwise *if they choose to do so.* According to compatibilism, there is no inconsistency in claiming both that I am able to do otherwise and that the past and the basic laws of nature together entail the action that I actually perform. Libertarians, by contrast, ask for more: to say of me that I am able to do otherwise requires that the actions which I actually perform are not entailed by the past and the basic laws of nature.[41]

Despite the arguments against the crucial role of this presumption in our practices of praising and blaming, I assume that the belief that those whom we praise or blame could have done otherwise is indispensable for these practices.[42] Recalling the distinction between different levels of moral practice introduced in Chapter 2, the language-games in which doubt is cast on the importance of that assumption are located at the level of critical reflection upon our moral deliberation. At the level of habitual moral practice, the connection between moral blame and the possibility that what one is blamed for could have been avoided is not called into question. There, absent special circumstances such as, for instance, duress or the influence of a drug, we assume that it was up to the agent which action out of the alternatives he chose to perform.

Likewise, we consider that it is up to us whether we now stand up or continue to remain seated, given that we are not tied to a chair, paralysed or subject to any similar impairment. While we take ourselves and others not to be morally responsible for being blown into another person by the wind, thereby causing harm, we ascribe moral responsibility to someone who, without being forced by nature or other people, assaults another person. Legal practice is also instructive here. The assumption that people can act otherwise than they actually do functions as an 'axis' within deliberations over whether or not a particular offender was able to act otherwise in a particular case and is therefore fully responsible or not.

It is not merely praising, blaming, ascribing moral responsibility and legal practice which presuppose the assumption that people can act differently from how they actually do. Moral and indeed all kinds of rules would appear pointless if people were not able to choose those

---

[41] See Timothy O'Connor, 'Free Will,' in *The Stanford Encyclopedia of Philosophy*, ed. Edward N. Zalta (2014).

[42] For an argument against the crucial role of this belief see for example R. Jay Wallace, *Responsibility and the Moral Sentiments* (Cambridge, Mass. and London: Harvard University Press, 1994), pp. 7 f.

actions that accord with the rules. In such a case, it would merely be a coincidence if actual behaviour coincided with the behaviour prescribed by a rule.[43]

5.5   The heterogeneity of the examples

The examples discussed thus far reveal both similarities and differences. Let us focus on the differences for the moment. The last example is obviously different in that it is not an example of a moral belief. Another example of something non-moral that stands fast in our moral language-games is the fact that human beings are vulnerable to pain.

'People are free to do otherwise' seems to differ also in another respect from the other examples considered. It seems at least that doubt is not unintelligible in this case. Philosophical explanations of this freedom lack the ridiculousness of philosophical explanations of the wrongness of killing. We seem to understand what it means to think that people could not have acted differently than they actually did. It seems possible for example to follow the fatalist in her way of thinking. This appears to distinguish the case from, for instance, the proposition that 'It is bad to harm innocent people'. However, while I think that doubt is more intelligible in the freedom case, I also want to point out that there are limits to our ability to imagine that no one has that freedom. As I see it, it is something that we can imagine as an abstract, but not as a real possibility. By imagining something as a 'real possibility' I do not mean that what we can thus imagine could actually be the case, but that we are able to imagine vividly what life would be like if human beings lacked that freedom, and how it would feel to believe this. However, others seem to have different intuitions in this respect. (Proponents of the view that the ability to do otherwise is an illusion would say that life does not look any different if we imagine people as lacking that freedom.)

---

[43] I am not claiming that we in fact have the capacity to do otherwise (understood in the libertarian sense), but that it is certain for people that human beings have that capacity. I admit that this view is disputed and that a compatibilist might argue that, while people indeed take for granted in practice the ability to do otherwise, the content of what they take for granted should be seen in the counterfactual and not the categorical sense. I thank Nigel Pleasants for pointing this out to me. This whole debate is highly complex and addressing it in detail would go beyond the scope of this book. For a good anthology of the topic of free will see Gary Watson, ed. *Free Will*, 2nd ed., Oxford Readings in Philosophy (Oxford and New York: Oxford University Press, 2003).

The assertion 'We know that this child, who is about to undergo what would otherwise be painful surgery, should be given an anaesthetic before the operation' differs from examples such as 'Killing is wrong' and 'Lying is wrong' because it is a particular moral judgement about a relatively specific case. It is not convincing to claim that what Bambrough claims to know is already presupposed whenever he doubts or justifies a moral judgement. While the latter can be said about the obligation to avoid gratuitous suffering by another person when we have the means to do so, it is not true of the obligation to give an anaesthetic to a particular child. In addition, what Bambrough claims to know is certain only for those who are familiar with the effects of anaesthetics.

'Lying is wrong' is peculiar in that there are numerous contexts in which lying is regarded as unproblematic or even desirable. Thus, telling the truth about somebody's bad looks is usually regarded as rude, as is telling a person everything we think of her, including all the things we do not like about her.[44] In addition, there are also contexts in which it has become commonplace to tell lies, for example in sick notes. Thus, it is quite common among employees to pretend to be sick when the real reason why they cannot (or do not want to) go to work is not regarded as acceptable.[45] While such practices do not undermine the status of the wrongness of paradigm cases of lying as an object of moral certainty, they mark out a difference between this case and, for instance, the wrongness of harming innocent people. The fact that there are so many forms of lies – barefaced lies, white lies, polite lies, lying by omission, bluffing, half-truths, exaggerations, minimisations, perjury, and so on – reveals the complexity of the practice of lying and the diversity of the functions lying performs in society.

5.6   The alleged problem of exceptions to moral principles

As Pleasants emphasises, it is not the proposition 'Killing is wrong' that is the object of moral certainty, but the wrongness of killing in

---

[44] See Thomas Nagel, 'Concealment and Exposure,' *Philosophy and Public Affairs* 27, no. 1 (1998): p. 6.

[45] It should be noted that the real reason why a person cannot go to work may be one that is actually a good reason also from a moral point of view, but which is not accepted by his employer or by society as a whole. Examples of this include mental problems, or simply being overworked. The reason may also be an obligation that conflicts with his professional obligations, for example a family obligation or an obligation related to voluntary work or political activity.

paradigmatic cases.[46] This attitude cannot be put into propositional form: put simply, no proposition will encapsulate that attitude in all of its complexity. According to Pleasants' non-propositional account, 'basic certainty' is an attitude towards 'innumerable taken-for-granted states of affairs'.[47] The objects of this attitude play a foundational role in our epistemic and moral practices respectively.

If we conceive of moral certainty as non-propositional, as I think we should, we can avoid the problem of exceptions.[48] Many philosophers have been bothered by the fact that there are situations in which it is at least questionable whether acts of killing, lying, stealing and so forth are wrong. However, this is not problematic, because what is beyond doubt is not the proposition expressed by 'Killing is wrong' and the like, but the fact that killing and so on is wrong in paradigmatic cases. This certainty cannot be put in propositional form, but this should not be regarded as any kind of shortcoming. In most cases, competent moral agents are able to judge whether particular acts of killing are justified, even though they cannot formulate a proposition that encapsulates the entire content of their moral attitude towards killing.

One way of putting this is to say that formulations of moral principles are labels for complex ideas.[49] Despite the inability to provide a precise and compact formulation of, for instance, the rule requiring that promises must be kept,

> [a]nyone who understands the point of promising – what it is supposed to ensure and what it is to protect us against – will see that certain reasons for going back on a promise could not be allowed without rendering promises pointless, while other exceptions must be allowed if the practice is not to be unbearably costly.[50]

Here an appeal to judgement is being made. An understanding of the point of promising is a necessary prerequisite for judging whether breaching a promise is justifiable in particular cases. Whether we have understood the point of this practice is, in turn, revealed in our judgements about particular cases. Another even better way of describing the role of moral principles is to say that they function as incomplete

---

[46] Pleasants, 'Wittgenstein and Basic Moral Certainty,' p. 678.
[47] Ibid., p. 670.
[48] I thank Nigel Pleasants for drawing my attention to this point.
[49] Scanlon, *What We Owe to Each Other*: p. 199.
[50] Ibid., p. 200.

articulations of moral practices. According to this view, they are 'inelim- inably open textured summaries' of that which we 'know' if we have mastered those practices.[51]

Kober considers the fact that 'formulations of moral certainties are not absolutely exact' to be problematic. He refers to the possibility of questioning and refining a moral certainty within a discourse that is distinct from the practice for which that certainty is constitutive.[52] According to his conception of moral certainty, it holds for everything that functions as a certainty within a given moral language-game that there is another moral language-game in which it does not have this function.[53] Kober argues that a moral certainty, for instance the one expressed by the sentence 'Killing people is wrong', can be refined by for example distinguishing between killing in self-defence, tyranni- cide, manslaughter and murder and ascribing moral wrongness only to murder.[54] He envisages this as a process of 'refinement of a community's moral vocabulary'.[55]

However, far from involving a case of linguistic refinement, the formulation 'Murder is wrong' looks like a tautology. Furthermore, to adopt that formulation would not ultimately settle the dispute as to when a particular act of killing is morally permissible. Moreover, we would not regard all cases of killing that do not qualify as murder as permissible, and it is not the case that everyone agrees on what precisely counts as murder. Other formulations we might come up with in order

---

[51] Jay Garfield, 'Particularity and Principle: The Structure of Moral Knowledge,' in *Moral Particularism*, ed. Brad Hooker and Margaret Little (Oxford: Oxford University Press, 2000), pp. 198 f. Garfield is explaining and defending John McDowell's Wittgensteinian framework. McDowell is a famous example of a moral particularist who seeks support from Wittgenstein. See John McDowell, 'Virtue and Reason,' in *Mind, Value, and Reality* (Cambridge, Mass.: Harvard University Press, 1998); John McDowell, 'Non-Cognitivism and Rule-Following,' in *Wittgenstein: to Follow a Rule*, ed. Christopher M. Leich Steven H. Holtzman (London et.al.: Routledge & Kegan Paul, 1981). Unlike Dancy, who defends a more radical version of particularism, McDowell and Garfield ascribe a role to moral principles. Garfield, 'Particularity and Principle: The Structure of Moral Knowledge,' pp. 181 and 198.

[52] Kober uses 'discourse', 'practice', and 'language-game' interchangeably. Michael Kober, 'On Epistemic and Moral Certainty: A Wittgensteinian Approach,' *International Journal of Philosophical Studies* 5, no. 3 (1997): p. 366.

[53] Ibid., p. 376.

[54] Ibid., p. 375. Kober formulates this certainty as 'Killing people is evil', but I do not think that this difference in terminology is of any importance in this context.

[55] Ibid.

to encapsulate our complex attitudes towards killing, stealing and so on fare no better. A refinement of our formulations of moral principles will not enable us to get rid of counterexamples. While Kober seems to acknowledge this point, he nevertheless makes the mistake of giving too much weight to the formulations of moral certainties.

It has been argued that the view that there are exceptions to the wrongness of breaking promises and so on is mistaken.[56] According to Arrington, the fact that there are cases in which it is, all things considered, justified to break a promise does not imply that by breaking a promise in that case one is doing something morally right. What has been done remains wrong, although breaking the promise was the best possible thing to do. Arrington points to the feeling of unease that accompanies and follows such actions. His view echoes the tragic choices found in Greek tragedy, where it is impossible for the agent to avoid acting wrongfully.

I disagree with Arrington, because the issue of whether a particular course of action is right or wrong is not dependent solely upon whether it accords with any particular moral norm. It depends, for instance, not only on whether it amounts to the breaking of a promise, but also on whether it is an act of helping someone, hurting someone and so on. Moral norms are not isolated from each other. If for example I have promised a friend not to tell anybody where she was, and then find out that she is seriously ill and in urgent need of medical help, informing a doctor of her whereabouts might be the right thing to do. Unlike Arrington, I would not say that breaking a promise in such a situation could only be *the best possible* course of action under the circumstances. I would say that it could actually be *right*, given that the rightness and wrongness of an action are determined by a combination of situational features and interconnected moral norms.

I thus conclude that there are exceptions to the prohibitions on lying, killing and so on (and to the obligation to keep promises, to avoid gratuitous suffering and so forth), but that this fact does not pose a problem for the view that the wrongness of paradigmatic cases of prohibited types of action (or the rightness of acts that we are obliged to carry out) is beyond doubt for morally competent agents, as long as we stick to a non-propositional conception of moral certainty.[57]

---

[56] Robert L. Arrington, 'A Wittgensteinian Approach to Ethical Intuitionism,' in *Ethical Intuitionism: Re-evaluations*, ed. Philip Stratton-Lake (Oxford: Clarendon Press, 2002), pp. 278 f.

[57] The emphasis on the non-propositionality of certainty makes it unnecessary to include a *ceteris paribus*-clause in the formulation of a certainty.

5.7   Moral certainties as grammatical propositions

Some authors conceive of moral certainties as belonging to the grammar of moral language-games. Arrington, for instance, argues that 'It is wrong to tell a lie' is an example of a proposition of moral grammar.[58] Similarly, Kober states that moral certainties like '"Killing people is evil", "Helping others is right", [and] "All men and women have equal rights"' are, like 'epistemic' certainties, constitutive rules of language-games.[59] I argued in Chapter 3 that it is illuminating to compare the role of the sentences Wittgenstein reflects upon with the role of a grammatical proposition, but that the claim that all of them play that role seems to impose homogeneity on the examples that they do not display. I also pointed out that the view that the formulations of certainties express grammatical rules requires a broad conception of grammar, and I did not pursue any further the question as to whether we should conceive of objective certainty as 'grammatical' in this broad sense. I shall not go into this question in relation to moral certainty either, but shall further illuminate the role of formulations of moral certainties by comparing this role with that of a proposition which belongs to moral grammar.

5.7.1   Propositions defining what can be said in moral terms

A proposition such as 'Lying is wrong' seems to determine, along with other propositions, what can be meaningfully said in moral terms. It can be understood as telling us something about the meaning, that is the use, of the terms 'lying' and 'wrong'. Arrington argues that the proposition 'Lying is wrong' constitutes his concept of a lie and is moreover 'partially constitutive of [his] concept of morality'.[60] Basic moral commitments such as this one 'spell out [...] what morality is all about': 'Being moral *just is* not lying, not breaking promises, not hurting others unnecessarily, and the like.'[61]

The convincing view that being moral *just is* refraining from certain types of action does not commit us to the claim that 'Lying is wrong' and so on are grammatical propositions. It is also compatible with the position that those sentences express core elements of the agreement

---

[58] Arrington, 'A Wittgensteinian Approach to Ethical Intuitionism,' p. 279.

[59] Kober, 'On Epistemic and Moral Certainty: A Wittgensteinian Approach,' p. 373.

[60] Arrington, 'A Wittgensteinian Approach to Ethical Intuitionism,' p. 281. His account is relativistic in that what is constitutive of one person's concept of morality need not be constitutive of that of another.

[61] Ibid., p. 280, my italics.

over (moral) judgements, and that what they express are the axes around which our moral doubts and justifications turn. Our practices of criticising and justifying moral views, of assessing the moral status of an institution or a practice and so on presuppose a shared sense of what is morally right or wrong, good or bad in many cases. They presuppose moral bedrock practices, which are included among the constitutive elements of moral certainty. [62]

The view that we are dealing with propositions of moral grammar is supported by the fact that in learning what the word 'lying' means we also learn that it is morally wrong in most cases. Its moral wrongness cannot be separated from the meaning of 'lying'. In order to have fully mastered the concept of lying, we must have understood that lying is wrong.[63] Moreover, children learn the meaning of the term 'wrong' by learning that certain types of actions are wrong. The concept of moral wrongness can be explained by reference to the concepts of lying, hurting others, killing, stealing, cheating, and so forth, and is at the same time an integral part of an explanation of the concepts of lying, hurting others, and so on.

Contrary to the proposition 'Lying is wrong', 'Abortion is wrong' would not be conceived of as being part of the grammar of our moral language-games. On Arrington's view, it would be a proposition whose truth value depends on 'evidence and arguments', such as 'Premarital sex is wrong' and 'Marital infidelity is wrong'.[64] He sees a 'sharp contrast' between the two kinds of propositions and classifies the latter as 'empirical moral propositions'.[65] A difference between the propositions 'Lying is wrong' and 'Abortion is wrong' concerns the way we acquire the concepts of 'lying' and 'abortion'. Unlike the meaning of 'lying', we usually do not learn the meaning of 'abortion' during (early) childhood. It is a concept that we acquire only at a later stage in life. At that time, we have (hopefully) already mastered the concepts of 'right' and 'wrong'. 'Abortion is wrong' is not 'drilled [...] into [our] head'[66] by our parents and early teachers in the same way as 'Lying is wrong'. Adapting a formulation by Wittgenstein quoted in Chapter 3, we can say that we learn with the

---

[62] I would not exclude the possibility of arguing that a view of moral certainty as constituted by bedrock practices and bedrock agreement ultimately boils down to the view that moral certainty is grammatical in a broad sense of the term.

[63] See Arrington, 'A Wittgensteinian Approach to Ethical Intuitionism,' p. 281.

[64] Arrington, 'A Wittgensteinian Approach to Ethical Intuitionism,' p. 280.

[65] Ibid., p. 279.

[66] Ibid., p. 277.

same inexorability that lying is wrong as that this is a chair or that 2 x 2 = 4 (see OC 455).

However, the view that full mastery of a concept such as that of lying requires a person to have understood that actions falling under that concept are wrong does not imply that 'Lying is wrong' belongs to moral grammar. As Pleasants argues in his article on the persistence and aboli-tion of slavery, in the case of some practices, we are not taught what they are in a way that is value-neutral.[67] Slavery is a good example of this. Today children learn at the same time what sort of practice slavery is and that it is morally wrong. Pleasants contrasts this practice with the practice of animal exploitation (understood in a value-neutral sense), about which we typically learn in a supposedly value-neutral manner. We learn that animal products serve nutritional and other functions, and it is only later that we might begin to question animal exploitation. I think that what holds for an institutionalised socioeconomic practice such as slavery also holds for practices such as lying, stealing, killing and so on: by learning what kind of practice they are we also learn that they are wrong.

It should be noted that the case of abortion differs both from the prac-tices of slavery and animal exploitation. It is an example of a practice that, at this point in time, is taught mostly as being morally problem-atic, and in some places, and within some social groups, as being wrong. I doubt that anyone learns what kind of practice it is in a value-neutral way. However, since its moral status is contested, learning what abor-tion is does not go hand in hand with learning that it is either right or wrong, at least not in the majority of cases.

5.7.2   False moves are the exception

If interpreted as grammatical, propositions such as 'Lying is wrong' are removed from doubt because doubt cannot be cast on elucidations of the grammar of 'wrong' in the same way in which particular uses of the term 'wrong' can be doubted. Doubting what these propositions express would be comparable to doubting the correctness of the rules of chess and thereby doubting that chess is in general played correctly. As Wittgenstein points out, 'it has no meaning to say that a game has always been played wrong' (OC 496). False moves 'can only exist as the exception', because 'if what we now call by that name became the rule, the game in which they were false moves would have been abrogated'

---

[67] Pleasants, 'Moral Argument Is Not Enough: The Persistence of Slavery and the Emergence of Abolition,' p. 152.

(PI II, p. 227). We have no problem understanding the question as to whether a particular move in chess is correct, but the question 'Are the chess rules correct?' does not make sense. What holds for the rules of chess also holds for the grammar of our moral language-games: we cannot meaningfully question its correctness. We lack a standard for assessing the rules comprising that grammar because we do not have a more general concept of morality.[68] There are standards for assessing the rules of chess in terms of their consistency or their contribution to an interesting and enjoyable game, but there is no standard for assessing whether they are correct.

The distinction between doubting the wrongness of lying in general and doubting the wrongness of lying in any particular case does not have to be explained by reference to the grammatical status of some propositions. It can also be explained by reference to the fact that language-games are not only constituted by their rules but also by their point, their aims, their surroundings, and their certainties. Doubt cannot be cast on any of the constituent elements in the same way as it can be cast on the moves made within the game.

5.8 The acting underlying our moral language-games

Just like certainty regarding the empirical world, moral certainty is 'enacted'. It is displayed in 'how we live and conduct ourselves, how we respond to sad events and wrongful acts, and in what we say in the ethical propositions that we produce as expressions of sadness and condemnation directed at such events and acts'.[69] The naturalness of what formulations such as 'Lying is wrong' express is the naturalness of our acting – in this case of our acting as morally competent agents.[70] Williams' claim that '[t]he chain of justification terminates with what has become our second nature' seems to be true of the justification of moral judgements as well, though our first nature plays a role, too.[71] As it is constituted by bedrock practices which involve shared natural reactions, moral certainty is partly instinctive and partly the result of enculturation.

---

[68] Arrington, 'A Wittgensteinian Approach to Ethical Intuitionism,' p. 280.

[69] Pleasants, 'Wittgenstein, Ethics and Basic Moral Certainty,' p. 263.

[70] See Andreas Krebs, *Worauf man sich verlässt* (Würzburg: Königshausen & Neumann, 2007), p. 112.

[71] Meredith Williams, *Wittgenstein, Mind and Meaning* (London: Routledge, 1999), p. 169.

As will be argued in greater detail in the following chapter, the acting underlying our moral language-games can be understood in at least three different ways: as involving primitive reactions to pain or signs of distress, which are non-verbal and instinctive and can also be found among non-human animals; as the natural reactions of children and caregivers within the process of moral teaching and learning (for example a parent's expression of approval and affection in response to good behaviour, the cries of another child which has been hurt, the child's reaction to those reactions, and so on); as the immediate responses of morally competent agents. On the third interpretation, it includes spontaneous emotional reactions as well as the exercise of linguistic competence, both of which are animal in the sense that they do not require conscious thought. The capacity to engage in complex moral reasoning when confronted with situations that require it presupposes a general moral sensitivity. Wittgenstein himself provides an example of the fundamental acting on the first interpretation: 'In its most primitive form it [the behaviour towards someone with toothache; J.H.] is a reaction to somebody's cries and gestures, a reaction of sympathy or something of the form. We comfort him, try to help him' (CE, p. 381).

There is continuous development from the primitive forms of behaviour at the beginning of the acquisition of ethical language, which are closely related to our instinctive endowment, through to the complex forms of behaviour that characterise our moral language-games.[72] As Goodman, who seems to have been the first to try to draw an analogy between non-moral and moral certainty, argues, 'some moral activity, and the associated moral judgments are [...] as much a prototype of our way of thinking as is the belief that the world has existed for more than the last five minutes'.[73] As mentioned in Chapter 3, Wittgenstein provides the following example of such a prototype: 'to tend, to treat, the part that hurts when someone else is in pain; and not merely when oneself is – and so to pay attention to other people's pain behaviour' (Z 540).

We can thus adapt some of Wittgenstein's remarks in *Last Writings*: the important thing about moral certainty, and the most important expression of moral conviction, is the way one behaves. We therefore have to ask how it 'shows' that we are morally certain (see LW II, p. 21). This is apparent for example in how we react when we find out that someone whom we trusted has lied to us, for instance our parents. It also shows

---

[72] See Krebs, *Worauf man sich verlässt*, p. 114.
[73] Russell B. Goodman, 'Wittgenstein and Ethics,' *Metaphilosophy* 13, no. 2 (1982): p. 145.

in their response to our reaction. They try to justify why they did not tell us the truth, or reinterpret it as for instance an act of being silent on something as opposed to lying (lying by omission). Our certainty also manifests itself in feelings of shame and guilt. The certainty that killing is wrong is revealed in how we react to cases of killing we hear about, how we talk about killings and in our feelings for instance towards a murderer.

5.9 Differences between certainty regarding the empirical world and moral certainty

I hope to have convinced the reader that moral reasoning, discussion and argument presupposes moral certainty which is manifested in the way we make moral judgements, use ethical language, interact with each other and so on. However, I do not claim that we should conceive of this moral certainty in exactly the same way as we understand certainty regarding the empirical world. It is indispensable for any philosophical inquiry that aims to proceed in a Wittgensteinian spirit that the differences between the various cases are not overlooked. To quote Diamond again: 'Wittgenstein's method does not provide shortcuts'.[74] As was argued in Chapter 3, Wittgenstein does not provide us with a systematic account of objective certainty, but instead reflects on many different examples, the heterogeneity of which tends to be insufficiently acknowledged. It is thus plausible to assume that instances of moral certainty exhibit both internal differences and differences with cases of certainty regarding the empirical world.

Some differences between the two types of certainty have already been noted in the previous sections. I thus remarked that in the moral case, the demand for reasons in support of a certainty is more likely to elicit a strong emotional reaction such as outrage or consternation (see 5.3). In addition, attempts to put moral certainty into propositional form and attempts to provide reasons for the truth of these propositions have a major potential to cause irritation. They can offend us, hurt us or provoke outrage. Any person who persisted in asking us how we could be so sure that this was a tree would eventually get on our nerves, but someone who, while watching the news with us, asked us with all signs

---

[74] Cora Diamond, 'Wittgenstein, Mathematics, and Ethics: Resisting the Attractions of Realism,' in *The Cambridge Companion to Wittgenstein*, ed. Hans Sluga and David G. Stern (Cambridge and New York: Cambridge University Press, 1996), p. 239.

of seriousness why there was anything wrong with killing children would deeply disturb us. This second form of irritation has a different quality.

Another difference concerns the familiarity of propositions that are meant to express something that is certain. It seems that some of the moral propositions we have considered are much more commonly uttered than their non-moral analogues. They are, for instance, used for educational purposes (see 6.3.6) and frequently occur in philosophical and religious texts. By contrast, the sentence 'The earth has existed since long before I was born' can supposedly only be found in philosophical tracts and articles dealing with Moore's knowledge claims. Many of Moore's examples are not used within education. A child is not explicitly told that it is a human being and that it has a body. 'This is a hand', however, is used for educational purposes, which again shows the heterogeneity of Wittgenstein's examples. We say to a baby things like 'This is your little foot' and 'This is your little hand' but we do not say 'You have a body'. It also seems wrong to say that the fact that I have a body has been drilled into my head or that I learned it with the same inexorability as that this is a chair or that 2 x 2 = 4 (see OC 455). Unlike 'The earth has existed since long before I was born', the propositions 'This is your little foot', 'This is your little hand' and 'This is a chair' are easy to transmit to a child. Since 'The earth has existed since long before I was born' cannot be as easily transmitted, it is therefore left to be picked up by repeated exposure.[75]

While our familiarity with some formulations of moral certainties can be explained by reference to their occurrence in religious and philosophical texts and to their use in educational contexts, it must be stressed that they rarely arise in newspapers or political discussions. Moreover, we do not use a proposition such as 'It is wrong to tell a lie' when blaming someone for having lied to us or debating whether particular instances of lying are justifiable. Despite their familiarity, these propositions have little use in practice.

A further difference between moral and non-moral certainty has been suggested by Rummens who argues that, unlike moral certainties, 'basic (empirical) certainties' reflect how the physical reality imposes constraints on our actions. While human beings are unable to perform actions such as flying without any technical equipment or to walk through walls, they can – and in fact do – commit crimes.[76] This is how he formulates the contrast:

---

[75] I thank Danièle Moyal-Sharrock for pointing this out to me.
[76] Rummens, 'On the Possibility of a Wittgensteinian Account of Moral Certainty,' p. 20.

It makes sense to say that somebody who believes that killing is wrong can, in spite of that belief, still commit murder. In contrast, it makes no sense at all to say that somebody who believes that human beings do not have wings can, in spite of that belief, still jump out of the window and simply fly off.[77]

The parallel drawn between acting against the certainty that human beings do not have wings by jumping out of the window and simply flying off and acting against the certainty that killing is wrong by committing murder is not convincing. Since the moral certainty concerns the *wrongness* of killing and not the human *ability* to kill, acting in contradiction with it requires more than simply committing murder. It requires murdering someone in the conviction that this action is morally right, or at least not wrong.[78] More generally, acting against moral certainties requires acting in a way that reveals complete indifference or even a positive attitude towards killing, harming, stealing and so on. In a nutshell: moral certainty concerns what we *should not* do, not what we *cannot* do.[79] Therefore, the commission of crime is not indicative of the contradiction of moral certainties.

Someone whose actions over time reveals the attitude required for acting in contradiction with moral certainties is not regarded as sane. Such a person is comparable to someone who continuously treats everything around him with enormous hesitation, suggesting that he has doubts regarding the existence of chairs, tables, trees and so on. The difference between certainty regarding the empirical world and moral certainty is therefore also not correctly described by saying that, while it is possible to act sanely in contradiction with a moral certainty, this is not possible in relation to certainty regarding the empirical world.[80]

Rummens concedes that the fact that crime is committed merely shows that we can act contrary to our conscience and not that 'these "immoral" ways of acting can be promoted into alternative moral language-games

---

[77] Ibid.

[78] Pleasants criticises Rummens along the same lines in Nigel Pleasants, 'If Killing Isn't Wrong, Then Nothing Is: A Naturalistic Defence of Basic Moral Certainty.' *Ethical Perspectives* 22, no. 1 (2015): 197–215.

[79] Ibid.

[80] Danièle Moyal-Sharrock has described the difference in this way (in a comment on an earlier version of this chapter), arguing that I cannot act as if I did not have a body or as if the world did not exist without being considered mad, whereas I can sanely act in contradiction with moral certainties, for instance by committing a crime.

and their concomitant moral forms of life'.[81] That these ways of acting can be promoted into alternative moral language-games he argues, is shown by the possibility of immoral ideologies. However, the assumption that ideologies such as that of the Nazis could give rise to such fundamentally different moral language-games is implausible, because moral language-games are not unconstrained by certain 'facts of nature' (RPP I 48). That morally competent agents do not doubt that killing and harming innocent people is wrong is not arbitrary. Unlike Rummens, I think that the assumption that there is a plurality of radically incompatible moral language-games is highly implausible. As will be argued in Chapter 7, human nature and facts about the world impose limits on the possible differences between moralities.

Rummens claims that physical reality imposes a 'shared human behaviour', but not a 'shared moral behaviour', at least not in the same way. To put it this way is to suggest that the engagement in moral practices is not integral to the human form of life, which would be an unconvincing claim. However, Rummens uses the term 'human' in a rather narrow sense, namely to refer to the fact that we partake of a shared physical reality.[82] Later on in the text he allows for the possibility of an argument in favour of 'some minimal forms of moral agreement' lying 'at the bottom of our human language-game'.[83]

A further objection to Rummens concerns the heterogeneity of Wittgenstein's examples. For many of them it is not correct to say that certainty corresponds to physical constraints. Consider the propositions 'My name is L.W.' and 'The earth has existed since long before I was born'. Moreover, we have to be careful not to conceive of the relationship between facts and certainties in the wrong way. It is not the case that the fact that something is beyond doubt can be explained or justified by reference to physical constraints (see Chapter 7). I therefore conclude that certainty regarding the empirical world and moral certainty do not differ in the manner claimed by Rummens.

5.10 Implications for views of moral justification

If there are cases of moral certainty, moral foundationalists and coherence theorists are wrong in thinking that every moral belief requires

---

[81] Rummens, 'On the Possibility of a Wittgensteinian Account of Moral Certainty,' p. 145.

[82] Ibid., p. 146.

[83] Ibid., p. 23.

justification. My reflections on what I take to be such cases point to an alternative to those two theory families. According to the practice-based view of morality, moral judgements are neither justified by virtue of their coherence with other judgements, nor are they all based on some judgements that are self-evidently true, or self-justifying. Justification ranges from what is less certain to what is more certain, but any justification automatically stops at the point where there are no more reasons for doubt. Framed in terms of the axis-analogy, it may be asserted that any justificatory endeavour is part of the movement which determines the immobility of some moral (and non-moral) axes.

Our moral language-games are grounded in primitive reactions such as the spontaneous reaction to another person's suffering. Some philosophers have tried to provide explanations and justifications for judgements that are not moral claims open to doubt and justification, but strings of words reflecting an enacted certainty, the certainty with which competent moral agents interact with their environment, talk about matters of right and wrong, good and bad, and make moral judgements.

Justifying and evaluating actions and judgements – practices that we looked at more closely in Chapter 4 – are some of our more sophisticated practices, which presuppose what Williams calls 'bedrock practices'. They are thus not, as many moral philosophers assume, constitutive of moral practices in general. Bedrock practices include reactions that arguably mark the beginning of moral language-games, such as human reactions to pain, and shared evaluative tendencies that have been greatly influenced by evolutionary forces.[84]

5.11   Conclusion

At the beginning of this chapter, I presented an attempt to prove that we have moral knowledge and criticised it along the lines of Wittgenstein's critique of Moore. I took this as the starting point for an analogy between the certainty Wittgenstein was concerned with and moral certainty. I then explored the analogy by looking at examples of cases in which the wrongness of an act or a type of action is beyond doubt and justification. We saw that these cases resemble those Wittgenstein pondered

---

[84] For the influence of evolutionary forces on our basic evaluative tendencies see Sharon Street, 'A Darwinian Dilemma for Realist Theories of Value,' *Philosophical Studies* 127(2006): pp. 113 ff. I shall address evolutionary explanations of morality in Chapter 7.

in a number of respects. The wrongness of paradigmatic cases of killing, lying and so forth is as certain as the existence of our hands. Like Wittgenstein's examples, my examples of moral certainty are heterogeneous and reveal family resemblances. As a family, they moreover differ in some respects from the family of non-moral certainties. It follows from this view that moral foundationalists and coherentists alike are wrong in claiming that every moral belief requires justification.

I argued in relation to the alleged problem of exceptions that if we conceive of moral certainty as non-propositional, the fact that there are cases in which it might be right to lie, kill and so on does not pose a problem. Just like non-moral certainty, moral certainty manifests itself in the way we act. Its objects are not amenable to propositional formulation. A sentence such as 'Killing is wrong' does not encapsulate our complex attitude towards killing. It is an incomplete articulation of a complex practice.

At the root of our moral language-games lie primitive reactions such as the reaction to another person's suffering, and the immediate responses of morally competent agents. The following chapter will say more about the acting that grounds moral practices, considering the notion of moral competence in greater depth.

6
Moral Competence

6.1 Introduction

It was argued in the previous chapter that there are moral certainties, and that attempts to doubt or justify them cast doubt on the moral competence of the speaker. These certainties show themselves in the way morally competent agents act. Thus, how I treat other people and react to cases in which innocents have been harmed shows that the wrongness of harming innocents is beyond doubt for me. Language-games of moral deliberation and justification are rooted in primitive actions and reactions, such as sympathetic reactions to another person's suffering and unreflective acts of helping others. It is now time to look more closely at these actions and reactions, and at what I call moral competence, which I will discuss in relation to the notions of moral knowledge, virtue, skills and training.

As was pointed out in the discussion of Bambrough's proof, the word 'know' plays a vital role in moral language-games. We say that we know what the morally right thing to do is, or that we do not know whether what we have done was right. We ask questions such as 'Did he know that he was doing something wrong?' or 'Do you know what I ought to do in this case?' Unlike such common uses of 'know', philosophers have talked, for instance, about 'knowing the difference between right and wrong'.[1] It is thought to be this knowledge that characterises the virtuous person. But what kind of knowledge are we dealing with here?

---

[1] See for example Oswald Hanfling, 'Learning about Right and Wrong: Ethics and Language,' *Philosophy* 78, no. 303 (2003): pp. 25 f.; Gilbert Ryle, 'On Forgetting the Difference between Right and Wrong,' in *Essays in Moral Philosophy*, ed. A. I. Melden (Seattle: University of Washington Press, 1958), p. 147.

Is it a form of theoretical knowledge, perhaps even systematic theoretical knowledge?[2] To use Gilbert Ryle's distinction: is it a form of 'knowing that', or rather a form of 'knowing how'? Does it follow from the fact that the moral domain is rule-governed that moral knowledge consists in 'knowledge of universal generalizations'?[3] In this chapter, it will be argued that what matters most for moral agency is not the holding of propositional knowledge, that is 'knowledge-that', but what I call moral competence, which is a form of 'knowledge-how'.[4]

I shall first describe and discuss three cases that require the exercise of moral competence, followed by a rough general description of that competence. I will then present Ryle's critique of the 'intellectualist legend'[5] and draw an analogy between moral competence and practical skills. As Ryle shows, propositional knowledge of rules is not sufficient for knowing how to play chess and the like.[6] If we consider what moral

---

[2] That morality is aimed at achieving systematic, theoretical knowledge has been claimed, for instance, by Michael DePaul. Michael R. DePaul, *Balance and Refinement. Beyond coherence methods of moral inquiry* (London and New York: Routledge, 1993), p. 110.

[3] Jay Garfield, 'Particularity and Principle: The Structure of Moral Knowledge,' in *Moral Particularism*, ed. Brad Hooker and Margaret Little (Oxford: Oxford University Press, 2000), p. 178.

[4] The relationship between propositional knowledge and knowledge-how is a matter of dispute. Jason Stanley and Tim Williamson argue that knowledge-how is a species of knowledge-that. Having knowledge-how amounts to knowing certain propositions under 'a *practical* mode of presentation'. Jason Stanley and Timothy Williamson, 'Knowing How,' *The Journal of Philosophy* 98, no. 8 (2001): p. 429. For a critique of Ryle's distinction see also Paul Snowdon, 'Knowing How and Knowing That: A Distinction Reconsidered,' *Proceedings of the Aristotelian Society* New Series, 104 (2004). It is doubtful that much hangs on how the distinction is drawn: between knowledge-that and knowledge-how or between what is normally conceived of as knowledge-that and knowledge of a proposition under what Stanley and Williamson call a 'practical mode of presentation'. For such doubts see also Alison Hills, 'Moral Testimony and Moral Epistemology,' *Ethics* 120, no. 1 (2009): pp. 105 f. According to Tobias Rosefeldt, 'talk about practical modes of presentation is simply disguised talk about abilities'. Tobias Rosefeldt, 'Is Knowing-how Simply a Case of Knowing-that?' *Philosophical Investigations* 27, no. 4 (2004), p. 375.

[5] Gilbert Ryle, *The Concept of Mind* (Harmondsworth: Penguin Books, 1963), p. 29.

[6] Since Ryle has traditionally been thought of as defending philosophical behaviourism, it should be noted that I am not endorsing that view. I refer to him in this context because a large part of his account of intelligent capacities is instructive for thinking about moral competence, because he wrote two articles on virtue in which he emphasises the differences between virtue and knowledge-how and because he can be understood as 'walking some stretches of philosophical terrain down a parallel path' to Wittgenstein. Julia Tanney,

agency involves, we can see that propositional knowledge is not sufficient for knowing how to act well either. It will be argued that moral competence is acquired in a way which is similar to how the practical skills Ryle is concerned with are learned. I shall provide examples of what the learning process involves and discuss how moral training enables us to deal with novel cases, what role rules play in it, and what the roles of innate capacities and dispositions acquired through enculturation are respectively. Moral training is discussed in some detail because understanding the process through which we learn to be moral is crucial for understanding moral competence. As will be argued below, how we learn to be moral is moreover constitutive of what is being learned.

Drawing on Wittgenstein's famous rule-following considerations, I shall argue that the way we follow moral rules is the result of training. I shall address the role of rules in the exercise of moral competence and provide a refined understanding of the acting that underlies moral language-games. Finally, I shall reject the attempt to justify morality as a whole from a standpoint that is external to it.

6.2 Moral competence in context

Since I am interested in moral competence as it is revealed in practice, I shall start by describing three cases in which a person may be said to be exercising this competence. My concern is here not with moral competence or moral persons in the abstract, but with good friends, good fathers, good judges and such like. I shall ask what it is that the people in the examples can be said to know, and what stands fast for them. The examples are supposed to give the reader an idea of the variety of situations in which moral competence is exercised as well as the complexity of what it takes to be moral.

Scenario 1: friendship

Lydia is working on a paper which is due the next day when her friend Anna calls. Anna is crying. She just came home from the hospital where her father had died a few hours ago. Lydia, who is her closest friend, does not hesitate even for a minute but closes the computer, takes her

---

who emphasises the parallels between Ryle's and Wittgenstein's philosophy, also points to a possible interpretation of Ryle as not endorsing behaviourism, not even a weak form of it. Julia Tanney, 'Gilbert Ryle,' in *The Stanford Encyclopedia of Philosophy*, ed. Edward N. Zalta, Winter 2009 Edition, <http://plato.stanford.edu/archives/win2009/entries/ryle/>.

coat and leaves the house. She spends the rest of the day and the whole night with Anna, listening to her, consoling her and hugging her.

Scenario 2: parenthood

Christian is worried about his 16-year-old son Paul. Paul has become very reserved recently. He seems unhappy but refuses to talk to his father. Christian has been contacted by one of his teachers, who is also worried about him. He is tempted to go into Paul's room when he is not there in order to see whether he can find anything suspicious. He knows that Paul keeps a diary, and he thinks it might be a good idea to take a look at it as it might contain some hints that could help him find out what is wrong with him. Yet he hesitates since it does not feel right to violate his son's privacy. Christian decides to talk to a psychologist. He also tries to talk to Paul once again.

Scenario 3: rule of law mission

Philip and Keira are judges working for EULEX Kosovo, the European Union Rule of Law Mission in Kosovo. Their task is to participate in trials together with local judges in order to contribute to strengthening the legal system. Before coming to Pristina, they learned a bit of Albanian and read a couple of books about the history of Kosovo. Communication with the local judges proves to be difficult, due to language barriers, cultural differences and their role as the Western judges who supposedly know better and are able to teach the Kosovar judges how to conduct a law suit. Philip and Keira are at pains to show respect towards their Kosovar colleagues and to avoid arrogant behaviour. They try to leave leadership to the local judges and to intervene as little as possible.[7]

Lydia, Christian, Philip and Keira are all exercising moral competence. They find themselves in very different situations, all of which require a number of capacities such as sympathy, empathy, respect, the capacity to consider what is morally right, the ability to listen and the ability to console. Each context requires slightly different sensitivities and capacities. A person might be able to deal well with one of the situations, but not so well with another.[8]

---

[7] I chose this example because in 2011 I had the opportunity to attend a trial in Pristina and was shocked by the arrogance of the EULEX-judges.

[8] In addition, a person might care more about the moral requirements associated with one context than about those associated with another. Thus, he might, for instance, care more about being a good father than about being a good friend, or more about being a good friend than about making morally good consumer choices. While some of these priorities are surely morally justified, others might, depending on the context, be morally objectionable.

Lydia's behaviour, for example, exhibits, amongst other things, empathy, a capacity for moral judgement, the ability to listen and the ability to console, both verbally and through physical contact. The fact that she hurries to Anna rather than finishing the paper is part and parcel of what it means to be a good friend.

For the second example it is significant that Christian shows sensitivity to the different aspects of the situation he finds himself in. He does not give in to the temptation to violate his son's privacy by entering his room without permission and reading his diary. He deliberates about what he should do, weighing up different options, and decides to consult a psychologist before taking further action. He also keeps trying to talk to his son. His behaviour reveals, amongst other things, empathy, respect, sensitivity to moral reasons and capacity for moral judgement.

Philip and Keira prepared themselves before starting their job in Kosovo. They are aware of the difficulties associated with their task, and try hard to act in an appropriate way towards their local colleagues. The way they handle their task shows empathy and respect. It could be argued that a distinction should be drawn between moral and cultural competence. The latter may be understood as referring to empathy and respect in relation to people with a different cultural background. A culturally competent person in this sense is a person who is sensitive to cultural differences and the particular difficulties that can arise in interactions between members of different cultural groups. Thus, Philip and Keira are aware of the delicate nature of their situation. Their attitude and behaviour exhibits a sensitivity towards differences between their approach to jurisdiction and the rule of law and that of their local colleagues. During a trial, they act tactfully. Understood in this way, cultural competence is a species of moral competence.

If we think in terms of the knowledge that is relevant in each respective situation, what kind of knowledge would we say Lydia, Christian, Philip and Keira have? We could say that Christian knows that as a father, he is responsible for his underage son, and that his privacy ought to be respected. Is the knowledge we are referring to here propositional, and can it be taught like other propositional knowledge such as the knowledge that Germany lost World War II?[9] Would telling Christian that fathers are responsible for their underage children and that, absent special circumstances, privacy ought to be respected have

---

[9] By contrasting Christian's knowledge with the knowledge that Germany lost World War II, I do not want to claim that historical knowledge is exclusively propositional. The contrast here is with a piece of knowledge that can be learned by being told alone.

provided him with knowledge that could enable him to deal appropriately with a situation such as the one described? It seems obvious that to be told what the relevant moral principles are is not sufficient in order to know how to deal with the situation. I would claim that the relevant knowledge in this situation is the knowledge of how to deal with a particular conflict, the conflict between taking one's responsibility as a father seriously and respecting a child's right to privacy. To a great extent, that knowledge cannot be learned by being told, but only by doing, that is by experience. It is to a large extent practical knowledge in the sense that it is learned in this practical way. In order to avoid confusion, I shall refer to this practical knowledge as 'competence' or 'knowledge-how'.

Christian needs deliberative capacities and moral judgement. His knowledge that privacy ought to be respected is knowledge how to participate in certain practices, which displays a complexity that cannot be captured by the formulation of the principle 'Privacy ought to be respected' (obviously it is not always the case that privacy ought to be respected) (see sections 5.6 and 6.3.7). In addition, we would only praise Christian's way of handling the situation if he showed real concern for his son's well-being. A good father not only takes his responsibility seriously, but also loves his child and cares about him. He is not only concerned with (conflicting) duties, but also, and in fact first and foremost, with how to help his child about whom he is seriously worried.

In all three cases, there are some moral beliefs that are beyond doubt. For Lydia, it is beyond doubt that she has to help her friend and that this is more important than her paper. She does not even consider the option of staying at home and finishing the paper, leaving Anna alone with her grief. Her reaction to her friend's call is an example of an unreflective way of acting morally.[10] For Christian, it is certain that, absent countervailing reasons, it is wrong to violate his son's privacy. His deliberations are based on unreflective reactions to Paul's apparent unhappiness: he is worried and feels the need to help him. For Philip and Keira, it stands fast that it is wrong to act arrogantly. Their reflections on

---

[10] By 'unreflective' I mean that no process of reflection on the issue is involved. Lydia acts spontaneously, thereby revealing a degree of moral competence that can do without conscious reflection in situations like the one described. However, her way of acting may be described as reflective in the sense that she feels that running to help Anna is the right thing to do in that situation. I owe this point to Ike Kamphoff.

how to interact appropriately with their Kosovar colleagues are based on unreflective reactions involving empathy and respect.[11] The examples give a first impression of the variety of contexts in which moral competence is relevant, the various sensitivities and capacities involved in it and the role of unreflective actions and reactions. We need to ask with regard to those actions and reactions how they relate to our first and second nature, and to moral thought. However, before turning to these questions and to the way in which moral competence is acquired, I shall attempt to sketch out a general description of this competence.

A morally competent agent knows what morality requires in many concrete cases. He is able to evaluate situations morally, to grasp moral reasons, and to act in accordance with them. Furthermore, a person who possesses moral competence acts out of moral motives. He does not merely act in accordance with moral rules, but also *because* this is what morality requires.[12] He grasps moral reasons and is moved by them.

It is important for my understanding of moral competence that it involves emotional capacities. The dispositions that a morally competent agent has include the disposition to react in certain situations with moral feelings like pity, outrage, guilt or shame.[13] Furthermore, a morally competent agent is predisposed to condemn certain actions and forms of behaviour and to accept others and to praise people (as well as himself) for certain attitudes, actions or behaviour, whilst blaming them (as well as himself) for others. Highly abstract cognitive capacities that enable moral reasoning include capacities for planning, inhibition, understanding others' mental states and language. The ability to use language makes cognitive distancing possible and thus moral choices.[14] Recent work by neuroscientists provides evidence that despite the crucial role of emotional capacities, moral judgement depends criti-

---

[11] All three cases can of course be described in different ways. Depending on the description, different capacities and certainties will be relevant.

[12] See Aristotle, who argues that 'the acts that are in accordance with the virtues' are only 'just and temperate' if chosen by the agent 'for their own sakes'. This is one of three necessary conditions for an action to be just. Aristotle, *The Nicomachean Ethics*, trans. David Ross (Oxford and New York: Oxford University Press, 1998), II.4, 1105a17. See also Kant, who holds that an action is only moral, if it is done out of duty. Immanuel Kant, *Grundlegung zur Metaphysik der Sitten*, vol. IV, Akademie-Ausgabe (aa) (1785), pp. 397 f.

[13] For my use of the term 'disposition' see the following section.

[14] Valerie Stone, 'The Moral Dimensions of Human Social Intelligence. Domain-specific and Domain-general Mechanisms,' *Philosophical Explorations* 9, no. 1 (2006): p. 56.

cally on the social cognitive abilities that enable us to understand one another's mental states.[15]

Like moral practices themselves, the competence we need in order to participate in them can be understood as operating on different levels. The level on which we deliberate about moral problems can be distinguished from the level on which we exercise our moral capacities more spontaneously without engaging in any conscious reasoning. However, knowing how to reason in the face of moral conflicts forms part of the competence in question. When we are confronted with a situation in which we cannot easily and almost without reflection say what would be morally right, deliberation is required. Deliberating in order to solve a practical problem improves our moral competence, thereby also improving our moral intuitions. Unreflective action and conscious reasoning mutually influence each other.

Despite the frequency of immoral behaviour, most human beings possess a certain degree of moral competence. That someone is morally competent does not mean that he always does the right thing in moral terms. Moral competence allows for error and weakness of will.[16] Feeling, thinking and acting morally are integral parts of human life. Depending on age, experience and upbringing, people are more or less morally competent.

6.3   Competence and training

6.3.1   Ryle's critique of the intellectualist legend

Theoretical support for the view that moral agency requires first and foremost a number of different capacities can be found in Ryle's book

---

[15] See Kristin Preen and Hauke R. Heekeren, 'Moral Brains – Possibilities and Limits of the Neuroscience of Ethics,' in *Empirically Informed Ethics: Morality between Facts and Norms*, ed. Markus Christen et. al. (Berlin: Springer, 2013), p. 151; D. Kliemann et al., 'The Influence of Prior Record on Moral Judgment,' *Neuropsychologia* 46, no. 12 (2008); Liane Young et al., 'The Neural Basis of the Interaction Between Theory of Mind and Moral Judgment,' *Proceedings of the National Academy of Sciences of the United States of America* 104, no. 20 (2007); Liane Young and R. Saxe, 'The Neural Basis of Belief Encoding and Integration in Moral Judgment,' *NeuroImage* 40, no. 4 (2008); Liane Young and R. Saxe, 'An FMRI Investigation of Spontaneous Mental State Inference for Moral Judgement,' *Journal of Cognitive Neuroscience* 21, no. 7 (2009); Liane Young et. al., 'Neural Evidence for 'Intuitive Prosecution': The Use of Mental State Information for Negative Moral Verdicts,' *Social Neuroscience* 6, no. 3 (2011).

[16] The notion 'weakness of will' refers to cases in which a person does not do X, which would be the right thing to do, although she is convinced of the rightness of X.

The Concept of Mind, where he shows, amongst other things, that propositional knowledge of rules is insufficient in order for a person to be competent.[17] Ryle is concerned not with moral competence, but with practical skills. In two relatively unknown papers, he emphasises the differences between knowledge-how and 'knowing the difference between right and wrong'.[18] However, there are striking similarities between certain practical skills and moral competence, which means that it is worthwhile to draw an analogy between them.[19]

Ryle argues that propositional knowledge of rules is insufficient for a skill such as playing chess by stressing that 'the intelligence involved in putting the prescriptions into practice is not identical with that involved in intellectually grasping the prescriptions'.[20] As he is eager to point out, '[k]nowing how to apply maxims cannot be reduced to, or derived from, the acceptance of those or any other maxims.'[21] This must hold for moral maxims as well as for the kind of maxims he mentions.

Ryle's endeavour is to criticise the 'intellectualist legend', according to which an intelligent act has to be preceded by some mental process which makes it intelligent.[22] This legend seems to be effective in much traditional moral philosophising with its emphasis on conscious moral deliberation. Ryle rejects the view that following a rule is a two-step-procedure. We do not first cite the rule to ourselves, looking at some kind of mental image, and then apply it. When we perform an action with intelligence, wit, prudence or care, we are not doing two different things, one of which is an intellectual operation, but just one.[23]

---

[17] Ryle, *The Concept of Mind*, pp. 25–61. At various places in this chapter I shall also refer to empirical support for this view.

[18] Ryle, 'On Forgetting the Difference between Right and Wrong;' Ryle, 'Can virtue be taught?,' in *Education and the Development of Reason*, ed. R.F. Dearden, P.H. Hirst, and R.S. Peters (London and Boston: Routledge and Kegan Paul, 1972).

[19] I say 'certain' practical skills because not all practical skills are similar to moral competence in relevant respects. Skills that seem to involve mere routine, such as making coffee or brushing one's teeth, and skills that are to a large extent dependent on natural talent are not those to which I compare moral competence. See Julia Annas, *Intelligent Virtue* (Oxford and New York: Oxford University Press, 2011), p. 16.

[20] Ryle, *The Concept of Mind*, p. 49.

[21] Ibid., p. 32.

[22] For parallels between Ryle's and Wittgenstein's arguments see for example PI 31, 143–155 and 179–202.

[23] Ryle, *The Concept of Mind*, p. 40.

We are performing 'one operation *in a certain manner* or *with a certain style or procedure'*.[24] An intelligent action is the 'exercise of a skill'.[25] A skill, in turn, is 'a disposition, or a complex of dispositions', the exercise of which is a manifestation of the 'observances of rules or canons or the applications of criteria, but [...] *not tandem operations* of theoretically avowing maxims and then putting them into practice'.[26]

In explaining what he means by knowledge-how, Ryle makes use of the contested term 'disposition'. There is no agreement amongst philosophers about what dispositions are. I shall not discuss different philosophical accounts of dispositions here, for the simple reason that it would distract me too far from my main topic.[27] Following Andreas Kemmerling, I shall conceive of the 'intelligent capacities'[28] Ryle refers to as 'dispositions to correct behaviour'.[29] They are not 'single-track dispositions' like the brittleness of glass or a smoking habit, but 'higher-grade dispositions' or – a term not used by Ryle himself but common in the literature – 'multiple-track dispositions'.[30] Single-track dispositions are always manifested in the same reaction, whereas multiple-track dispositions are manifested in multiple ways. It is impossible to indicate all of their specific manifestations. In addition, we cannot provide either necessary or sufficient conditions for their manifestation in a particular situation.[31] These intelligent capacities are, like habits, a sort of 'second nature', although they differ from habits in that they are inculcated through training (as opposed to pure drill) and manifested in numerous ways.[32] Habits are single-track

---

[24]   Ibid., p. 48, my italics.

[25]   Ibid., p. 33.

[26]   Ryle, *The Concept of Mind*, pp. 33 and 46, my italics.

[27]   See for example David Malet Armstrong, Charles Burton Martin, and Ullin T. Place, *Dispositions: A Debate* (London: Routledge, 1996).

[28]   Ryle, *The Concept of Mind*, p. 42.

[29]   Andreas Kemmerling, 'Gilbert Ryle: Können und Wissen,' in *Grundprobleme der großen Philosophen – Philosophie der Gegenwart*, ed. Josef Speck (Göttingen: Vandenhoeck & Ruprecht, 1975), p. 163, my translation.

[30]   Ryle, *The Concept of Mind*, pp. 44 ff. See Kemmerling, 'Gilbert Ryle: Können und Wissen,' pp. 159 ff.

[31]   Kemmerling, 'Gilbert Ryle: Können und Wissen,' p. 161. We cannot specify a single, precisely defined form of behaviour in a precisely defined situation so that from the fact that someone exhibits this behaviour we can conclude that she has a particular multiple-track disposition. Likewise, we cannot specify a single, precisely defined form of behaviour that someone must follow in a precisely defined situation in order for him to have a particular multiple-track disposition.

[32]   Ryle, *The Concept of Mind*, pp. 42 ff. Although different from mere habits, intelligent capacities include an element of habit.

dispositions. A further important difference is that a person who exercises a capacity keeps learning and improving his skill. Ryle gives the example of a 'mountaineer walking over ice-covered rocks in a high wind in the dark' about whom he says: 'If he makes a mistake, he is inclined not to repeat it, and if he finds a new trick effective he is inclined to continue to use it and to improve on it.'[33]

In the manner described above, moral competence is like the intelligent capacities referred to by Ryle. Like a skilled piano player, a morally competent agent is characterised by dispositions that are manifested in multiple ways, for example in rescuing a drowning child and in not doing so, in the judgement that harming a particular person would be wrong and in the opposite judgement, in refraining from reading someone else's diary and in reading it. As will be argued below, the capacities that are characteristic of a morally competent agent are inculcated through training, which involves giving and receiving reasons.[34] Moreover, both the skilful piano player and the morally competent agent correct mistakes they have made and try to avoid them in future. They keep learning, and risk losing relevant capacities if they fail to continue to use them.[35]

Ryle presents an account of intelligent practice, stressing that it is 'not a step-child of theory'.[36] He argues that a chess player does not have to recite the rules of chess to himself before he makes a move. As far as a game like chess is concerned, knowing the content of the catalogue of rules, that is being able to cite them, is not equivalent to knowing *how* to play the game, which is being able to play chess. A person who knows all the rules of chess by heart may not be capable of actually playing the game. In particular, he may not be a good player who is able to devise good strategies which improve his chances of winning the game. What the chess player needs is not propositional knowledge – at least not primarily – but knowledge-how.

The same is true of the morally competent agent. Such an agent does not have to recite moral principles before she makes a moral judgement or performs an action that can be evaluated as morally good. I do not have to recite the rule that prohibits lying before I assess whether a particular

---

[33] Ibid., p. 42.

[34] Moral competence also involves some innate capacities. I shall address these in section 6.3.9.

[35] See Annas, *Intelligent Virtue*, pp. 13 ff. Julia Annas draws an analogy between *virtues* and practical skills. For the relationship between my notion of moral competence and virtue see note 48 below.

[36] Ryle, *The Concept of Mind*, p. 27.

act of lying was right or wrong, or before I tell someone the truth in a situation where this has negative consequences for me. In addition, a person who has learned a long list of moral rules by heart may not be capable of making correct moral judgements in concrete cases and of actually acting morally. A good example is someone who suffers from an antisocial personality disorder. These psychopaths or sociopaths, as they are often called, are not characterised by the fact that they lack propositional knowledge. They may not verbally reject the proposition 'Murder is evil' and yet show through their actions that they find nothing wrong with murder. People with this disorder are defined not as lacking general reasoning abilities, but as lacking the capacity to respond with feelings like empathy and guilt. Since they lack these capacities, psychopaths do not care about the harmful consequences their actions have for others.[37] They 'primarily lack certain emotions: sympathetic pleasure at another's happiness, dismay at another's sorrow, remorse at having brought trouble to another'.[38]

One important consequence of Ryle's view of an intelligent action is that we cannot tell from looking at one single action alone whether it amounts to the exercise of knowledge-how. Two acts of, for example, giving an answer to a multiplication problem can be indistinguishable even though one of them is given at random and the other results from the exercise of mathematical competence.[39] This leads us to assume that what makes one of these actions an intelligent one is some kind of secret act going on within a person's mind.[40] We tend to look for the

---

[37] For empirical research on psychopathy see for example R. J. R. Blair, 'A Cognitive Developmental Approach to Morality: Investigating the Psychopath,' *Cognition* 57 (1995); J. Blair et al., 'Neuro-Cognitive Systems Involved in Morality,' *Philosophical Explorations* 9, no. 1 (2006): p. 18; R. J. R. Blair, 'Moral Judgment and Psychopathy,' *Emotion Review* 3 (2011); Jonathan Haidt, 'The Emotional Dog and its Rational Tail: A Social Intuitionist Approach to Moral Judgment,' *Psychological Review* 108 (2001): p. 824; Christopher J. Patrick et al., 'Emotion in the Criminal Psychopath. Startle Reflex Modulation,' *Journal of Abnormal Psychology* 102 (1993). In the American Psychiatric Association's *Diagnostic and Statistical Manual of Mental Disorders* it says: 'Persons with this disorder disregard the wishes, rights, or feelings of others. They are frequently deceitful and manipulative [...] Individuals [...] also tend to be consistently and extremely irresponsible [...] [They] show little remorse for the consequences of their acts. They may be indifferent to, or provide a superficial rationalization for, having hurt, mistreated, or stolen from someone.' *Diagnostic and Statistical Manual of Mental Disorders*, third ed. (Washington, D.C.: American Psychiatric Association, 1980). Quoted in Adam Morton, *On Evil* (New York and Oxon: Routledge, 2004), p. 48.
[38] Morton, *On Evil*, p. 48.
[39] See Ryle, *The Concept of Mind*, p. 40.
[40] See ibid., p. 33.

intelligence with which the act is performed 'in the head', and not in the act itself. Yet that is where we should look. Being 'second natures or acquired dispositions', competences like knowing how to calculate or how to play chess are both acquired and revealed through practice.[41]

Whether a person knows how to play chess can only be judged by looking at the moves he actually makes on the board:

> His knowledge-how is exercised primarily in the moves that he makes, or concedes, and in the moves that he avoids or vetoes. [...] It is not what he does in his head or with his tongue, but *what he does on the board* that shows whether or not he *knows the rules in the executive way of being able to apply them.*[42]

Here Ryle emphasises the fact that a chess player knows the rules in the 'executive' way in order to point out that propositional knowledge of rules would not be sufficient. We can only come to know rules in the executive way by learning them in practice, for example by practising chess. In addition, in order to understand intelligent performances like the moves of a chess player we must to some extent be competent in that practice.[43] We do not need to be good chess players ourselves, but we cannot understand what the chess player is doing if we do not know at all how to play chess.

It also holds for moral competence that we can only judge whether somebody has it by looking at how she acts: how Lydia reacts to her friend's phone call, how Christian behaves towards his son, how Philip and Keira handle their task. Also the capacity for moral reasoning is revealed by the way people act. As Williams puts it: 'understanding requires public manifestation of mastery of the practice'.[44] Both Ryle and Wittgenstein make this point which, whilst neither of them has so argued explicitly, can be extended to moral understanding. Moreover, understanding the moral value of other people's actions no doubt requires some degree of moral competence. I do not have to be like mother Theresa in order to understand what an exceptionally virtuous person she was, but I would not be able to appreciate her character if I lacked moral competence altogether.

---

[41] Ibid., pp. 41 f.

[42] See Ryle, *The Concept of Mind*, p. 41, my italics.

[43] See ibid., p. 54.

[44] Meredith Williams, *Wittgenstein, Mind and Meaning* (London: Routledge, 1999), p. 199.

One reason for being taken in by the intellectualist legend is that human beings learn many things by learning explicitly formulated rules. This way of learning is often more efficient than learning to do something without learning rules.[45] As mentioned above, there are propositions which are usually uttered only in the context of teaching a practice to someone. However, it does not follow from this that once we know how to do the thing in question, we need to think of explicitly formulated rules every time we exercise our knowledge-how. That said, it must be added that in some cases, learning the role of explicit formulations of rules tends to be overestimated and misunderstood. Moral learning is an example of this (see 6.3.6).

An objection has been raised against the analogy with practical skills that, unlike skills, moral dispositions or virtues have a motivational character.[46] Bernard Williams writes that '[o]ne can be a good pianist and have no desire to play, but if one is generous or fair minded, those qualities themselves help to determine, in the right contexts, what one will want to do'.[47] A morally competent agent is not only *able* to act, think and feel morally, but is also motivated to exercise these capacities. Since having moral dispositions implies the desire to act in certain ways, Thomas conceives of them as virtues *in opposition to* skills.[48] However, after further consideration it does not seem to be true that skills and virtue differ in this way. Both a morally competent or virtuous agent and

---

[45] I thank Beate Sachsenweger for drawing my attention to this point.

[46] See for example Bernard Williams, *Ethics and the Limits of Philosophy* (London and New York1985), p. 9, and Alan Thomas, *Value and Context: the Nature of Moral and Political Knowledge* (Oxford: Clarendon Press, 2006), p. 213, note 49. Here a short note on the relationship between my notion of moral competence and the notion of virtue is necessary. What I call a morally competent agent has a lot in common with the virtuous person as conceived of for example by Annas. Both are characterised by a number of dispositions, including emotional dispositions, both have developed these dispositions in practice and both are motivated to act well. The main reasons why I do not use the terminology of virtue ethics are that I am primarily concerned with morality as being about our behaviour towards others, rather than with the question as to how an individual can live the most fulfilling life (although of course the two questions overlap to a certain extent), and that my focus lies on the capacities that moral agency requires. Because what virtue ethicists such as Annas say about the learning of virtue is equally valid for the acquisition of moral competence as I conceive of it, I shall sometimes use the labels virtue and moral competence interchangeably.

[47] Williams, *Ethics and the Limits of Philosophy*, p. 9.

[48] Thomas, *Value and Context: the Nature of Moral and Political Knowledge*, p. 213, note 49.

a skilled piano player are not always motivated to exercise their competence. Empirical studies show how people become less moral towards the end of the day as they get tired.[49] Moreover, no pianist can most of the time, or even permanently, not want to practise, since playing the piano well requires many hours of practice every day.

An observable difference between virtue and skills concerns their social embeddedness. While we generally demand moral behaviour from people, we do not demand that they play the piano well or build nice furniture. A piano teacher might demand from a particular pupil that after all of the lessons she has had she plays well; however, there is no general requirement of this kind.[50]

According to Ryle, a crucial difference between our knowledge of the difference between right and wrong and knowledge-how is that the former 'does not get rusty'. The notions of being out of practice, forgetting and decay are said to be out of place here.[51] Ryle rightly notes that it would be odd to excuse my selfish behaviour by saying that I have not practiced being unselfish for a while, or to say that I forgot the difference between right and wrong. 'Forgetting' is not applicable to what we know when we know that difference. According to Ryle, this is because 'to have been taught the difference is to have been brought to appreciate the difference'. This appreciation includes an 'inculcated caring, a habit of taking certain sorts of things seriously'.[52]

His point here is subtle. He argues that 'we do not keep up our honesty by giving ourselves regular exercises in it', in order to emphasise that 'drill[ing] ourselves into good habits and out of bad habits' should not be equated with the exercises we do in order to make sure that our Latin or our tennis does not get rusty. He does not deny that there is such a

[49] See for example Roy F. Baumeister, Mark Muraven, and Dianne M. Tice, 'Ego Depletion: A Resource Model of Volition, Self-Regulation, and Controlled Processing,' *Social Cognition* 18 (2000); Christopher M. Barnes et al., 'Lack of Sleep and Unethical Conduct,' *Organizational Behavior and Human Decision Processes* 115, no. 2 (2011); Dan Ariely, *The (Honest) Truth About Dishonesty: How We Lie to Everyone – Especially Ourselves* (New York: HarperCollins Publishers, 2012); Robert Kahneman, *Thinking, Fast and Slow* (New York: Farrar, Straus and Giroux, 2011), pp. 41–44. I am grateful to Tsjalling Swierstra for drawing my attention to this research by psychologists and behavioural economists.

[50] I owe this point to Tsjalling Swierstra.

[51] Ryle, 'On Forgetting the Difference between Right and Wrong,' p. 150.

[52] Ryle, 'On Forgetting the Difference between Right and Wrong,' p. 156. I think that it applies also to people with a certain skill that they appreciate the difference between good and bad piano playing, good and bad strategies in chess and so on.

thing as moral deterioration, but rejects its assimilation to 'declines in expertness, that is, to getting rusty'.[53]

I think that Ryle overstates the difference. First, it would be odd to speak about forgetting even in relation to many skills. Consider cases such as knowing how to play the piano or knowing how to ride a bike. We can say that we might unlearn these things, although the latter seems to be very difficult to unlearn.[54] Secondly, I would argue that 'moral deterioration' is in many respects similar to getting rusty. That someone becomes, let's say, less courageous can be due to the fact that he has not been in challenging situations for a long time. As regards the moral or character virtues which, according to Aristotle, are acquired by practising them, it makes perfect sense to say that a lack of practice following their acquisition can lead to a person becoming less virtuous. As Aristotle writes, 'men become builders by building and lyre-players by playing the lyre; so too we become just by doing just acts, temperate by doing temperate acts, brave by doing brave acts'.[55] It requires 'some level of routine practice' to maintain the expertise that has been achieved. There is an element of habit in virtue as well as in skills. Even the fully virtuous person has 'to work to maintain her virtue'.[56]

The discussion of Ryle's account of knowledge-how and its relevance for our understanding of moral agency has included a number of references to the process of learning. That process is crucial in order to understand what being moral involves. The following section will therefore examine the way in which we learn to be moral, thereby showing how moral training is related to the content of what is being learned.

6.3.2 Can virtue be taught?

Like all other language-games, moral language-games need to be learned (see PI 249). But how do we learn them? Whether virtue can be taught is an old philosophical question. Those who think that it can, have different ideas about how it is taught. Ryle, for instance, thought that

---

[53] Ibid., pp. 150 f.

[54] Like cycling, moral behaviour seems to be rather difficult to unlearn. In both cases this difficulty might be explainable by reference to certain biological features of human beings. I thank Jeroen Hopster for pointing this out to me.

[55] Aristotle, *The Nicomachean Ethics*: 1103a33–1103b3.

[56] Matt Stichter, 'Virtues, Skills, and Right Action,' *Ethical Theory and Moral Practice* 14, no. 1 (2011): p. 82. For a more detailed critique of Ryle see Julia Hermann, 'Learning to be Moral,' in *What Makes Us Moral: On the Capacities and Conditions for Being Moral*, ed. Bert Musschenga and Anton van Harskamp (Dordrecht et al.: Springer, 2013), pp. 213 ff.

virtue is taught in a way that differs both from the teaching of facts ('teaching by dictating') and from that of skills ('teaching by training').[57] Yet despite some differences between the ways in which skills and virtue are acquired, some important similarities were underestimated by Ryle. As some virtue ethicists have noted, the analogy between virtues and practical skills is particularly helpful when it comes to the development of virtue.[58] Like skills, virtues can only be developed in practice. Aristotle pointed out that both involve 'learning by doing'.[59] As I shall argue below, becoming morally competent involves a significant amount of training similar to that involved in the acquisition of practical skills.

Wittgenstein's later work includes numerous appeals to cases of learning. Such appeals are particularly frequent in *On Certainty*. Thus, by looking closely at the way in which moral practices are learned, we remain in the spirit of Wittgenstein's investigations. Moreover, Wittgenstein gives training a central place in his account of rules and rule-following. It is the process of training through which a connection is established between the expressions of rules and the way we react to them (PI 198). Wittgenstein's arguments imply that being trained into a moral practice is the *conditio sine qua non* for the normativity and the necessity of moral rules, that is for the fact that there is a distinction between correct and incorrect applications and for the fact that moral rules have normative force.[60] In addition, they show that the learning process is constitutive of what is being learned.[61] Thus, we cannot understand morality and moral competence without considering the process through which we learn to be moral.

Reflecting on how human beings learn to be moral is also another way of thinking about the acting that grounds moral language-games. As we shall see below (6.3.9), moral teaching and learning begins with certain 'natural' reactions, such as a parent's expression of displeasure in response to the bad behaviour of her child. Moreover, when he starts to acquire moral competence, the child does not doubt the moral judgements of his teachers. Just like learning other things, learning to be moral requires initial trust in the teacher, as well as in the context in which the learning takes place, for instance one's family.[62] Doubt and

---

[57] Ryle, 'Can virtue be taught?,' p. 326.
[58] Annas, *Intelligent Virtue*: pp. 16 ff. Matt Stichter, 'Ethical Expertise: The Skill Model of Virtue,' *Ethical Theory and Moral Practice* 10, no. 2 (2007): p. 184.
[59] See Aristotle, *The Nicomachean Ethics*: 1103a32–b2.
[60] See Williams, *Wittgenstein, Mind and Meaning*, pp. 167 f.
[61] Ibid., pp. 206 ff.
[62] See Annas, *Intelligent Virtue*, p. 52.

opposition come only later, when the child has already acquired some degree of moral competence.

The theoretical arguments concerning moral education that I put forward in the following sections should not be understood as grounding the moral practices we come to participate in, that is they do not serve as a justification for those practices. As was argued in Chapter 5, moral practices are grounded in action.

6.3.3 Moral and other kinds of training

What I refer to as 'moral training' should not be understood as being separable from the learning and teaching of other things. Just as moral practices overlap with other practices, moral training overlaps with other kinds of training, for example the training involved in learning one's native language. Those who teach us to be honest, fair and so on do so 'not in separate lessons, but in the ways they teach us [...] other things and in the way they act themselves, giving us examples and role models to follow (and to avoid)'.[63] Training in the moral use of language is associated with training in the use of language for other purposes. Children learn to use language for moral purposes, for example in order to make moral judgements, ascribe responsibility to someone, morally praise or blame someone and so on when becoming competent speakers in general. As Hanfling argues, 'the language of right and wrong, vice and virtue' is part of a child's native language which, as long as it is normal, it will pick up necessarily. It is, mainly, by being spoken to by competent speakers and by being present when they talk to each other that language, including moral language, is acquired.[64]

It might be objected that I have so far failed to distinguish between learning to be moral or virtuous and learning to use language, and moral language in particular. However, the two cannot be strictly separated. It is by learning how words such as 'right', 'wrong', 'good', 'bad', 'honest'and 'fair' are used that children learn what *is* right, wrong and so on, and by that they also learn to act well. It is by learning the meaning of words such as 'steal', 'lie', 'harm' and so forth that they learn that stealing, lying, harming and so on are wrong, thereby also learning to behave morally.[65] We learn to use moral language by learning to use language in general, and we learn what morality requires partly by learning to use

---

[63] See Annas, *Intelligent Virtue*, p. 21.

[64] Hanfling, 'Learning about Right and Wrong: Ethics and Language,' p. 25.

[65] Hanfling, 'Learning about Right and Wrong: Ethics and Language,' pp. 35 f. and 30 f.

language, both moral and non-moral.[66] Learning what morality requires involves learning to act well.

It follows from this view of the development of moral competence that it is not the case that children are *taught* not to steal, lie and the like. Instead, they pick up the meaning of 'steal', 'lie'and so forth when learning their native language, and once they are able to use these words correctly, they thereby know that stealing, lying, and so on are wrong.[67] However, mastery of moral language is something special in that it has an 'emotive element' that already characterises the learning process. When learning moral language, children develop certain emotional dispositions such as the disposition to feel guilty or ashamed when they have acted wrongly.[68] Learning how to use moral language thus goes hand in hand with learning to act morally. How this works will be explained below.

Some readers might be unhappy about the term 'training' in this context, since it is associated with the drilling of animals. Wittgenstein certainly used this term in order to highlight the dimension of the education of human beings that is exemplified by the way we drill animals. However, as Ryle notes, although training involves a certain amount of drill, the two are not identical.[69] Drill consists in the 'imposition of repetitions' and is used for inculcating habits.[70] The capacities involved in moral competence, however, are not habits, although they involve an element of habit and are often exercised habitually. Moral training involves more than getting someone to perform certain actions automatically, without conscious thought. It involves giving and receiving reasons, and does not establish mere automatisms. However, particularly in the early stages, imitation plays a crucial role, and moral judgements are adopted without being questioned, and without being identified with.[71]

---

[66] Valerie Stone stresses the importance of the ability to use language for moral agency. Small children who do not yet have this ability have difficulties resisting environmental demands, because they cannot distance themselves from their immediate circumstances. Stone, 'The Moral Dimensions of Human Social Intelligence. Domain-specific and Domain-general Mechanisms,' p. 56.

[67] Hanfling, 'Learning about Right and Wrong: Ethics and Language,' pp. 30 f.

[68] Ibid., p. 28.

[69] Ryle, *The Concept of Mind*, pp. 42 f.

[70] Ibid., p. 42.

[71] See Sabina Lovibond, 'Ethical Upbringing: from Connivance to Cognition,' in *Essays for David Wiggins: Identity, Truth, and Value*, ed. Sabina Lovibond (Oxford, UK, and Cambridge, Mass.: Blackwell, 1996), p. 84. I am indebted to Sabina Lovibond who encouraged me to highlight the difference between training and mere drill.

Unlike pure drill, moral training and training in a practical skill such as playing the piano involve habituation but do not result in mere habits or routine.[72] As is argued by Julia Annas with respect to virtue, its development requires 'time, experience, and habituation', 'but the result is not routine but the kind of actively and intelligently engaged practical mastery that we find in practical experts such as pianists and athletes'.[73]

6.3.4   What is involved in moral training

What does learning the difference between right and wrong involve? What are crucial components of the development of moral competence? Let us look more closely at what it takes to become morally competent agents, thereby also comparing the development of moral capacities with the development of (some) practical skills.

Moral teaching and learning start in early childhood. Moral education is undertaken not only by parents or other primary caregivers[74], but also by grandparents, nannies, teachers, friends, and ultimately by society as a whole.[75] While initially the relation between child and parents plays a crucial role in the process of moral development, friends and school become relevant at a later stage.[76] Moral education is, to a large extent, not provided by any one particular person. Rather, interactions with others, including being spoken to by competent speakers, provide a 'training-ground' for the development of moral competence.[77]

The ability to take up the moral point of view cannot be merely or primarily the result of prescriptive teaching of moral principles, which

---

[72] See Annas, *Intelligent Virtue*, p. 15.

[73] Ibid., p. 14.

[74] For the sake of simplicity I shall sometimes only refer to the parents.

[75] The view that moral education is undertaken by society as a whole goes back to the ancient Greeks.

[76] See Monika Keller, 'Moralentwicklung und Moralische Sozialisation,' in *Moralentwicklung von Kindern und Jugendlichen*, ed. Detlef Horster (Wiesbaden: VS Verlag für Sozialwissenschaften, 2007), pp. 40 ff. In countries with very short maternity leave such as France and The Netherlands, nursery school teachers and nannies already play an important role at a very early stage. As Herman Philipse pointed out to me, in traditional China grandparents play a central role.

[77] It should be noted that, of course, children also learn immoral behaviour like lying, deceiving and so on. Within the peer group, they learn both morally correct and morally incorrect behaviour. Through interacting with others they may acquire not only the disposition to react with feelings like pity and empathy, but also the disposition to feel envy or jealousy. I thank Beate Sachsenweger for stressing this point.

lies at the centre of rationalist accounts of moral education.[78] As the sociologist Michael Rustin stresses, the essence of moral learning is 'not intellectual subscription to abstract precepts, but a process of learning-within-a-situation, from experience and example, in which the implications and effects of feelings and actions can be reflected on with others'.[79]

Human beings develop moral competence through practice, as a result of interactions with others, and in particular through the experience of conflict. Parents and other adults repeatedly correct the child's behaviour, both verbally and – especially at the beginning – by physical interference. They take away the toy that has been taken from another child and give it back to that child, stop their child from pulling another's hair, encourage him to share his toy blocks, tell him not to hit another child with his toy car, and so on. In addition to functioning as a corrective, they serve as a model. In performing actions like helping others and sharing, they communicate to the child an idea of what moral behaviour looks like. Training moreover includes pointing to paradigmatic cases, talking about moral questions, reading out stories that stimulate moral reflection, and so on.

The actions and reactions of other children are important too. At nursery, toddlers are confronted with the needs and desires of others, which may conflict with their own, and they experience how some actions evoke signs of pleasure and others the reverse. Here are some examples: a baby grabs the toy block another baby is playing with. A baby hits another baby with a toy and the baby hit cries out loud. One baby smiles at another baby and touches him gently, making that other baby smile as well.

In the process of learning to be moral, the child comes to think and feel in certain ways, and to develop certain attitudes. She learns to take the interests of others into account, and to put herself in their shoes. As McDowell argues, one learns 'to see situations in a special light, as constituting reasons for acting'.[80] That we see for example the unsuc-

---

[78] See for example Laurence Kohlberg, *Essays on Moral Development* (San Francisco: Harper & Row, 1981).

[79] Michael Rustin, 'Innate Morality: A Psychoanalytic Approach to Moral Education,' in *Teaching Right and Wrong: Moral Education in the Balance*, ed. Richard Smith and Paul Standish (Staffordshire: Trentham Books, 1997), p. 87.

[80] John Henry McDowell, 'Are Moral Requirements Hypothetical Imperatives?,' in *Reason, Value, and Reality* (Cambridge, Mass.: Harvard University Press, 1998), p. 85.

cessful attempt of an older man to reach something on a higher shelf in a supermarket as a reason to help him is the result of training.[81]

Children learn 'to associate various emotional responses with objects of moral evaluation, for example, [...] to have feelings of guilt and resentment toward certain of one's own actions and the actions of others'.[82] This can partly be explained by a process of conditioning, involving caregivers' responses to good and bad behaviour. Acts of sharing and helping, for instance, elicit signs of affection and approval, while bad behaviour elicits the reverse.[83] Moreover, caregivers say things like 'Aren't you ashamed of what you've done?' or 'You should be ashamed!', accompanied by a suitable facial expression, thereby contributing to the development of a tendency to have feelings of shame, remorse or guilt after having acted wrongly.[84]

The development of emotional capacities can further be explained by reference to a form of moral education called 'induction'.[85] It involves for instance an attempt by a parent whose child has hurt another child to make her imagine what it would feel like to experience similar harm. Induction, which highlights the distress of the victim as well as the action that caused it, 'has been found to contribute to the development of guilt and moral internalization in children'.[86] According to the moral sentimentalist and virtue ethicist Michael Slote, parents do not only deliberately make their child more sensitive to the feelings of others. Inductive training also involves what he calls 'a kind of empathic osmosis'. The parents demonstrate an empathic concern, for example for the child who was hurt, which can be directly understood by the child. The kind of modelling involved in this empathic osmosis differs from that advocated by most educational theorists in that it is non-deliberate and possibly unconscious. It can also be expected to occur at

---

[81] This view is compatible with the view that we have some innate altruistic dispositions. Training is needed in order for such dispositions to develop into full-blown moral capacities. Not everyone sees such an attempt by an older man as a reason to help.

[82] Mark Timmons, *Morality without Foundations: A Defense of Ethical Contextualism* (New York: Oxford University Press, 1999), p. 217.

[83] See Hanfling, 'Learning about Right and Wrong: Ethics and Language': p. 28.

[84] See ibid.

[85] M. L. Hoffman, *Empathy and Moral Development. Implications for Caring and Justice* (Cambridge: Cambridge University Press, 2000), p. 10.

[86] M. L. Hoffman, *Empathy and Moral Development. Implications for Caring and Justice.*

times where induction is not used and a child simply notices a parent's empathic concern and caring attitude.[87]

6.3.5 The ability to deal with new cases

Remarkably, the kind of moral training human beings enjoy enables them to recognise the morally relevant aspects of a novel situation and to make judgements. Despite the fact, highlighted by Larmore, that training and moral rules taken together are not sufficient to determine in what way moral judgement is exercised, this underdetermined faculty has been developed in the course of training.[88] In fact, the workings of a skill never seem to be entirely explicable by reference to rules and training. Let us consider once more the ability to play chess. A competent player has not been acquainted with all possible situations during training. He will have to exercise his competence in novel circumstances, and is able to do so. Ryle points out that unlike drill, training enables people to react to new situations.[89] It must be remembered that it is characteristic of intelligent capacities that in exercising them we keep on learning. Annas explains the ability to deal with novel cases by reference to the fact that teaching and learning to be virtuous, like teaching and learning certain skills, involves giving and receiving reasons und thus understanding why a given action is virtuous.[90] Similarly, Alison Hills argues that what explains our ability to draw the right conclusion or give the right explanation in novel cases is our appreciation of the reasons why a given action is right or wrong.[91]

The explanations conveyed within moral education clearly distinguish it from pure drill or conditioning. Moral learning includes reflection, together with others, on 'the implications and effects of feelings and

---

[87] Michael Slote, *Moral Sentimentalism* (Oxford and New York: Oxford University Press, 2010), p. 20. Moral sentimentalism is a meta-ethical view according to which morality is somehow grounded in emotions ('moral sentiments' in the terminology of philosophers such as David Hume and Adam Smith). It is an alternative to rationalism, which is the dominant position.

[88] Charles Larmore, *Patterns of Moral Complexity* (Cambridge et al.: Cambridge University Press, 1987), p. 18. This does not mean that innate moral dispositions are of no importance for moral judgement. During moral training, innate dispositions are developed further. Capacity for moral judgement involves, for instance, a capacity for empathy, which is developed out of an innate disposition (see 6.3.9).

[89] Ryle, *The Concept of Mind*, pp. 42 ff.

[90] Annas, *Intelligent Virtue*, pp. 19 and 23.

[91] Hills, 'Moral Testimony and Moral Epistemology,': p. 102.

actions'.[92] Adults usually do not simply tell children not to do certain things, but provide reasons: 'It hurts her if you pull her hair'; 'If you do not give him back his toy, he will get upset'. However, I do agree with Hanfling that a child's moral development does not depend on her being given moral lectures.[93]

If successful, moral training results in dispositions to respond immediately, without thought, in situations where this is required. As Morton points out, 'a large part of being a good, responsible participant in social life consists in being able to know, *immediately*, what the right things to do are'.[94] The immediate response of a morally competent agent – for example an immediate judgement when confronted with Singer's pond example – is unlike a rote habit in that it is intelligent because it is educated.[95] Such a response is 'flexible and innovative'.[96] It seems as if the conscious thoughts involved in a judgement made by someone who is not yet competent have disappeared. They have 'effaced themselves', as Annas puts it.[97] A morally competent agent judges immediately that she ought to jump into the pond to save the child, and acts accordingly. In a slightly different situation, she would presumably act differently. If, for instance, she were very far from the child but saw someone else standing on a landing stage much closer to the child, she would tell that person to rescue the child and run to the landing stage in order to help.[98]

6.3.6   Rules and the acquisition of moral competence

What role do rules and instructions play in moral training? According to the well-known model of moral expertise developed by Dreyfus and Dreyfus, their role is crucial at the first stage of moral learning. The authors conceive of a child as learning moral rules prior to being able to judge in a concrete situation whether violating them would be justified. They provide the example of a child who follows the rule 'Never lie' by not lying in any circumstances whatsoever until he faces a dilemma we know from Kant: the choice between telling the truth, thereby betraying a friend's

---

[92] Rustin, 'Innate Morality: A Psychoanalytic Approach to Moral Education,' p. 87.
[93] Hanfling, 'Learning about Right and Wrong: Ethics and Language,': p. 31.
[94] Morton, *On Evil*, p. 55.
[95] See Annas, *Intelligent Virtue*, pp. 28 f.
[96] Annas, *Intelligent Virtue*, p. 29.
[97] Ibid., pp. 28 f.
[98] There are of course many situations which are more complex. In such situations, the agent deliberates. Successful moral training also results in the capacity to deliberate about what the right thing to do is in a situation in which this is not obvious.

whereabouts to a killer, or lying about where the friend is. (The authors admit that the example is 'greatly oversimplified and dramatic'.) Only upon confrontation with this serious dilemma does the child realise that whether it is morally right or not to tell the truth is context-dependent. The experience of regret and guilt after having told the truth and said where the friend is to be found makes the child realise that moral rules need to be contextualised. The next step for the child is to seek maxims like 'Never lie unless someone might be seriously hurt by telling the truth'. In acting according to such maxims, the child will again experience negative moral feelings. It is only with presumably a lot of experience that the child (who might by then have become an adolescent or an adult[99]) would be able to judge, without appeal to either rules or maxims, in a concrete situation whether lying or telling the truth is the morally right thing to do, and thus have reached the stage of ethical expertise.[100]

The first thing that is striking is that the authors assume that at the very beginning of her moral development, the child is already able to react with the appropriate moral feelings. The authors do not comment on this, but obviously presuppose that we are either already born with these emotional capacities or that they somehow develop prior to the initial stage of moral development (which is an odd assumption). While negative moral feelings play a crucial role in their account of the development of ethical expertise, these authors do not discuss how the capacity to have these feelings when appropriate is itself developed.[101] As I see it, the development of emotional moral capacities goes hand in hand with the development of the ability to judge what is morally right in particular situations. We develop these capacities in the course of concrete experiences, and feelings and judgements affect each other. The capacity for moral judgement is not a distinct faculty but involves emotional capacities, for instance a capacity for empathy.[102]

---

[99] Dreyfus and Dreyfus do not say anything about this.

[100] Hubert L. Dreyfus and Stuart E. Dreyfus, 'Towards a Phenomenology of Ethical Expertise,' *Human Studies* 14, no. 4 (1991): p. 237.

[101] As Herman Philipse pointed out to me, it is possible to refer to evolution here, but I want to stress once more that the (evolved) moral dispositions with which humans are born are not fully developed moral capacities. Feeling guilty after having acted wrongly is something that children have to learn (see 6.3.4).

[102] For this critique see also Hermann, 'Learning to be Moral,' pp. 218 ff. Empathy has been investigated from many different angles. For an interdisciplinary collection of texts examining the idea that empathy is central to morality see Heidi L. Maibom, ed. *Empathy and Morality* (Oxford and New York: Oxford University Press, 2014).

Dreyfus and Dreyfus' description of how the child seeks maxims that embody exceptions to the rule followed initially echoes the attempts of moral generalists to reformulate moral principles with the aim of removing counterexamples. Given that it is in concrete situations that children learn that lying is wrong, the view that they initially follow the rule 'Never lie' by not lying in any circumstances whatsoever is implausible. I doubt that this rule figures in moral education at all. Children are not told never to lie, but they are asked to tell the truth when something has happened that needs elucidation, and corrected when they are caught lying in a particular case. In addition, they are told that it was wrong for their sister to lie, or that their friend ought not to have lied to the teacher. They learn that whether telling the truth is morally right or not depends on the context by learning the rightness and wrongness of instances of truth telling in such contexts. It should moreover not be forgotten that there are also cases in which children are told to lie, for instance to say that they are late for school because of the traffic although the real reason is that their parents slept in, or to say 'Thank you for this beautiful cardigan' despite the fact that the cardigan is awful. The fact that children are asked to lie in particular circumstances already at an early age does not fit well with Dreyfus and Dreyfus' description.

What, then, is the role of moral rules? As Jay Garfield points out, we use universal moral principles to point to the relevant similarities between cases. At the same time, we are aware of the fact that there are exceptions and that the generalisations 'derive their content from the more basic particular facts and similarity relations they capture'. Moreover, generalisations play a role in my account of moral training because the paradigm cases referred to during training must be identified and 'characterized as satisfying relevant moral descriptions'.[103] If, for instance, an adult describes particular behaviour as an example of modesty, she commits herself to the claim that all materially similar behaviours in materially similar contexts are modest.[104] Moral principles are moreover used in order to emphasise the wrongness of a particular instance of lying, stealing and so on. In addition to correcting the child's behaviour, the adult utters a moral rule such as 'Lying is wrong': 'You ought to have told me that it was you who broke the cup and not your

---

[103] Garfield, 'Particularity and Principle: The Structure of Moral Knowledge,' p. 200.

[104] Garfield, 'Particularity and Principle: The Structure of Moral Knowledge,' p. 200.

sister! Lying is wrong.' In such a case, the function of the utterance of the rule is not to teach the child that lying is always wrong, but to stress the wrongness of this particular instance of lying.

I also want to point out that the role of the rule 'Do not lie' differs from that of the rule 'Do not steal', and both differ from that of other rules. As we saw above, some forms of lying have a positive function in society. There are differences between moral rules with regard to the frequency with which they are used in moral education and with regard to the ways in which they are used. In addition, the role of moral rules differs depending on the broader context. Many children are presumably never told by their parents or teachers not to kill innocent human beings, while some, for instance in the context of civil war, are told to kill particular people and to refrain from killing others. It depends on the context which moral rules are taught (explicitly) and how. In a society in which equality between men and women has been largely achieved, the rule 'Men and women are equal' will play a different role in moral education than in a society in which many institutions still manifest inequality between the sexes. These few examples provide sufficient indications of how cautious we have to be with generalisations.

The general claim I want to make is that moral rules are not at the centre of moral teaching and learning. We learn to participate in moral practices and thereby become able to abstract rules from those practices. The practice is prior to the rules in two senses: first, we are initially trained to follow patterns of behaviour that merely conform to rules rather than being trained actually to obey rules.[105] Secondly, moral rules or principles function as incomplete articulations of moral practices. They are mere 'summaries' of that which we 'know' if we have mastered those practices.[106] Thus, the principle 'We ought to help friends in need' falls short of articulating the 'knowledge' revealed by Lydia's behaviour. Likewise, 'We ought to treat members of other cultures with respect' is no more than a summary of the complex practice it aims to articulate. I shall elaborate on our mastery of these complex practices in the following section.

---

[105] See Williams, *Wittgenstein, Mind and Meaning*, pp. 194 f., for the distinction between three different forms of regularity: 'rule-conforming behavior', 'rule-obeying behavior' and 'pattern-governed behavior'. To say of a person that she is obeying a rule is to say that she is following it intentionally.

[106] Garfield, 'Particularity and Principle: The Structure of Moral Knowledge,' pp. 198 f.

6.3.7   Rules and the exercise of moral competence

It has been argued by Andy Clark that those summaries of moral practices fulfil crucial functions within both collective and individual moral reasoning. According to Clark, in the same way as the emphasis on explicitly endorsed moral principles, the emphasis on practical wisdom – as may be found for instance in the work of Dreyfus and Dreyfus – fails to capture the 'subtlety, power and complexity of human moral intelligence'. Linguistic tokens of moral principles have two important roles to play: that of a 'medium of collaborative effort' and that of a 'source of new stable entities standing-in for complex patterns and relations'.[107]

I shall explain their role as a 'medium of collaborative effort' first. Moral reasoning and decision-making is to a large extent not undertaken by individuals in isolation, but together with others. Moral debates concerning for instance whether euthanasia or stem cell research should be allowed are collaborative efforts at negotiating a course of action that meets with the needs of different individuals and groups. Within such negotiations, linguistic formulations of moral maxims and principles play a role. Despite being only summaries, these formulations are 'the tools that enable the co-operative explorations of moral space'.[108] However, it must be stressed that these formulations do not include sentences that manifest attempts to articulate a moral certainty. Participants in moral debates do not attempt to formulate certainties, but the debate reveals that for instance the wrongness of killing as such is taken for granted. The fact that the formulation of a rule enters a moral debate shows that we are not dealing with a certainty.

The second role of formulations of moral rules identified by Clark is the more fundamental one. Unlike the first role, it concerns individual moral reasoning. According to Clark, those formulations are part of that which enables individual brains to engage in abstract moral thought by serving to reduce complex patterns to regularities that are tractable and can be learned.[109] They make learning based on experience and examples possible, and in mature moral thought they function as 'tools for focusing, holding steady, and refining moral understanding'.[110] Clark criticises Dreyfus and Dreyfus for limiting their role to that of a tool for the novice.

---

[107] Andy Clark, 'Word and Action: Reconciling Rules and Know-How in Moral Cognition,' in *Moral Epistemology Naturalized*, ed. Richmond Campbell and Bruce Hunter (Calgary, Alberta, Canada: University of Calgary Press, 2000), p. 279.

[108] Andy Clark, *Moral Epistemology Naturalized*, p. 274.

[109] Ibid., p. 275.

[110] Ibid., pp. 277 f.

It should be stressed that moral principles are not independent of one another and that in situations of conflict, we thus do not weigh up independent principles. This can be explained by reference to the fact that, as Clark admits, formulations of moral rules cannot capture the complexity of what competent agents know. Understanding moral principles such as the prohibition on killing, the obligations to keep one's promises and secrets, and the duty to help, amounts to the ability to participate in certain practices, including linguistic practices. Practices such as entrusting another person with a secret, making a promise, making moral judgements and so on are not distinct but overlapping, and morally competent agents engage in many of them at the same time. On the basis of this view, we can expect fewer situations of moral conflict than we would from the perspective of a position starting from independent moral principles which are the object of propositional knowledge.

Moral competence involves the mastery of these overlapping practices. In order to know, for instance, whether it is justifiable to disclose a secret in a particular case, we have to know the point of the practice of having secrets and entrusting someone with a secret, which cannot be understood independently of the point of other practices such as the practice of promising, as well as the practice of helping friends. For a morally competent agent, the particular situation does not involve independent moral principles such as the obligation to keep a secret and the duty to help a friend, which have to be weighed up against each other. By contrast, her recognition of the first obligation is dependent on recognition of the other, and vice versa.[111] If she keeps a secret, thereby refraining from helping a friend who needs her help urgently, where this is not connected to unbearably high personal costs and the person whose secret would be disclosed would not be seriously harmed, her behaviour does not reveal an understanding of the point of keeping a secret.[112] We do not learn moral norms in isolation and their meaning, conceived of as their role in our practices, cannot be understood in isolation.

---

[111] This view does not amount to radical particularism. I am not claiming that there is no role for moral principles, but that such principles are interconnected and that they are summaries. I thank Herman Philipse for pressing me to clarify this.

[112] It follows from the arguments in the previous chapter (5.6) that this does not amount to a complete list of exceptions. Ertz provides a similar account of the interdependence between the virtues. He uses Wittgenstein in order to argue for Plato's unity of the virtues. Timo-Peter Ertz, *Regel und Witz. Wittgensteinsche Perspektiven auf Mathematik, Sprache und Moral* (Berlin and New York: de Gruyter, 2008), p. 232.

A good example of a competence that does not require much explicit knowledge of rules is the ability to speak one's native language. Almost everyone is acquainted with the phenomenon whereby a person who is not a native speaker knows linguistic rules that the native speaker has never been aware of. I speak German in a grammatically correct way without knowing many of the rules which people learn in German classes. Usually, we learn a number of rules at school which we later forget, but there are many rules that no native speaker ever learns explicitly. It is thus both possible that I had propositional knowledge of linguistic rules at one time, which I lost later on in life, and that I am able to write and speak in a grammatically correct way without explicitly knowing the linguistic rules. Many German students have to wait until their first classes in Latin until they explicitly learn certain rules of the German language (although their German does not necessarily improve after that). Nevertheless, knowing these rules can be useful, for example when teaching foreigners.

6.3.8 Training and rule-following

We come to follow moral rules by being trained into a moral practice.[113] Moreover, we come to follow rules of (moral) language by being trained into a linguistic practice. Wittgenstein argues that there is a connection between training and rule-following in relation to non-moral rules (his examples include the rule 'Add 2' and the rule expressed by a sign-post), but his argument is also relevant for the moral domain. As Baker and Hacker note, the concept of following a rule is central to 'many distinctively human activities', and we use it in clarifying issues ranging from 'metaphysics to the laws of logic, from mathematics to morals'.[114] A crucial passage is paragraph 198 of the *Philosophical Investigations*: 'Let me ask this: what has the expression of a rule – say a sign-post – got to do with my actions? What sort of connexion is there? – Well, perhaps this one: I have been *trained* to react to this sign in a particular way, and now *I do so react to it*' (PI 198, my italics). Wittgenstein counters the objection that the connection in question is merely causal by asserting that his formulation 'indicated that a person goes by a sign-post only in so far as there exists a regular use of sign-posts, a custom'.[115]

---

[113] See Williams' general claim that we become rule-followers by being trained into a social practice. Williams, *Wittgenstein, Mind and Meaning*, p. 167.

[114] G. P. Baker and P. M. S. Hacker, *Wittgenstein: Rules, Grammar and Necessity*, 2nd, extensively rev. ed. (Chichester, U.K. and Malden, MA: Wiley-Blackwell, 2009), p. 156.

[115] The original reads: '[...] sich Einer nur insofern nach einem Wegweiser richtet, als es einen ständigen Gebrauch, eine Gepflogenheit, gibt.'

This passage contains the core of Wittgenstein's alternative to the Platonist conception of rules and rule-following, according to which a rule, for example an algebraic formula, determines by itself, *considered in isolation*, all its correct future applications in advance (see PI 186 ff.). This view implies a conception of meaning as an entity which can be grasped 'in a flash' (PI 138). Although intuitively appealing, that conception is problematic for a number of reasons: it implies that human minds, which are finite, can grasp infinitely many applications, it makes it hard to explain the fact that we sometimes apply rules wrongly, it leads to a regress of interpretations[116] and to a collapse of the distinction between correct and incorrect applications.[117] On Wittgenstein's alternative view, a rule means something only insofar as there is a practice in which it is followed, which involves agreement over judgements as to what counts as compliance with the rule and thus as doing the same. (Wittgenstein's example of the pupil who follows the rule 'Add 2' as we do up to 1000 and then continues by writing down 1004, 1008 and so forth serves to show that, considered in isolation, a rule cannot fix what doing the same as before is in any given case.[118]) This agreement is not a criterion of correctness, but without it there would be no distinction between correct and incorrect and thus no

---

[116] For different interpretations of the regress Wittgenstein is concerned with see for example Ertz, *Regel und Witz. Wittgensteinsche Perspektiven auf Mathematik, Sprache und Moral*, pp. 14 ff.; James Tully, 'Wittgenstein and Political Philosophy. Understanding Practices of Critical Reflection,' in *The Grammar of Politics. Wittgenstein and Political Philosophy*, ed. Cressida J. Heyes (Ithaca, NY: Cornell University Press, 2003), pp. 38 f.; Williams, *Wittgenstein, Mind and Meaning*, pp. 159 ff.

[117] For this last consequence see Williams, *Wittgenstein, Mind and Meaning*, p. 160.

[118] This is the scenario described by Wittgenstein:

> [A] pupil has mastered the series of natural numbers. Next we teach him to write down other series of cardinal numbers and get him to the point of writing down series of the form
>
>   0, n, 2n, 3n, etc.
>
> at an order of the form '+n'; so at the order '+1' he writes down the series of natural numbers. – Let us suppose we have done exercises and given him tests up to 1000.
>
> Now we get the pupil to continue a series (say +2) beyond 1000 – and he writes 1000, 1004, 1008, 1012. (PI 185)
>
> In what follows, the pupil reacts to the teacher's objection with lack of understanding. He denies having done anything different from what he had done before. He seems to understand the order 'Add 2' as we would understand the order 'Add 2 up to 1000, 4 up to 2000, ...'.

rule-following.[119] Wittgenstein refers to this agreement when he writes that 'there is a way of grasping a rule which is *not* an *interpretation*, but which is exhibited in what we call 'obeying a rule' and 'going against it' in actual cases' (PI 201). The standard for correctness is not independent of the actual practice, that is of the applications of the rule, as it is assumed by Wittgenstein's opponent.[120]

In order to explain what it is to continue in the same way and thus to follow a rule, we have to refer to the process of training.[121] That we follow the rule the way we do is the result of training and thus a contingent fact.[122] There is no logical contradiction involved in thinking that people might react differently, for example, to the rules of addition, and to the way we are taught to apply them at school; however, we cannot imagine what it is like to react to them in those other ways (see PI 206 and RFM IV 29).[123] For us, following the order 'Add 2' by writing down 1004 after 1000 is not a genuine alternative. That we write 1002 after 1000 and that this is uniformly judged to be the way the order is meant is not a matter of mere convention, as Stroud convincingly argues.[124] This means that we did not choose this way of judging out of alternatives. (I shall return to this point in the following chapter.)

As a matter of fact, there is conformity within 'matter-of-course-reactions'. We share, so to speak, a 'sense of the obvious'.[125] This agreement is part of the 'natural history of human beings' (PI 415), and thus part of the constitutive surroundings of rule-governed practices (see Chapter 2). If it were absent, we would not be able to make sense of a rule. This shared sense of the obvious is revealed by what Williams calls

---

[119] The version of the so-called community-view of rule-following that I endorse is not vulnerable to the objection that the community-view claims that actual agreement provides the criterion for correctness. For this objection see Baker and Hacker, *Wittgenstein: Rules, Grammar and Necessity*, pp. 150 f. and 155. The community-view holds that rule-following requires not merely that an act is performed on multiple occasions but also that it is performed by a group of people. The latter requirement is denied by Baker and Hacker. See ibid., pp. 149 ff. Wittgenstein's remarks are ambiguous with regard to this point, but to me the view that rule-following presupposes *shared* practices seems to be more convincing overall.

[120] See Williams, *Wittgenstein, Mind and Meaning*, pp. 158 f.

[121] Ibid., p. 205.

[122] See Barry Stroud, 'Wittgenstein and Logical Necessity,' *The Philosophical Review* 74, no. 4 (1965): pp. 513 f.

[123] Barry Stroud, 'Wittgenstein and Logical Necessity,' pp. 509 f.

[124] Ibid., pp. 511 ff.

[125] Williams, *Wittgenstein, Mind and Meaning*, p. 202.

'bedrock rule-following', or 'bedrock practices'.[126] These are behaviours that are 'pattern-governed', but not instances of rule compliance, that is behaviours that are not performed because the agent recognises and follows a set of rules, but 'because they conform to, or contribute to, a complex social pattern'.[127] In the moral case the shared sense of the obvious is manifested for instance in the universal reaction to Singer's pond example. ('Of course we ought to save the child from drowning in such a situation.')

It has been objected by Simon Blackburn that the pupil envisaged by Wittgenstein has no moral analogue. The 'mental life' of that pupil, says Blackburn, may be impossible to describe and to imagine, but we can only too well imagine 'the mental life of someone who parts company on hard ethical cases'.[128] Wittgenstein's remarks on rule-following do not have the relevance for ethics that John McDowell and others take it to have, because they deal exclusively with cases in which 'everything is a matter-of-course' and 'disputes do not break out' (PI 240). '[E]thical evaluations or descriptions, and in particular 'hard cases', argues Blackburn, 'are often not at all a matter-of-course'.[129]

To this it may be objected that, despite the existence of 'hard cases', much of moral rule-following is a matter-of-course. Focusing on the hard cases conceals this fact. Moreover, we could not even speak about rule-following in ethics if there were no bedrock practices. Although we can imagine what goes on in the mind of a person who judges differently from us in a hard case, say someone who disagreed with our view on the moral permissibility of euthanasia, the 'mental life' of someone who reacted to moral training by for instance judging every second murder she hears about to be morally permissible is just as unimaginable as is that of the pupil who continues the series after 1000 with '1004', '1008' and so on.

The idea that we come to share the same sense of the obvious through training sheds further light on the phenomenon of moral certainty. Propositions that manifest attempted articulations of those certainties seem to state something that is obvious. Their obviousness can now be explained partly by reference to the training through which we acquire

---

[126] Williams, *Wittgenstein, Mind and Meaning*, pp. 168 and 202.

[127] Ibid., p. 195.

[128] Simon Blackburn, 'Reply: Rule-Following and Moral Realism,' in *Wittgenstein: to Follow a Rule*, ed. Steven H. Holtzman and Christopher M. Leich (London et. al.: Routledge & Kegan Paul, 1981), p. 170.

[129] Ibid.

moral competence. Moral certainties acquire their status through the way we act towards them, which is partly fixed by the training we have received.[130] Another part of the explanation refers to our evolutionary history. It is not arbitrary that we treat the wrongness of killing and lying as certainties, but do not for instance do likewise in relation to the proposition that helping others is wrong. Moral certainty is a complex combination of biological and social factors.[131] It is the interplay between innate moral dispositions and dispositions that result from enculturation, to which I now turn.

6.3.9   Innate capacities and capacities that are the product of moral learning

Are all of the 'natural' moral actions and reactions part of our second nature, that is the result of training, or do some of them belong to our first nature? The behaviour towards someone with toothache, as described by Wittgenstein, is an example of a primitive reaction which is natural in the sense of first nature: 'In its most primitive form it is a reaction to somebody's cries and gestures, a reaction of sympathy or something of the form. We comfort him, try to help him (CE, p. 381)'.[132] I think that it is plausible to conceive of this primitive response to pain as an example of a reaction that marks the beginning of moral language-games. The distress felt by a parent who hears her baby crying has a clear biological function and is at the same time, I would argue, fundamental for the capacities that characterise a good parent. Returning to one of the cases described at the beginning of this chapter, Christian's feelings of unease at his son's situation can be seen as natural reactions to signs of him not being well, which might ultimately be rooted in the distress felt when he was crying as a baby. This 'original' feeling of distress is crucial for reproductive success. This, however, does not imply

---

[130] See Williams, *Wittgenstein, Mind and Meaning*, p. 200. Williams writes about a rule that it 'is made a guide, or standard, for action *by* our acting towards it in ways that are fixed by our training'.

[131] While Pleasants conceives of moral certainty as innate, Brice argues that it is exclusively the result of enculturation. Nigel Pleasants, 'If Killing Isn't Wrong, Then Nothing Is: A Naturalistic Defence of Basic Moral Certainty,' *Ethical Perspectives* 22, no. 1 (2015): 197–215. Robert Greenleaf Brice, 'Mistakes and Mental Disturbances: Pleasants, Wittgenstein, and Basic Moral Certainty,' *Philosophia* 41 (2013). I thank Herman Philipse for urging me to acknowledge that references to training do not exhaust explanations of (moral) certainty.

[132] Whenever I use the term 'natural' without further specification, it should be clear from the context whether it refers to first or second nature.

that the fact that it is crucial for reproductive success justifies the moral language-games that developed from it.

As was suggested in the previous chapter, there is continuous development from the primitive forms of behaviour at the start of ethical language acquisition (which are closely related to our instinctive endowment) to the complex forms of behaviour that characterise our moral language-games.[133] Hanfling describes these primitive forms of behaviour in his article about ethics and language: since it is a 'fact of human life' that children are sometimes a nuisance, and since such behaviour is troublesome for parents, they react to it naturally by expressing displeasure.[134] Likewise, they naturally express pleasure when their children behave well. Before telling a child verbally not to do something, we react to acts of the respective sort by, for instance, expressions of pain and physical prevention. For instance, I cry out when my six-month-old baby grabs my nose, boring her fingernails into my skin, and I stop her from continuing to do so by taking her hand and holding it. When I see that she is about to do the same to another baby at the crèche, I take her hand or move her away from the other child. This is followed by an explanation of why she should not do this, referring to the pain caused. I already start explaining this at a time where she probably does not yet understand my words at all, believing that only in this way will she gradually come to understand and behave accordingly. Here again, the difference between moral training and mere conditioning becomes manifest. However, initially physical prevention and the primitive expression of pain presumably do most of the educatory work. Moreover, the reactions of other babies form part of the natural reactions that feature at the beginning of moral learning.

There is no consensus regarding the exact interplay between nature and enculturation in moral development. It is widely believed by psychologists and evolutionary theorists that human beings are born with 'dispositions to develop capacities for living and cooperating with others', such as 'sensitivity to fairness and unfairness in the distribution of food and other resources, and to cheating in claims to distribution', as well as the capacity to recognise situations in which the use of violence is inappropriate.[135] While we are not born with any full-blown moral capacity, it is part of our natural endowment that we are disposed to develop such capacities

[133] See Andreas Krebs, *Worauf man sich verlässt* (Würzburg: Königshausen & Neumann, 2007), p. 114.
[134] Hanfling, 'Learning about Right and Wrong: Ethics and Language,' p. 30.
[135] Morton, *On Evil*, p. 41.

to some degree, if our environment gives us the slightest chance to do so. As Annas argues, everyone is in principle capable of becoming virtuous, but some are brought up in an environment that poses great obstacles for the development of virtue. Feelings of affection and sympathy, which children have as a matter of their first nature, are by their very nature capable of being developed, for instance by parental encouragement.[136] It is only rarely that a child appears to have had no opportunity at all to develop these capacities. These rare cases involve situations where a child experiences only aversion and violence, and his longing for love is always rejected.[137] The experience of love and (parental) care is a crucial component of the process in which we become morally competent.

We are not the only animals that seem to be born with the disposition to have social emotions.[138] Thus, we share the impulse to help others with certain other primates. It appears that chimpanzees have 'retributive emotions' and 'punish negative actions with other negative actions'. Such reactions and behaviour could be called 'precursors' of moral reactions and behaviour. Observations of these primates support the 'long tradition, going back to Aristotle and Aquinas, which firmly anchors morality in the natural inclinations and desires of our species'.[139]

However, what can be found in other primates can only be called 'premoral' behaviour. For example, the full development of the capacity for empathy in a human being requires a form of sentimental education that clearly has no parallel in the non-human animal world. Moreover, we have some highly abstract cognitive capacities which make our morality 'unique in the animal kingdom' (the capacities for planning, inhibition, understanding others' mental states, and language).[140] Stone argues that

---

[136] See Hanfling, 'Learning about Right and Wrong: Ethics and Language,': p. 31.

[137] See Gary Watson, 'Responsibility and the Limits of Evil: Variations on a Strawsonian Theme,' in *Agency and Answerability. Selected Essays*, ed. Gary Watson (Oxford: Clarendon Press, 2004). Watson provides a shocking example of someone who grew up in this way and ended up as a ruthless killer. See also Morton's description of the development of violent personalities. Morton, *On Evil*, pp. 35 f.

[138] I take moral emotions to be a subgroup of social emotions. There is no sharp boundary between moral emotions and emotions that are social but not moral.

[139] Frans de Waal, 'Morally Evolved: Primate Social Instincts, Human Morality, and the Rise and Fall of "Veneer Theory",' in *Primates and Philosophers. How Morality Evolved*, ed. Stephen Macedo and Josiah Ober (Princeton and Oxford: Princeton University Press, 2006), pp. 18 ff.

[140] Stone, 'The Moral Dimensions of Human Social Intelligence. Domain-specific and Domain-general Mechanisms': pp. 56 ff.

these capacities enable us to 'engage in a wide range of moral judgements and behaviours'. While 'our ancient social instincts are the driving force of morality', the cognitive capacities concerned expand the range of behaviours which can be driven by those instincts. This is Stone's modification of Darwin's claim that 'our moral sense depends on [our; J.H.] intellectual capacities'.[141] That humans have those capacities can be said to belong to the constitutive 'surroundings' of moral language-games. In combination with the intellectual capacities mentioned, our emotional capacities make us 'a moral animal'.[142]

6.3.10   The acting at the bottom of moral language-games

These reflections on moral teaching and learning provide us with a refined conception of the acting that lies at the root of moral language-games. They point to at least three ways in which we can think of that acting. First, we can conceive of it as involving primitive reactions to pain or signs of distress, such as the reaction described by Wittgenstein. These reactions are non-verbal and instinctive, and can also be found among non-human animals. Secondly, we can conceive of the natural reactions featuring at the beginning of moral learning as grounding moral language-games: a parent's expression of approval and affection in response to good behaviour, the cries of another child who has been hurt, the first child's reaction to those reactions, and so on. Thirdly, the acting underlying moral language-games can be interpreted as the immediate responses of morally competent agents. Here

---

[141] Stone, 'The Moral Dimensions of Human Social Intelligence. Domain-specific and Domain-general Mechanisms'. See also Charles Darwin, *The Descent of Man and Selection in Relation to Sex* (New York: Modern Library, 1871), pp. 73 and 471 f. Darwin believed that if non-human social animals had intellectual capacities comparable to those of humans, they would develop a similar, but not an absolutely identical, moral sense. A creature's moral sense depends on its ecology. See William Fitzpatrick, 'Morality and Evolutionary Biology,' in *The Stanford Encyclopedia of Philosophy*, ed. Edward N. Zalta, Fall 2014 Edition, <http://plato.stanford.edu/archives/fall2014/entries/morality-biology/>.

[142] Stone, 'The Moral Dimensions of Human Social Intelligence. Domain-specific and Domain-general Mechanisms': p. 63. Since I take emotions to involve cognitive capacities (see introduction, note 58 above), the contrast is not between emotional and cognitive capacities, but between emotional and *highly abstract* cognitive capacities. For the 'animal dimension' of human morality see also Julia Hermann, 'Man as a Moral Animal: Moral Language-Games, Certainty, and the Emotions,' in *Language, Ethics and Animal Life: Wittgenstein and Beyond*, ed. Michael Burley, Niklas Forsberg, and Nora Hämäläinen (New York: Bloomsbury (formerly Continuum Publishing), 2012), pp. 122 f.

we are concerned with second nature, and with agreement in moral judgements.

All three ways of interpreting the underlying acting – which should not be regarded as mutually exclusive, but rather as mutually complementing– are conducive to achieving a better understanding of morality. They enable us to see that morality, like language, 'did not emerge from some kind of ratiocination' (OC 475).

Let me at this point summarise the core of my practice-based view: (1) morality is based on practice in the sense that moral justification and deliberation presuppose shared natural reactions and immediate responses by morally competent agents; (2) we learn to be moral through practice; (3) moral agency requires a complex competence that needs to be practised throughout an agent's entire life; (4) the actions of a morally competent agent manifest moral certainty.

6.4   Rejection of the attempt to justify morality as a whole

On the basis of the understanding of moral competence laid out in this chapter, I am now able to reject the philosophical demand for a justification of morality as a whole from a standpoint that is external to it. I shall address the question 'Why be moral?' and argue that, as understood by the philosopher, it does not have to be taken seriously. I shall argue against the philosophical conception of the amoralist as someone who is morally competent but at the same time not moved by moral concerns. The main aim of this section is to show how it follows from the practice-based view that the demand to justify morality from an external standpoint is pointless and that morality is irreducible.

The demand for a justification of morality as a whole is motivated by the desire to silence the moral relativist, the sceptic and the nihilist. They deny respectively that it is possible justifiably to make moral judgements about practices of other cultures, that moral knowledge is possible and that moral truths exist.[143] The question 'Why be moral?' seems to make perfect sense. We could imagine a response to it which merely pointed out inconclusive reasons in favour of compliance with moral norms. However, the response asked for is one that is capable of convincing every rational person of the authority of morality. If an account of morality aims to convince every rational person, it seems

---

[143] See Jeffrey Stout, 'On Having a Morality in Common,' in *Prospects for a Common Morality*, ed. Gene Outka and John P. Reeder Jr. (Princeton, N.J: Princeton University Press, 1993), p. 215.

that it must be based on non-moral premises. This impression rests on the assumption that no moral convictions are shared by all rational human beings.

6.4.1   'Why be moral?'

The question, 'Why be moral?' has a long history. It has concerned philosophers since the Ancient Greeks. Plato addressed it in a number of dialogues, in particular in his *Republic*.[144] There have been several attempts to answer it, and the history of philosophy also includes a number of arguments seeking to refute such attempts, including for instance arguments that accuse the respective philosophers of committing some version of the 'naturalistic fallacy'.[145] Nevertheless, the demand is still alive within contemporary philosophy. I shall not present and discuss the arguments of other philosophers, but use the resources provided by my account of morality in order to reject this justificatory demand.

Sinnott-Armstrong notes that the question 'Why be moral?' is 'too short to be clear'.[146] Both 'why' and 'moral' can be taken to mean different things. I am concerned with the question as it is put by the philosopher, and I take it to refer to reasons for caring about moral norms. These reasons do not necessarily have to be self-interested. The question can thus be reformulated as 'Why should we care about morality?' To begin with, I would like to contrast this use of the question with its occurrences in everyday life. When the question as to why one has to comply with moral norms arises in (non-philosophical) practice, it is motivated by the experience that moral obligations conflict with non-moral interests.[147] Let me give an example. I promised my friend

---

[144] The first systematic expression of the question in Western philosophy can be found at the beginning of Book II of Plato's *Republic* (357b).

[145] The classical sources for these arguments are David Hume and G. E. Moore. David Hume, *A Treatise of Human Nature*, ed. L. A. Selby-Bigge, 2nd revised ed. by P. H. Nidditch (Oxford: Clarendon Press, 1978), p. 469. G.E. Moore, *Principia Ethica* (London: Cambridge University Press, 1903). We can be said to commit the naturalistic fallacy if we reduce a moral concept like 'good' to non-moral concepts such as 'pleasurable', or if we infer an 'ought' from an 'is'. The former refers to Moore, and the latter to Hume.

[146] Walter Sinnott-Armstrong, 'Moral Skepticism,' in *The Stanford Encyclopedia of Philosophy*, ed. Edward N. Zalta, Fall 2011 Edition, <http://plato.stanford.edu/archives/fall2011/entries/skepticism-moral/>. Sinnott-Armstrong distinguishes between two meanings of 'moral' in 'Why be moral?': 'Why should I be a moral person?' and 'Why should I do moral acts?'

[147] See Charles Larmore, *The Autonomy of Morality* (Cambridge and New York: Cambridge University Press, 2008), p. 88.

that I would help her move house on Sunday, but when the day comes, the weather is very nice and I would much prefer to go to the beach. This is a harmless case, but such examples add up, and we encounter situations in which it is very inconvenient for us to comply with moral rules. In asking ourselves in a particular situation whether we actually have to do what morality requires and cannot simply disregard moral claims, thereby asking for reasons to be moral, we are not reflecting from an extra-moral standpoint.

There are also more general conflicts between personal interests and moral requirements. If, for instance, Max did not spend any time and money helping people who are worse off than he is, he would be richer and could do more of the things he enjoys, such as buying books, travelling, entertaining friends, and so on. The question why he, as a rich and successful person, should use part of his income to support developmental projects or social initiatives in his home town and spend his summer holidays working as a volunteer in an old people's home instead of flying to the Riviera becomes even more pressing, given the limited impact that individual action has in relation to the world's suffering. In such cases, we feel the force of moral obligations. It is *because* we feel it, together with the force of interests other than the interest to live up to these demands, that we sometimes end up asking ourselves why, and whether, we should actually be moral. We might answer it positively in some cases, and negatively in others.

In the examples provided above, the question 'Why be moral?' makes sense. It is used in the language-games that are 'its original home' (PI 116). Within those contexts, the question is accompanied by the 'typical antecedents and consequences' (RPP II 345).[148] The philosopher, however, has taken the question 'out of its home'. As he understands it, it is comparable to the question as to why it should not be the case that our senses always deceive us. There is no serious non-philosophical reason for it.[149] This is one of the cases where 'language goes on holiday' (PI 38).

I intended my discussion of the role of moral justification in Chapter 4 to show that our practices of morally justifying actions, judgements, institutions, and so on perform a function in our lives. This function is constitutive of them. Moral justification serves, amongst other things,

---

[148] Wittgenstein here talks about the 'typical antecedents and consequences of doubt'.

[149] See Kurt Bayertz, *Warum überhaupt moralisch sein?* (München: C. H. Beck, 2004), p. 27.

to legitimise, to avoid blame, to gain acceptability for our behaviour amongst our fellow human beings, and to reach agreement. By contrast, the function of philosophical attempts to answer the question 'Why be moral?' is not clear.

Although there is no sharp boundary between non-philosophical moral practices and philosophical practices, moral philosophical questions that seem to lack any relevance for our daily affairs are dubious. If they are to illuminate our understanding of morality, questions raised at the level of critical reflection upon moral reflection and deliberation (level 4, see Chapter 2) must somehow be anchored in the lower levels of moral practice. What can the philosophical way of asking why we should be moral possibly contribute to a better understanding of morality?

In Chapter 4, I argued that the distinction between epistemic and moral justification is not applicable to moral beliefs. Thus, it appears that the demand for a justification of morality as a whole amounts to the demand for a *moral* justification of morality. However, what does it mean to morally justify morality? It would have to mean justifying morality by reference to a higher order morality. However, the assumption that such a justification is needed leads to an infinite regress. If we have to justify our first order morality, we also have to justify the second order morality appealed to in order to justify the first order morality, and so on. Therefore, the question of whether morality is *really* moral makes no sense. As Arrington notes, we do not have a more general concept of morality to appeal to.[150]

Moreover, since morality as a whole belongs to those practices that are characteristic of the human form of life, asking for a justification of it amounts to asking for justification of what humans are. Stroud points out that '[t]o ask whether our human practices or forms of life themselves are "correct" or "justified" is to ask whether we are "correct" or "justified" in being the sorts of things we are'.[151] He refers in particular to the practices of calculation and inference, but our engagement in moral practices is no less central to the human form of life. We do not decide to make moral evaluations 'any more than we decide to be human beings as opposed to trees'.[152] While it makes sense to ask for

---

[150] Robert L. Arrington, 'A Wittgensteinian Approach to Ethical Intuitionism,' in *Ethical Intuitionism: Re-evaluations*, ed. Philip Stratton-Lake (Oxford: Clarendon Press, 2002), p. 280.

[151] Stroud, 'Wittgenstein and Logical Necessity,' p. 518.

[152] Ibid. Stroud says this about our ways of calculating and inferring.

justification of particular moral practices and views, the demand that morality as a whole should be justified is pointless.

6.4.2   To whom do we justify?

Who is the addressee of philosophical answers to the question 'Why be moral?' Should such a person be described as someone who is not susceptible to any moral considerations? Does she consider our moral practices as a matter of curiosity, wondering why we feel morally obliged to do certain things and to refrain from others, why we evaluate the actions of others as well as our own, have feelings of shame and guilt, and so on?[153]

Within everyday practice, attempts to justify a moral judgement, an action or an institution are directed at persons whom we expect will accept the authority of morality. We conceive of our opponents as persons who are morally competent, which implies that they generally accept moral requirements. If we had the impression that our opponent lacked this competence, we would presumably give up, concluding that our efforts would be in vain. Yet some philosophers think that they have to provide a theory capable of convincing an amoralist, understood as someone who is not moved by any moral concerns whatsoever. A philosopher like Peter Stemmer, whose sanction-based moral theory recently received much attention in Germany, conceives of the amoralist, whom he calls a moral sceptic, as someone who presents an intellectual challenge by forcing us to provide an answer to the question as to why it is rational to act morally.[154] The answer we are asked to provide should not be based on any moral premises, because the addressee has positioned herself outside of morality and we cannot expect any concessions from her.[155] Like other proponents of sanction-based accounts of morality, Stemmer thinks that the authority of moral norms cannot be explained without reference to the sanctions associated with them. He assumes that people

---

[153] 'Why' here refers to explanatory reasons.

[154] See Peter Stemmer, *Handeln zugunsten anderer. Eine moralphilosophische Untersuchung* (Berlin and New York: de Gruyter, 2000), p. 38. Other philosophical attempts to justify morality as a whole from an extra-moral standpoint include Bayertz, *Warum überhaupt moralisch sein?*; David Gauthier, *Morals by Agreement* (Oxford and New York: Clarendon Press and Oxford University Press, 1986); Michael von Grundherr, *Moral aus Interesse: Metaethik der Vertragstheorie* (Berlin and New York: de Gruyter, 2007).

[155] See Bayertz, *Warum überhaupt moralisch sein?*, p. 26.

act morally in order to avoid moral sanctions, which according to his narrow conception of sanctions consist in social exclusion.[156] Stemmer's view implies that in order to transform a person who has so far not been moved by any moral considerations into a person who believes that she should act morally, it is sufficient to provide an argument as to why it is rational to act morally which does not rely on any moral assumptions. He thus seems to presuppose that the amoralist does not lack any competence, since competence cannot result from the acceptance of an argument.[157] However, any attempt to convince such a person through argument of the authority of moral norms is doomed to failure.

It must be recalled that the justification of moral judgements or norms necessarily refers to moral reasons, which can only be appreciated from a moral point of view, and that in order to take up such a point of view, moral competence must have been developed through training. If we conceive of knowledge of right and wrong as involving a complex competence, human beings will not be able to respect moral norms through a process of reasoning alone. No theory – however sophisticated – can do the job. They need to develop the respective capacities. Since we would not judge someone to be a morally competent agent if she were not in general moved by moral concerns, the philosophical conception of the amoralist as a morally competent agent who refuses to accept moral norms is inconsistent. Whether someone possesses moral competence is revealed through practice. To quote Williams again: 'understanding requires public manifestation of mastery of the practice'.[158] A person whose actions displayed a complete ignorance of the interests and feelings of others could not be regarded as morally competent. In addition, given the close connection between emotions and moral judgements suggested by scientific studies, it seems that a person who gave no weight to moral considerations within her

---

[156] Stemmer, *Handeln zugunsten anderer. Eine moralphilosophische Untersuchung*: pp. 101 and 152. This narrow conception of sanctions excludes inner sanctions as well as for example contempt and the withdrawal of trust. For a discussion of Stemmer's position see also Julia Hermann, 'Die Praxis als Quelle moralischer Normativität,' in *Moral und Sanktion. Eine Kontroverse über die Autorität moralischer Normen*, ed. Eva Buddeberg and Achim Vesper (Frankfurt and New York: Campus, 2012), pp. 138 ff.

[157] It seems that if there were anything like moral competence for Stemmer, it would consist solely in the insight that it is in one's own interest to act morally.

[158] Williams, *Wittgenstein, Mind and Meaning*, p. 199.

judgements would lack certain emotional capacities.[159] Thus, the idea of the amoralist only appears to be consistent if we conceive of her as a sociopath.[160]

6.4.3   The irreducibility of morality

The view that the philosophical demand for an argument for morality based on non-moral premises is deeply mistaken is supported by the way moral education works. Let us once more return to our moral training. In learning to distinguish between right and wrong, children learn that their own interests are not the primary criterion for what may and should be done. They are taught that the interests of others need to be taken into account within reasoning about how to act, not because this is in one's own interest but because those interests have to be considered in their own right.

For example, a father does not tell his child Simon not to take Kelly's toy because this would be contrary to Simon's self-interest. Instead, he explains to him that this toy belongs to Kelly and that he is not therefore allowed to take it without permission. The father thereby indirectly explains to his child the institution of property. He might further say that Kelly would be very unhappy if Simon took her toy, appealing to Simon's concern about others' well-being and thereby also to emotional capacities like empathy. Thus, he would be appealing to the moral idea that the well-being of others is important. If Simon has not yet developed such a concern for others, which means that he has also not yet developed certain emotional capacities, he might not accept what his father tells him and simply scream or cry. More

---

[159] See for example Blair, 'Neuro-Cognitive Systems Involved in Morality'; Blair, 'Moral Judgment and Psychopathy'; J.D. Greene, 'Emotion and Cognition in Moral Judgment. Evidence from Neuroimaging,' in *Neurobiology of Human Values*, ed. J. P. et al. Changeux (Berlin: Springer-Verlag, 2005); J.D. Greene and J. Haidt, 'How (and Where) Does Moral Judgment Work?,' *Trends in Cognitive Sciences* 6(2002); Haidt, 'The Emotional Dog and its Rational Tail: A Social Intuitionist Approach to Moral Judgment'; Liane Young et al., 'Damage to Ventromedial Prefrontal Cortex Impairs Judgment of Harmful Intent,' *Neuron* 65, no. 6 (2010).

[160] See Jesse J. Prinz, 'The Emotional Basis of Moral Judgments,' *Philosophical Explorations* 9, no. 1 (2006): p. 38. That the attempt to convince an amoralist as he is understood by the philosopher would be pointless is also indicated by the fact that we do not first acquire moral competence and then subsequently require motivation. See Annas, *Intelligent Virtue*, p. 28.

situations of that sort would gradually lead him to develop the required emotional capacities as well as a concern for the needs and interests of others.[161]

It might be objected against this example that Simon's father could indeed refer to Simon's self-interest, arguing that he should not take Kelly's toy because he would not want Kelly to take his toy either. This, however, is itself a moral argument that cannot be reduced to pure considerations of self-interest. It does not follow that Simon should not take Kelly's toy from the fact that he would not want her to take one of his toys. The argument is based on the idea that you should not treat others in ways you would not want to be treated yourself. As familiar as this idea might sound to us, it is certainly hard to understand for small children. I would not expect Simon to be very impressed if his father were to invoke such an argument. Understanding and accepting something like the 'golden rule', presupposes recognition of the interests and feelings of others, the ability to put oneself in their shoes, and so on. In spite of the fact that it is a basic feature of the moral reasoning of a morally competent agent, it requires capacities which a small child has not yet developed. The notion of what one wants for oneself serves as a criterion for how others should be treated. The reason for treating them this way is not that it serves our own interests.

Our moral education of children indicates that the rightness or wrongness of actions is always explained partly by reference to other moral beliefs. A child will only understand that a certain act is wrong if it already holds other moral beliefs and has at least a rudimentary capacity to think and feel morally. Moral training advances the further development of capacities that are already there to a certain extent. If a child's moral competence is not yet sufficiently developed, it will not be convinced that the respective action is wrong, but disagreement with his parents will be part of what makes it develop that competence further.

Moral training results in certain ways of feeling, thinking and acting which are not supported by reasons. To say that they are the result

---

[161] Let me add that the father of course also praises the behaviour of his child at times, and that the child does not only behave badly. It is merely for the sake of argument that I focus here on morally wrong behaviour on the part of the child and on the blame and criticism of the father.

of training is not tantamount to justifying them, since it does not invoke reasons. From a moral standpoint, Simon's father has reasons for objecting to Simon's behaviour, but he does not take up that standpoint on the basis of reasons.[162] If we refer to his own moral training, we refer to the way his ways of reasoning and reacting were *caused*. We do not, thereby, refer to *reasons* for them. In this case, asking for reasons would be unreasonable. Acting on reasons means that there is a rational connection between the action and certain beliefs. Wittgenstein emphasises the difference between reason, or 'ground', and cause: '"The certainty that the fire will burn me is based on induction." Does that mean that I argue to myself: "Fire has always burned me, so it will happen now too?" Or is the previous experience the *cause* of my certainty, not its ground?' (PI 325; see also OC 130 f., 429 and 474). Similarly, we do not argue to ourselves that the interests of others matter in their own right because, say, this is what we were taught by an authority.

A religious person might believe that the interests of others matter in their own right because every individual is an image of God. Yet there is still something more fundamental than that belief, which is not based on reasons, that is his conception of morality in terms of God's demands. It might be objected that he has reasons for doing so, for example that there are many arguments in favour of God's existence and that his existence makes it necessary to ground morality in him. However, belief in God is ultimately not based on reasons. Believing in God provides someone with a wide range of reasons for believing certain things and for rejecting others. Yet when someone has to defend his faith, he will run out of reasons at some point.[163]

There is moreover another sense in which morality is irreducible. The fact that we come to think in moral terms as a result of training does not mean that our moral thoughts are *about* that training.[164] Similarly, if our moral beliefs are shaped by evolved emotional dispositions, this does not mean that they are beliefs about those dispositions. The content of morality cannot be reduced to considerations about reproductive

---

[162] He can give reasons for why morality is a good thing, but these reasons would not be morally neutral and would not be any more certain than the belief that morality is authoritative.

[163] This is admittedly a highly complex topic which would need more careful consideration.

[164] I owe this point to Barry Stroud.

success, self-interest, and so on, no matter what caused morality to be an integral part of human life in the first place. To reduce morality in this way would be to commit the naturalistic fallacy.

6.5 Conclusion

This chapter has elaborated on the notion of moral competence, paying particular attention to the way in which it is acquired. Drawing on Ryle's distinction between 'knowing how' and 'knowing that', moral competence has been compared with certain practical skills. Many such skills are acquired in ways that resemble the ways in which human beings learn to be moral. During the course of moral training, we come to think, feel and act in certain ways. We come to follow moral rules, but this rule-following is to a large extent unconscious. Explicit formulations of moral principles are incomplete articulations of complex practices and have a limited role both in the acquisition of moral competence and in its exercise. During moral training, innate moral dispositions are developed into full-blown moral capacities.

This account of moral competence and training shows that moral language-games are grounded in action in at least three different ways: they rest on primitive responses that are not specifically human; at the start of moral language acquisition certain natural reactions play a crucial role; sophisticated moral language-games such as justifying and evaluating actions and judgements presuppose bedrock practices, that is thoughtless moral action that is the result of training. Those bedrock practices provide a link between the notion of moral competence and that of certainty. Moral bedrock practices reveal a shared sense of the obvious, which plays an explanatory role in an account of moral certainty. For morally competent agents, the wrongness of paradigmatic cases of killing, stealing, lying and so on is obvious. Being obvious, they are beyond reasonable doubt and not susceptible to justification. The actions of morally competent agents reveal moral certainty. This certainty is both a matter of training and of biological makeup.

Moreover, it has been argued that morality is irreducible. It cannot be grounded in anything outside of our moral practices, and its content cannot be reduced to anything non-moral like reproductive success. It does not make sense to attempt to justify morality from an external standpoint. A person who is unable to grasp moral reasons or who refuses to accept them will not be convinced by any argument in favour of a moral conviction. The addressees of moral justification are situated within moral practices, which they arrive at through a process of moral training. According to the anti-intellectualist stance taken in this book, the philosophical conception of the amoralist as someone who knows the difference between right and wrong but does not care about it is inconsistent. The way in which the practice-based view allows for the criticism of moral practices will be addressed in the following chapter.

7
Objections

7.1 Introduction

In this chapter, I shall address what seem to me the two main possible objections to the practice-based view: the objection that it amounts to a form of moral relativism and the claim that it is utterly conservative. These two objections are closely connected. I shall reject them by arguing (1) that the practice-based view allows for the justified moral critique of practices of people with different cultural affiliations, (2) that it does not make our own moral views and practices immune from criticism and (3) that it can account for moral change and progress.

7.2 The threat of moral relativism

7.2.1 The objection

It might be objected against the practice-based view that, given the role ascribed to moral training and the account of moral certainty, it amounts to a form of moral relativism. The critic can formulate his objection as follows: you argued that moral rightness and wrongness are relative to moral practices. The standards for establishing the correctness of moral judgements and the moral status of actions are internal to those practices. According to your account, the process of learning to be moral is constitutive of what is being learned, and moral training plays a role in explaining why some things are certain for morally competent agents. This commits you to cultural relativism. Your view implies that we have to refrain from judging the moral practices of members of other cultures, since they were trained to be moral in different embedded contexts, thus coming to accept different moral norms and to treat different moral beliefs as certain. Having been trained in different cultural contexts, they do not play the same moral language-games as we do.

I shall reject this objection by arguing that moral practices do not coincide with cultures, that intercultural moral dialogue is possible and that intercultural moral agreement exists. I shall argue against the possibility of radically different moralities, drawing on Wittgenstein's view of the relationship between language-games and facts, the existence of moral universals and possible evolutionary explanations of such universals.

7.2.2   Practices do not coincide with cultures

Let me start my defence against the charge of relativism by stressing that the view that moral rightness and wrongness are relative to moral practices does not commit me to the claim that they are relative to time and place or, more specifically, to culture.[1] It is possible to engage in the same practice at different times and in different places, and practices can transcend cultural boundaries. Moral practices are no exceptions in this regard. People from different cultural backgrounds gather to discuss moral questions, or conduct such discussions on the internet. The practice of making moral judgements does not reveal any commitment to relativism. It seems to be part of the grammar of moral concepts like 'right' and 'wrong', 'good' and 'bad' that their application is not restricted to members of one's own culture or group.[2]

For example, most people today think that slavery is morally wrong, as well as the practice of burning witches and killing aged parents. We do not refrain from judging these practices to be wrong or bad, irrespective of whether or not they complied with the moral standards endorsed at the time and in the place they occurred. We do not consider that slavery is morally wrong here today, but that it is so independently of time and place, although we acknowledge that it was commonly judged to be a necessary institution until the end of the 18th century.[3]

It also has to be noted that the boundaries between cultures are fluid, and that people 'identify with and are identified as belonging to

---

[1] According to the definition provided by Lukes in his recent book on the subject, moral relativism is 'the idea that the authority of moral norms is relative to time and place'. Cultural relativists take it to be relative to culture. Steven Lukes, *Moral Relativism* (New York: Picador, 2008), p. 18.

[2] I have so far described the standpoint of the participant in moral practices, which can be distinguished from the observer's standpoint (see 2.5.2). See ibid., pp. 19 ff.

[3] However, as shall be argued below, moral practices can change over time (7.3.3).

multiple culturally defined groups – local, national, ethnic, religious, and countless others – and [that; J. H.] they relate to them in multiple ways'.[4] The countless virtual communities make the picture even more complex. In the face of this complexity, caution is required when using the terms 'culture' and 'cultural relativity'. In many contexts, references to cultural differences simply obscure the multiple affiliations people have. However, there are contexts in which such references are sufficiently precise. If, for instance, I refer to cultural differences in relation to the debate about so-called 'Asian values' (see 7.2.3), the reader will understand what I mean. In the following I shall mainly use the term 'people with different cultural affiliations', instead of 'members of other cultures', as to mean that there is a low level of overlap between their multiple cultural affiliations and our own.

7.2.3 The possibility of intercultural moral dialogue

It does not follow from the claim that the authority of moral norms is relative to moral practices that we should refrain from making moral judgements about the practices of people with different cultural affiliations. This would only follow were those people considered to have radically different moral practices or, to use the game-metaphor again, were they considered to play our moral language-games in a radically different way, in which case the question would arise as to whether they were still playing the same games.

But why should we think that their moralities are radically different? The existence of moral disputes across borders seems to count in favour of the assumption that we are able to understand each other, even if we come from different cultural backgrounds. Thus, it does not appear, for instance, that the members of a certain political regime do not understand what it means when they are said to violate human rights. Moreover, we understand at least in part the way they try to justify their actions, for instance their references to economic exigencies and relations of priority between different types of human rights.

Take as an example a hypothetical dispute between a Chinese official and a representative of a human rights organisation. The representative tells the official that it is morally wrong to impose severe restrictions on the freedom of speech. The official disagrees, providing a justification which the human rights advocate does not accept. The justification draws on reasons such as the aim of achieving economic stability and the alleged priority of economic and social rights over civil and political

---

[4] Lukes, *Moral Relativism*: p. 119.

rights. In order for this to be a case of real disagreement, the two parties would have to play the same language-game.[5] Whether they do depends partly on what their dispute is about and what the prospects of reaching agreement are. As will be argued below, their disagreement might be caused by conflicting factual beliefs (7.2.4).

If the Chinese official in the example refuses to accept a moral norm which functions as a certainty for the member of the human rights organisation, it is possible that their moral frameworks may be radically different. However, this is not the only option. The Chinese official might not have understood what the human rights advocate meant by his formulation of that norm. He might also not *want* to engage in moral reasoning, thinking that this would not support his interests or those of the government he represents. This leaves the possibility that Chinese citizens might agree with the human rights defender. As Willaschek points out, cases in which people affected by a practice which we regard as immoral themselves reject that practice provide starting points for intercultural moral criticism.[6] We would at least have to show that the parties to the dispute do not treat the same moral judgements as being beyond doubt in order for them to be justified in claiming that their disagreement is unreal, or that the human rights advocate is not entitled to judge the respective practice in moral terms.

The arguments of the Chinese philosopher Xiaorong Li support the view that there is common ground for an intercultural debate about human rights and that disagreements are therefore real.[7] Arguing that what are often referred to as 'Asian values' (an alleged system of values that centres on the community) are compatible with the belief in universal human rights, Li points to an ongoing intercultural dialogue concerning the validity of such rights. That dialogue starts from a minimal basis of agreement that practices such as genocide, slavery and racism are wrong. She rejects the claim that universal human rights conflict with

---

[5] Thanks to the possibility of translation and the existence of English as a global *lingua franca*, playing the same (moral) language-game does not require membership of the same language community.

[6] Marcus Willaschek, 'Moralisches Urteil und begründeter Zweifel. Eine kontextualistische Konzeption moralischer Rechtfertigung,' in *Argument und Analyse. Ausgewählte Sektionsvorträge des 4. internationalen Kongresses der Gesellschaft für analytische Philosophie*, ed. Andreas Beckermann und Christian Nimtz (http://gap-im-netz.de/gap4Konf/Proceedings4/Proc.htm, 2002), p. 639.

[7] Patrick Hayden, *The Philosophy of Human Rights* (St. Paul, MN: Paragon House, 2001), pp. 402 ff. I refer to Li's essay "'Asian Values' and the Universality of Human Rights', which is reprinted in Hayden's book.

the value of the community, arguing that appeals to such conflict rest on the 'conceptual manoeuvre' of equating the community with the state and the state with the current regime. The appeal to the importance of protecting the community conceals the regime's interests in restricting freedom of expression, freedom of association and other civil and political rights. Li argues that, far from being destructive of communities, rights guaranteeing individual freedom contribute to their flourishing. Thus, the possibility to engage in deliberations which are open and public enables vulnerable social groups to 'voice their concerns and expose the discrimination and unfair treatment they encounter'.

Li's view finds support in the work of the Indian economist, philosopher and Nobel Prize winner Amartya Sen, who ascribes a positive role to civil and political rights in the prevention of famines and other economic and social catastrophes.[8] Sen rejects the idea of 'Asian values' on the grounds that Asian traditions are heterogeneous, and argues that the constituent elements of the idea of human rights exist also in Indian and Chinese traditions.[9]

7.2.4   The prospects for intercultural moral agreement

In order for intercultural dialogue to exist, at least minimal agreement on moral matters is required. However, some people deny the existence of such agreement even among members with similar cultural affiliations. Before turning to the issue of intercultural moral agreement, I shall briefly consider the case of 'intra-cultural' agreement. It cannot be denied that moral disagreement exists also within society. However, it is based on widespread agreement regarding moral matters. We disagree, for instance, about whether euthanasia is morally permitted or even required in certain cases, whilst agreeing on the moral demand to respect human dignity, that it is unacceptable to ask a doctor to kill an old relative because we would prefer to go on a holiday instead of looking after him, and that it is necessary to refrain from legalising a practice which increases the likelihood of such cases, and so on. There is disagreement over whether the legalisation of euthanasia is likely to

---

[8] Amartya Sen, 'Development: Which Way Now?,' *Economic Journal* 93, no. 372 (1983). Amartya Sen, *Resources, Values and Development* (Cambridge, MA: Harvard University Press, 1997). Amartya Sen, 'Human Rights and Asian Values,' *The Sixteenth Morgenthau Memorial Lecture on Ethics and Foreign Policy*, Carnegie Council on Ethics and Foreign Affairs, available at http://www.carnegiecouncil.org/publications/archive/morgenthau/254.html (1997).

[9] Amartya Sen, 'Human Rights and Asian Values.'

lead to an increase of cases like that, whether it is a means to advance what has been called 'humane dying', how likely it is that a law permitting euthanasia in specified cases might be abused, how clearly such cases can be specified, and so on. Disagreement about the moral permissibility of a law permitting euthanasia can thus be traced back to disagreement about non-moral questions. The example suggests that the disturbing moral disagreements we observe are often caused by disagreements about the likelihood of certain consequences, the best way of achieving a given moral end, and so on.

What then are the prospects for moral agreement between people whose cultural affiliations display relatively little overlap, for example between non-Muslim German citizens and religious Iranian Muslims? Do we find sufficient conformity in their moral judgements, or is it at least likely that such conformity can be achieved? I suppose that both groups agree that it would be morally wrong for a member of the other group to inflict harm on them, for instance. Both will also regard it as morally (and not only morally) prohibited to try to encroach upon the other's territory. And they both surely believe that they have the right to expect certain behaviour from others, both from members of their own group and those of the other group, and that they are morally justified in protecting themselves from attack. I would add that they also commonly condemn actions like the following: deceiving others for one's own advantage, stealing something which one likes but cannot afford, killing someone in order to come into possession of an inheritance, or allowing someone to bleed to death who could have been rescued.[10]

Thus, it is possible to point to instances of moral agreement between people with apparently very different world views. The undoubtedly numerous moral disagreements between them may, like the euthanasia case discussed above, be partly the result of conflicting views about what the best means to a given end is, for example the end of enabling the members of a society to live a good life. Some of them might also rest on different opinions about the biological differences between men and women, the role of the state, the need for human beings to live within hierarchical structures, and so on.

Similarly, James Rachels argues that what at first sight appears to be a difference between values is often in fact a difference between factual

---

[10] However, this is complicated by the fact that a society or group often distinguishes between the ways in which members and non-members may be treated. I shall return to this below (7.2.5).

beliefs, religious beliefs and physical circumstances.[11] These are factors which, alongside values, make up the customs of a society. Therefore, it does not follow from the fact that there are different customs that the members of the respective societies have conflicting values. It is argued by Rachels that in many cases factual beliefs contribute more to the differences between customs than values.

This view is supported by the example of the traditional Eskimos, whose customs differed drastically from those we have in the Western world. As explorers who came into contact with the traditional Eskimo society reported, infanticide was a common practice in that society.[12] Especially female babies were often killed by their mothers. Contrary to initial appearances, this does not reveal that the Eskimos did not care about their children or lacked respect for human life. If we consider the particularly rough physical circumstances in which the Eskimos lived, we see that the differences between their values and ours are much smaller than we may think, and that the reason why their practices differ drastically from ours is that 'life forced choices upon them that we do not have to make'.[13] For instance, Eskimo mothers nursed their babies for at least two to four years, often even longer, and therefore could only have a limited number of infants.[14] Moreover, the harsh climate forced them to be nomads, and an Eskimo mother was not able to carry more than one baby.[15] Female babies were particularly likely to be killed because of the fact that girls could be expected to leave their parents after marriage and because the Eskimo society was in desperate need of men, who were the main food providers and often died during hunting.[16] However, before killing a child, parents would usually offer it for adoption. 'Life is hard and the margin of safety small' is a postulate which has been extracted from reports of Eskimos' beliefs and practices. A corollary of this postulate is their

---

[11] James Rachels, 'The Challenge of Cultural Relativism,' in *Exploring Ethics: An Introductory Anthology*, ed. Steven M. Cahn (New York and Oxford: Oxford University Press, 2009), pp. 41 f.

[12] Peter Freuchen, *Book of the Eskimos* (London: Arthur Barker Limited, 1962), pp. 97 f.

[13] Rachels, 'The Challenge of Cultural Relativism,' p. 42. See also E. Adamson Hoebel, *The Law of Primitive Man* (New York: Harvard University Press, 1968), pp. 67 ff.

[14] Hoebel, *The Law of Primitive Man*: p. 74. Freuchen, *Book of the Eskimos*: p. 98.

[15] Freuchen, *Book of the Eskimos*, pp. 37 ff.

[16] Hoebel, *The Law of Primitive Man*, p. 75.

belief that '[u]nproductive members of society cannot be supported'.[17] This shows the dynamic relationship between factual assessments and evaluative judgements. Apart from the practice of infanticide, the postulate mentioned above is expressed by the practices of 'senilicide', 'invalidicide' and suicide.[18]

Examples like this provide a reason to be optimistic about the existence of intercultural moral agreement, which makes an intercultural practice of making moral judgements possible (further reasons for such optimism will be given in the next section). Such agreement forms the basis for real intercultural moral disagreement, that is, disagreement which cannot be denied by claiming that the parties play different games. However, the extent to which human beings agree on moral matters is ultimately an empirical question which is difficult to settle.

Despite the fact that many disagreements which prima facie appear to relate to moral beliefs are actually disagreements over certain factual or other beliefs, genuine moral disagreement exists. One example is disagreement regarding the just distribution of wealth in a society. The view that an equal distribution amongst all members of society would be just conflicts with the view that a distribution is just if and only if the members of society who contribute more to the society's wealth receive more than those who contribute less. Both of these views can be supported by reasons, and the conflict between them cannot be reduced to a conflict between factual or other non-moral beliefs. Although the disagreement concerned might be associated with conflicting beliefs as to whether equality of opportunity could ever exist, it is a moral disagreement about what we consider to be just. Two people who agree that it is impossible to create conditions under which everyone would have the same opportunities may still disagree over the question as to whether an equal or unequal distribution is just.

Disagreements of this kind are characteristic of moral practices, and are among the driving forces behind the advancement of these practices. We deal with these forms of disagreement in different ways. First, we often try to find practical compromises, for example an unequal distribution which compensates for individual disadvantages of a certain kind. Second, we continue to discuss those issues, trying to find further reasons and questioning the reasons already provided. Conflicting views

---

[17] Ibid., p. 69.
[18] Ibid., p. 76.

of what is fair or just drive the discussions about how to create a just society, both within the national borders and beyond.

7.2.5 Human nature, evolution and moral universals

7.2.5.1 Natural limits of moral diversity

The view that there can be moral agreement among people with different cultural affiliations and that justified moral criticism is possible is supported by the fact that the content of morality is constrained, amongst others, by human nature.[19] This holds despite the fact that

> [s]ometimes, when we look at all that ethnography and history have recorded about customs and institutions, it seems as though there had developed varieties of moral judgment so different from one another as to force the conclusion that there is no common human nature but only a multitude of human natures.[20]

Anthropologists have, at different points in time, emphasised cultural differences and that which is universally human. During the 19th century, the emphasis was placed on what all human beings have in common. The emphasis shifted towards cultural differences at the beginning of the 20th century and then back to the common elements in the second half of that century.[21]

In the previous chapter it was stated that, like counting and inferring, moral practices belong to those practices which are essential for human beings.[22] I mentioned Stroud's interpretation of Wittgenstein's special form of conventionalism about necessity regarding practices such as

---

[19] The term 'human nature' has been used in three different ways: to refer to the biological and psychological features shared by all human beings, to that which all human beings equally develop or acquire, and to cultural differences. Robert Redfield, 'The Universally Human and the Culturally Variable,' in *Ethical Relativism*, ed. John Ladd (Belmont, CA: Wadsworth Publishing Company, 1973), p. 134. I shall use the term to refer both to innate dispositions and to those capacities that every human being acquires, independently of the cultural context in which he is brought up.

[20] Ibid., p. 130.

[21] Robert Redfield, in *Ethical Relativism*, pp. 132 f.

[22] For the claim that there are such essential practices see Andreas Kemmerling, 'Regel und Geltung im Lichte der Analyse Wittgensteins,' *Rechtstheorie* 6 (1975): p. 125.

calculating and inferring, which is illuminating also for our moral practices (see 6.5.2). Let me therefore return to Stroud's view.

According to Stroud, Wittgenstein is neither a standard nor a radical conventionalist about necessity.[23] His conventionalism does not imply that we could have chosen to have different mathematical practices, for example to count and infer differently.[24] Our practices would be mere conventions if there were genuine alternatives for us, which there are not. Yet inhabitants of the earth with a very different 'natural history' (RFM I 142 and PI 415) could engage in practices of a very different nature to our own.[25] Our practices of counting, inferring, and so on are contingent and at the same time 'somehow "constitutive" of mankind'.[26] We cannot imagine what it would be like to be someone for whom 2 + 2 is not 4.[27] Likewise, we could not simply have chosen for instance the principle that human beings should be harmed as much as possible, although it is conceivable that creatures who were *very* different from us in terms of natural and moral history might have endorsed such a principle.[28] I shall return to this below.

Wittgenstein writes that 'thinking and inferring (like counting) is of course bounded for us, not by an arbitrary definition, but by *natural limits* corresponding to the body of what can be called the role of thinking and inferring in our life' (RFM I 116). He states that 'what we call "counting" is an important part of our life's activities [...] Counting (and that means: counting like this) is a technique that is employed

---

[23] Barry Stroud, 'Wittgenstein and Logical Necessity,' *The Philosophical Review* 74, no. 4 (1965). That he is a radical conventionalist has been claimed by Michael Dummett. Michael Dummett, 'Wittgenstein's Philosophy of Mathematics,' *The Philosophical Review* 68, no. 3 (1959): p. 329.

[24] Stroud, 'Wittgenstein and Logical Necessity,' p. 513. See also Kemmerling, 'Regel und Geltung im Lichte der Analyse Wittgensteins,' p. 125.

[25] 'What we are supplying are really remarks on the natural history of human beings; we are not contributing curiosities however, but observations which no one has doubted, but which have escaped remark only because they are always before our eyes' (PI 142).

[26] Stroud, 'Wittgenstein and Logical Necessity,' p. 514.

[27] Ibid., p. 509. See RFM IV 29.

[28] I refer to 'moral history' separately here, although what Wittgenstein refers to as our natural history should be understood as including our history as 'moral animals'. As Baker and Hacker note, the natural history of human beings is 'the history of a convention-forming, rule-following, concept-exercising, language-using animal – a cultural animal'. G. P. Baker and P. M. S. Hacker, *Wittgenstein: Rules, Grammar and Necessity*, 2nd, extensively rev. ed. (Chichester, U.K. and Malden, MA: Wiley-Blackwell, 2009), p. 221.

daily in the most various operations of our lives' (RFM I 4, my italics). He also points to certain 'physical' and 'psychological facts' that make such a technique possible (RFM VII 1). His point is that the function of certain activities human beings engage in imposes constraints on these activities. Given the functions of the practice of counting, there are limits to what would still count as being an instance of counting. We can extend this point to moral practices and argue that they are similarly limited by their role in our life. In the light of that role, a practice featuring agreement on the rightness of killing and the virtuousness of ruthless behaviour would not be recognisable as moral.

7.2.5.2 *The relationship between moral language-games and facts*

Wittgenstein remarks about the relationship between language-games and facts that '[i]f we imagine the facts otherwise than as they are, certain language-games lose some of their importance, while others become important. And in this way there is an alteration – a gradual one – in the use of the vocabulary of a language'. He asks: 'Indeed, doesn't it seem obvious that the possibility of a language-game is conditioned by certain facts?' This question is followed by the remark that '[in] that case it would seem as if the language-game must show the facts that make it possible. (But that's not how it is.)' (OC 63 and 617 f.). By pointing to the gradual alteration of the use of the vocabulary of a language, Wittgenstein points out that our language-games and their rules are not arbitrary. However, the facts that condition the use of our concepts are not 'written into the concepts'. They are 'part of the framework within which our language-games are played'.[29] We can easily envisage how some moral language-games would become less important if, for instance, human beings were only vulnerable to pain under very specific conditions or if most of us were self-sufficient.

Just as the 'procedure of putting a lump of cheese on a balance and fixing the price by the turn of the scale would lose its point if it frequently happened for such lumps to suddenly grow or shrink for no obvious reason' (PI 142), jumping into a lake fully dressed and taking a child out of it would lose its point if the water could not harm the child. The procedure described by Wittgenstein would under those circumstances not be an act of weighing, and the act of jumping into a lake fully dressed and taking a child out of it would not be an act of rescuing a child. Similarly, telling a potential employer that one has a

---

[29] Baker and Hacker, *Wittgenstein: Rules, Grammar and Necessity*, p. 212.

lot of experience in the area one wants to work in when in fact one has none at all would not be an act of lying if people did not believe what others said anyway and instead of listening to the words merely paid attention to their body language.

Wittgenstein does not explain how language-games are rooted in facts in the sense of stating a hypothesis about a causal relationship between those games and certain facts:[30]

> But I am not saying: if the facts of nature were different we should have different concepts. That is a hypothesis. I have no use for it and it does not interest me. I am only saying: if you believe that our concepts are the right ones, the ones suited to intelligent human beings; that anyone with different ones would not realise something that we realise, then imagine certain general facts of nature different from the way they are, and conceptual structures different from our own will appear *natural* to you.
>
> Remarks on the *Philosophy of Psychology* I 48

In the above quote, Wittgenstein criticises the view that the concepts we actually have are the right concepts in the sense that there are no alternative concepts that would be equally adequate for intelligent human beings. According to his alternative view, it is not the case that our concepts are the right ones, but that the obtaining of certain general natural facts makes our conceptual structures seem natural to us.[31] If we were to conduct a thought experiment and imagine some of these facts being otherwise, different conceptual structures would seem natural, and we would thus be able to understand how other concepts could be equally adequate (see also RC III 293). I agree with Stroud, who understands Wittgenstein as pointing to the fact that 'our having the concepts and practices we have is dependent upon certain facts which might not have obtained'.[32]

---

[30] Ertz objects to this, arguing that the change of certain facts of nature in fact changes our concepts. Timo-Peter Ertz, *Regel und Witz. Wittgensteinsche Perspektiven auf Mathematik, Sprache und Moral* (Berlin and New York: de Gruyter, 2008), p. 61.

[31] Wittgenstein presumably uses the term 'conceptual structures' in order to refer to something less specific than concepts. I am grateful to Beate Sachsenweger for some inspiration in relation with the interpretation of this quote.

[32] Stroud, 'Wittgenstein and Logical Necessity,' p. 516. See also ———, Stroud, 'Concepts of Colour and Limits of Understanding,' in *Wittgenstein On Colour*, ed. Frederik A. Gierlinger and Stefan Riegelnik (Berlin and Boston: De Gruyter, 2014).

Instead of offering a hypothesis, Wittgenstein describes some of our language-games and their alteration, which he portrays as going hand in hand with an alteration of facts. The facts 'no one has doubted and which have only gone unremarked because they are always before our eyes' (RFM I 142 and PI 415) include, for instance, the fact that our rulers do not have the property of shrinking to half their length when they are taken from one room to the other (RFM I 140). They also include certain abilities human beings have.[33] What Wittgenstein is doing can be described as pointing to obvious facts which make the adoption of certain concepts and rules useful for us, thereby not implying that we simply choose them.[34] He does not aim to provide a transcendental argument for the possibility of our language-games.

In the moral case, the facts on which our having the concepts and practices we have depends include the vulnerability of human beings, their dependence on others, the scarcity of goods, and evolutionarily evolved capacities and traits such as the capacity for empathy and the trait of caring for one's children.[35] These facts, which as Wittgenstein says condition the possibility of the game, are part of the surroundings of our moral practices and as such belong to their constituent elements. As it is constituted partly by these facts, morality is 'somehow "constitutive" of mankind'.[36]

This gives us good reasons to think that the different moral codes that are observable across space and time have enough in common for it to be possible to object to practices which are embedded in a different society or institutional setting. As Willaschek rightly notes, it is often the case that we find norms and values in other cultures to which we can appeal in criticising a practice common in the respective culture.[37] Due to the common features of human beings and the physical circumstances they live in, it is likely that certain moral judgements are shared by all human beings. We share our 'first nature' with all other human beings, as Krebs notes. Therefore, it is very unlikely that we could ever encounter people 'whose ways of acting and certainties are entirely alien

---

[33] See Stroud, 'Wittgenstein and Logical Necessity,' p. 514.

[34] See Baker and Hacker, *Wittgenstein: Rules, Grammar and Necessity*, p. 211.

[35] One of Wittgenstein's own examples of something that is simply given or belongs to the 'facts of living', as he calls it, is the fact that we 'take an interest in others' feelings' (RPP I 630).

[36] Stroud, 'Wittgenstein and Logical Necessity,' p. 514.

[37] Willaschek, 'Moralisches Urteil und begründeter Zweifel. Eine kontextualistische Konzeption moralischer Rechtfertigung,' p. 639.

to us'.[38] Human action occurs under conditions which are to a certain extent similar.[39] However, the facts that are constitutive of a practice as part of its surroundings do not justify morality. Nor do the functions of morality play a justificatory role.[40] As was argued in the previous chapter (6.4), no ultimate justification of morality is possible.

7.2.5.3   Moral universals

That certain moral judgements are shared by all human beings is also argued by anthropologists today. Examples of these 'moral universals' include the prohibitions on lying and murder, restrictions on the use of violence, the rule that infants must be protected, and the incest taboo.[41] It looks as if certain rules are necessary for a viable society. For instance, given the fact that babies can only survive if adults take care of them, a society could not maintain itself if it did not protect its offspring. As Rachels points out, '[i]nfants that are *not* cared for must be the exception rather than the rule'.[42]

---

[38] Andreas Krebs, *Worauf man sich verlässt* (Würzburg: Königshausen & Neumann, 2007), p. 118, my translation.

[39] There are of course also big differences between the circumstances in which people live, which correspond to differences in moral norms. Despite not having had different fundamental moral values, the traditional Eskimos had very different norms regulating sexual behaviour. Their sexual morality was extremely lax, which is at least partly explicable by reference to the fact that since a traditional Eskimo had usually only one set of clothes, people were usually naked at home. Freuchen, *Book of the Eskimos*, pp. 81 f.

[40] In terms of justification, practices are autonomous, as Ertz argues. He illustrates this point by considering the example of the practice of arithmetic, which is not justified by the several functions it has. One of its functions is that of producing kettles which are likely to last. Although 'the point of calculating consists partly of the fact that kettles which have been calculated correctly, i.e. in accordance with the rules of mathematics, are in general more durable than kettles which have been calculated wrongly', the criterion of correctness is not the durability of the kettle. Ertz, *Regel und Witz. Wittgensteinsche Perspektiven auf Mathematik, Sprache und Moral*, pp. 8 f., my translations. The German original states: 'Der Witz des Rechnens besteht unter anderem darin, dass Kessel, die richtig (d.h. gemäß den Regeln der Mathematik) berechnet wurden, im Allgemeinen besser halten als solche, die falsch berechnet wurden. Das Kriterium der Richtigkeit ist allerdings nicht das Halten des Kessel, und daher hat der Zweck des Rechnens keine begründende Funktion für die Institution des Rechnens.'

[41] See Rachels, 'The Challenge of Cultural Relativism,' p. 43; Redfield, 'The Universally Human and the Culturally Variable,' pp. 140 f.

[42] Rachels, 'The Challenge of Cultural Relativism,' p. 43.

Despite appearances to the contrary, Stroud's point that certain practices or rules are inconceivable is applicable to morality. Initially, it appears to be conceivable what the consequences would be if, for instance, people generally thought that killing were morally right, and acted accordingly. It would be something like Hobbes's war of all against all, or perhaps even lead to the destruction of mankind. Yet it follows from this that we cannot imagine a community in which people followed such a rule. The rule in question seems inconceivable as part of any moral code. In a similar thought experiment, Rachels invites us to imagine a society which did not value truth telling. How can people communicate if they have no reason to assume that others are telling them the truth? There would obviously be no point in asking anyone anything if we had no reason to presume that the person would respond truthfully. Absent communication however, a complex society could not exist.[43]

In addition to the fact that norms like the prohibition of murder can be found in all viable human societies, there is a widespread distinction between an in-group to which this prohibition and other moral rules apply and an out-group to which they do not apply, or do so to a lesser extent. This distinction between in-group and out-group, which is of course morally objectionable, is common in the moral history of humankind. For instance, according to Ifugao law, which rests primarily on the principle of kinship, killing strangers is permissible.[44] To provide a less exotic example: in the United States, after 9/11 followers of Islam were perceived by many non-Muslim American citizens as members of the out-group. Moreover, in the name of the war on terror, basic constitutional rights were suspended for Muslims suspected to be terrorists.

7.2.5.4 *Evolutionary explanations*

One plausible explanation for the existence of moral universals is our evolutionary history. The development of a 'capacity for normative guidance', that is a capacity to make and act upon normative judgements, might be explicable by appeal to 'natural selection pressures in the distant past'. This capacity might be 'an adaptation that evolved

---

[43] Rachels, 'The Challenge of Cultural Relativism,' p. 43.
[44] Hoebel, *The Law of Primitive Man*, pp. 100 ff. The Ifugao belong to the non-Christian tribes that inhabit the island of Luzon, which forms part of the Philippines. See Roy Franklin Barton, 'Ifugao Law,' *American Archaeology and Ethnology* 15, no. 1 (1919).

in connection with social coordination, cooperation and stability'.[45] Moreover, it seems plausible that not only this general capacity, but also more specific tendencies such as a sense of fairness, resentment towards swindlers and care for one's children are traits that have evolved through natural selection due to their adaptive effects. Also the widespread existence of rules that regulate violence and sex might be explicable by reference to evolutionary hypotheses.[46]

The rule that infants have to be protected can be explained by reference to 'kin selection', an evolutionary strategy that promotes the reproductive success of an organism's relatives, even at significant cost to itself, in that the organism might sacrifice its own life.[47] Evolutionary success consists in an increase of the percentage of one's own genes in future generations.[48] This cannot be achieved solely by traits that cause greater reproductive success for oneself but also by traits that cause such success for members of one's kin group, since they also carry our genes. Given a human infant's remarkable dependence on others, the trait of caring for one's offspring must be expected to be one that has been strongly selected within human beings.[49]

Kin selection is also helpful in explaining helping behaviour towards non-kin for two reasons: first, organisms must be able to recognise kin, and natural selection might have opted for a rather simple proximate mechanism such as 'Help those with whom you interact frequently'. Second, the pressures of natural selection might have pushed in the direction of using the psychological and physiological structures involved in helping family members for new tasks such as the task of helping people beyond one's family.[50]

---

[45] William Fitzpatrick, 'Morality and Evolutionary Biology,' in *The Stanford Encyclopedia of Philosophy*, ed. Edward N. Zalta, Fall 2014 Edition, <http://plato. stanford.edu/archives/fall2014/entries/morality-biology/>. Note that it is also possible that only our non-moral intellectual capacities may be adaptations, and that the capacity for normative guidance is a by-product of them, in which case the role of natural selection for this capacity would be indirect.

[46] William Fitzpatrick, 'Morality and Evolutionary Biology,' in *The Stanford Encyclopaedia of Philosophy*.

[47] See Charles Darwin, *The Origin of Species* (London: John Murray, 1859); William D. Hamilton, 'The Genetical Evolution of Social Behaviour' I and II, *Journal of Theoretical Biology* 7 (1964).

[48] Michael Ruse, *Taking Darwin Seriously: A Naturalistic Approach to Philosophy* (Oxford: Basil Blackwell, 1986), p. 219.

[49] Richard Joyce, *The Evolution of Morality* (Cambridge, MA and London, England: The MIT Press, 2006), p. 20.

[50] Richard Joyce, *The Evolution of Morality* (Cambridge, MA and London, England: The MIT Press, 2006), p. 20.

The evolved tendency to privilege members of one's own group over others might also explain the frequency of in-group/out-group distinctions in our moral history.[51] The Darwinian 'expects a stronger sense of moral obligation to those who are in the same moral pool as we, than to others'.[52] However, as beings capable of autonomous moral reasoning, we can reflect on our evolved tendencies and the behaviour to which they have led, and judge certain patterns of behaviour as unjustified. This has been the case for restrictions of moral consideration to members of one's in-group, as the idea of inalienable human rights testifies. Thus, we can see that there is scope for moral progress.

The view that creatures that are very different from us could have radically different moral rules can be interpreted as 'counterfactual moral relativism for deeply different courses of human evolution'.[53] Had humans evolved in a radically different way, the content of their moral judgements would probably have looked very different.[54]

7.2.5.5 *The imposition of a shared moral behaviour*

I can now reply to Rummens (see Chapter 5) that 'physical reality' does to a certain extent 'impose "a shared moral behaviour"'.[55] Rummens suggests that, unlike certainties regarding the empirical world, moral certainties are not 'closely connected with the way our actions as human beings are embedded in an external physical reality'.[56] He takes this as a reason for concluding that an account of moral certainty might not be able to avoid the charge of relativism. However, moral certainties such as the fact that inflicting gratuitous suffering on innocents is wrong are closely connected with certain facts about human nature. The first nature that we all share can be said to impose shared moral judgements.[57] Rummens refers to a 'plethora of moral language-games that deny some or even most of the moral certainties we take for granted', arguing that this shows the lack of constraints in the moral case. One of his examples

---

[51] Fitzpatrick, 'Morality and Evolutionary Biology.'

[52] Ruse, *Taking Darwin Seriously: A Naturalistic Approach to Philosophy*, p. 240.

[53] Fitzpatrick, 'Morality and Evolutionary Biology.'

[54] It must be noted that the normative and meta-ethical implications of findings in evolutionary biology and psychology are anything but straightforward.

[55] Stefan Rummens, 'On the Possibility of a Wittgensteinian Account of Moral Certainty,' *The Philosophical Forum* 44, no. 2 (2013): p. 144.

[56] Stefan Rummens, 'On the Possibility of a Wittgensteinian Account of Moral Certainty,' *The Philosophical Forum* 44, no. 2 (2013): p. 144.

[57] Pleasants replies to Rummens in the opposite way, namely by denying that either moral or non-moral behaviour is imposed by physical reality. Nigel Pleasants, 'If Killing Isn't Wrong, Then Nothing Is: A Naturalistic Defence of Basic Moral Certainty,' *Ethical Perspectives* 22, no. 1 (2015): 197–215.

of such a radically different moral language-game is that of the Nazis. Yet despite the boundless cruelty that took place under that regime, I would not conceive of the Nazis as having played a radically different moral language-game. Instead, I am inclined to think that what makes it look as if they did is their ability to overcome their natural barrier against killing innocents by regarding them as sub-human. Pleasants suggests that the citizens of Nazi Germany learned to accept far more exceptions to the prohibition on killing than are usually allowed.[58] Nazi German society 'learned to suspend that certainty for large categories of people'. In a short period of time, the in-group shrank rapidly.

As was argued in Chapter 5, acts of killing do not undermine the certainty that killing is wrong. The language used to describe Jews and other groups that were to be eliminated, the justifications given for their elimination, the efforts made to distance people from those who were killed and from the process of killing itself, and the brainwashing necessary for people to support this horrific ideology – all of this supports the view that Nazi Germany did not have radically different moral certainties.

These reflections on the limits of moral diversity mean that my claim that the moral standpoint a person adopts is relative to the moral training she has gone through is less objectionable. The moral standpoints of people brought up in different parts of the world will not differ radically, although significant differences can be expected to exist, which can indeed create moral conflicts that are difficult to resolve. We have good reasons to believe that there are universal moral norms, which are not justified by certain natural facts, but which together with these facts constitute moral practices.

Let me summarise my response to the objection of relativism: moral practices, to which moral rightness and wrongness are relative, do not coincide with cultures. There is intercultural agreement on moral matters, which makes real intercultural disagreement and justified intercultural moral critique possible. The possibility of different moralities is limited by human nature, certain common facts about the world we live in and the functions morality has in human life. Given these constraints on moral practices, the fact that a person's moral outlook is relative to her moral education does not imply that it is illegitimate to judge from a moral perspective the behaviour of people brought up in different contexts.

---

[58]   Ibid.

7.3 The objection of conservatism

7.3.1 The objection

It is a well-known objection to coherence theories of moral justification that they are utterly conservative, and do not achieve more than a systematisation of our moral prejudices. Similarly, it might be objected against the practice-based view that it does not go beyond those moral judgements which we already hold, thus leaving no scope for moral change and critique of existing moral practices. A criticism accusing this approach of advocating moral conservatism may object that the account is conservative for two reasons. First, it argues that some moral beliefs are beyond doubt for morally competent agents. By thus immunising certain moral beliefs against possible criticism, the possibility of fundamental moral change and critique is excluded. Secondly, it is asserted that the process of moral learning is constitutive of that which is being learned. This implies that people will be unable to look critically at what they have learned and to depart from the views of their teachers and the society they live in, that is they will not be able to criticise the contexts in which they acquired moral competence.[59] Thus, the practice-based view falls short of explaining cases of fundamental moral critique and instances of moral change and progress, such as the abolition of slavery (at least to a great extent, see Chapter 5), the improvement of the status of women in many parts of the world, the abolition of death penalty in many countries, the Universal Declaration of Human Rights after the end of World War II, and so on.

7.3.2 The possibility of critique

The assumptions that there are moral certainties and that our moral standpoint is partly constituted by the process of learning to be moral do not exclude the possibility of criticism of elements of the moral practices we engage in. They do not commit me to conservatism. As Pleasants points out, the moral certainty of the wrongness of paradigmatic cases of killing 'has nothing to do with the certainty of someone who is convinced that their moral and political opinions and judgements are infallibly correct'. This certainty is rather 'an attitude towards [...] killing that underlies everyone's – conservative, liberal

---

[59] See Julia Annas, *Intelligent Virtue* (Oxford and New York: Oxford University Press, 2011), p. 53.

or radical – moral opinions and judgements'.[60] Any criticism of moral views and practices turns around some axes of moral certainty. There is ample scope to object, for instance, to specific institutionalised practices of killing, such as the killing of animals, and to views about particular cases of killing, for example abortion or the killing of bystanders in a military operation. Far from advocating a form of moral conservatism, I intend to highlight the framework within which reasonable moral criticism operates.

According to the practice-based view, standards of critique are internal to moral practices. They are not practice-independent facts and thus not independent of their actual applications.[61] It is the existence of such internal standards which makes critique both possible and mandatory. For the reasons mentioned above (6.4), it does not make sense to criticise morality as a whole, although particular moral views and practices can and should be subjected to criticism, if there are good reasons for criticising them. What counts as a good reason is relative to our practice of making moral judgements.

The worry that, if our ability to adopt a moral standpoint and the content of our moral convictions is crucially dependent on our moral education, we shall be unable to criticise the contexts in which we learned to be moral, can be rebutted by pointing once again to the way in which moral training differs from training that results in rote habits (see 6.3.5). Moral education involves not only conditioning, but also explanations and reflection upon what is moral and why. In learning to be moral, we come to understand why some acts are right and others are wrong, why something is a justifiable instance of lying and something else is not, and so on. Moreover, like someone who exercises a practical skill, a person who exercises moral competence keeps learning and improving her competence (see 6.3.1). Since the learning process is open-ended, we can realise at any stage that certain views that were inculcated in us by our parents or certain practices common in our society are wrong. As Annas emphasises in her account of virtue, learning to be virtuous involves becoming an autonomous judge who is capable of reflecting critically on the things taught.[62] She calls one

---

[60] Nigel Pleasants, 'Wittgenstein and Basic Moral Certainty,' *Philosophia* 37 (2009): p. 679.

[61] Examples of philosophers who consider moral standards to be external to moral practices include robust moral realists and people who think of morality in terms of God's commands.

[62] Annas, *Intelligent Virtue*, pp. 52 ff.

crucial component of the learning of virtue the 'drive to aspire'.[63] As moral learners, we want to understand what we are being taught, and we aim to be better than our teachers. Thanks to the drive to aspire, we become critical moral judges who call into question certain behaviour by our parents, teachers and fellow citizens and some of the moral norms they adhere to. We do not start by questioning what we are told is right or wrong, good or bad, because if we did, we would not be able to learn anything, but we do begin questioning at a later stage. In a nutshell: we learn to be moral in a way that enables us to reflect critically on what we have learned.

But what about the possibility of a radical critique of our moral practices? Is a critique like that attempted by Nietzsche conceivable on my account? Nietzsche advocates a 'revaluation of all values', arguing that our values belong to a slave morality which has been invented by the weak.[64] I take it to be crucial for the alternative values he defends that they are not suitable for human beings.[65] This is shown by the fact that they conflict radically with the moral feelings human beings normally develop, and for which there are plausible evolutionary explanations. The 'overman' for whom Nietzsche's values would be suitable differs significantly from the human beings that populated the earth in his day and those who inhabit it today.[66] Nietzsche himself is said not to have lived up to his own ideals. We are told that he felt pity even for animals, which means that he was incapable of avoiding contradiction of his theoretical views in practice.[67] I agree with Ertz that morality is ultimately bound to a realistic estimation of human nature.[68] Therefore, there are limits on what can count as a plausible philosophical critique of existing moral values and practices.

---

[63] Ibid., p. 25.

[64] Friedrich Nietzsche, *Ecce Homo*, ed. Walter Kaufmann, trans. Walter Kaufmann and R. J. Hollingdale (New York: Vintage, 1967), II:9. *On the Genealogy of Morality*, trans. M. Clark and A. Swensen (Indianapolis: Hackett, 1998), I:13.

[65] A similar claim is made by Philippa Foot: '[…] it is only for a different species that Nietzsche's most radical revaluation of values could be valid. It is not for us as we are, or are ever likely to be.' Philippa Foot, *Natural Goodness* (Oxford 2001), p. 115.

[66] Friedrich Nietzsche, 'Thus Spoke Zarathustra,' in *The Portable Nietzsche*, ed. Walter Kaufmann (New York: Viking, 1954).

[67] See Rüdiger Safranski, *Nietzsche. Biographie seines Denkens* (München and Wien: Carl Hanser Verlag, 2000).

[68] Ertz, *Regel und Witz. Wittgensteinsche Perspektiven auf Mathematik, Sprache und Moral*, p. 230.

7.3.3   The possibility of moral change and progress

The possibility of critique is associated with the possibility of moral change and progress.[69] An approach in the spirit of *On Certainty* is able to account for changes even in basic moral convictions. On Wittgenstein's epistemological account of basic beliefs, there is indeed scope for such a fundamental change. He expresses this possibility by means of the metaphor of the river-bed (OC 96–99) (see 3.2.4). Let me explain how my account allows for (fundamental) moral change. In order to do so, I shall first consider the possibility of change within basic epistemic beliefs. Here an example of a belief which has been beyond doubt for a long time but then lost its status is the belief that nobody has ever been on the moon. When Wittgenstein wrote the notes later published as *On Certainty*, it was inconceivable for him that human beings might go to the moon. Wittgenstein refers to this conviction several times (for example OC 111 and 117). When ordinary people started thinking that it might be technically possible to go to the moon, the object of the statement 'Nobody has ever been on the moon' became a falsifiable empirical proposition. Today it is a false proposition, which might at best be believed by a child who does not know anything about space travel, or by a person who doubts all reports of expeditions to the moon. The transformation of a 'hard' into a 'fluid' proposition amounts to the transformation of a 'world view' (OC 95 f.).[70] The world view in which it is possible to fly to the moon is significantly different from one in which this possibility is excluded. If it now turned out that there were life on other planets, this would change our world view completely.

As we know, our moral world view has also undergone such funda-mental changes. What now serves as an axis of moral reasoning for a large group of people, the requirement that all human beings be respected, used to be a contested claim. There have even been times and places where it was not made at all. Thus, until the 18th century slavery

---

[69] The examples of moral change provided in this section are examples of change that we evaluate positively, and it is in this sense that I use the term 'moral progress'. Of course moral change can also cut the other way. The notion of moral progress raises several questions: What is moral progress? What are the criteria for establishing such progress? Is there not only local, but also overall moral progress? Answering these questions would go beyond the scope of this study.

[70] 'World view' is my translation of 'Weltbild'. 'World-picture', the translation chosen by the official translators in order to distinguish it from 'Weltanschauung', does not convey the full meaning of the German term. I would translate 'Weltanschauung' as 'ideology'.

was regarded as naturally right. Human beings were believed to differ in nature and worth.

But how are changes in our moral world view possible? How do moral beliefs lose their status as certainties? In Wittgenstein's metaphorical formulation, how do fluid propositions harden, and hard ones become fluid (see OC 96)? One explanation refers to factual changes in the environment of moral practices. Changes in the world like climate change or technological development affect our moral practices, and thereby the content of our moral rules. For example, in a time where pollution poses a threat to future generations, it is morally required of each of us that we care about the environment. By driving an old car, producing large amounts of rubbish and travelling enormous distances by plane we are, absent justificatory circumstances, doing something morally wrong. Flying was not morally relevant 60 years ago. The fact that we now have knowledge about the long term effects of pollution has changed our moral practices.

Another example is knowledge of the relationship between smoking and cancer. Today, in most Western societies it is considered to be morally wrong to smoke in the presence of young children. Most people did not judge such behaviour to be bad or wrong, say, 60 years ago. At a time where people did not know much about the risks of smoking, no moral rules were violated by smoking in the presence of children. The campaign against smoking is a recent phenomenon, even more recent than the fight against climate change.

Gradual changes in moral practices are therefore caused by changes in their surroundings. Since a practice is partly constituted by the facts surrounding it, changes in the realm of these facts are *ipso facto* changes to the practice. A practice which is partly constituted by certain knowledge about the risks of smoking is not identical with one that lacks this constitutive element. Technological development, climate change, new health risks and so on, are factors that cause moral change.[71]

It might be objected that, on this account, fundamental moral change cannot be the result of a process of reasoning, but only the causal effect of

---

[71] There is for example the phenomenon of 'techno-moral change', the co-shaping of technology and moral norms and values. See Marianne Boenink, Tsjalling Swierstra, and Dirk Sternerding, 'Anticipating the Interaction between Technology and Morality: A Scenario Study of Experimenting with Humans in Bionanotechnology,' *Studies in Ethics, Law, and Technology* 4, no. 2 (2010). Tsjalling Swierstra and Jozef Keulartz, 'Obesity in 2020: Three Scenarios on Techno-Social-Ethical Co-Evolution,' in *Genomics, Obesity and the Struggle over Responsibilities*, ed. Michiel Korthals (Dordrecht: Springer Academic Publishers, 2011).

factual changes. And indeed the account leaves no scope for reasonable doubt regarding moral norms that function as axes of moral reasoning. If we have grounds to question or even reject a moral norm, this norm can no longer be said to function as an axis. At this point, it has already lost its special status, assuming that it ever had it. However, the change in status cannot only be affected by changes in the surroundings of the practice, but also by changes within the beliefs that determine the immobility of the axes. As was argued in Chapter 3, fixed propositions are held by other beliefs, which are open to doubt and thus to justification (see 3.2.6). Changes within those beliefs can have the effect that a proposition that has long been treated as a certainty is no longer treated as such. It can thus result from a process of reasoning – although not from a process of doubting the relevant certainty – that a moral norm loses its status as one that is beyond reasonable doubt from a moral point of view.

As Pleasants stresses, the case of slavery is not only an example of moral progress, but can be regarded as 'the paradigmatic case of radical moral criticism, which was successful to such an extent that not only were attitudes changed fundamentally, but the object of criticism itself abolished'.[72] Until the late 18th century, the moral legitimacy of slavery was taken for granted. Pleasants points out that criticism were merely sporadic and not taken seriously. This corresponded with a near complete lack of justification for slavery. Aristotle's defence of it marks an exception. As Pleasants convincingly argues, the fact that after centuries in which slavery was considered to be natural and necessary, large numbers of people turned against that practice, resulting in its abolition cannot be explained by moral argument alone. In order to become effective, moral argument requires 'certain social, material and practical conditions'. In particular, it requires the existence of a plausible alternative, which in the case of slavery was wage labour. The ability to point to an alternative that is available and superior lifts objections to a harmful institutionalised practice 'out of the realm of merely moralistic expression and into that of efficacious radical social criticism'.[73] Thus, it was partly due to a change in the surroundings of moral practices, namely the emergence of wage labour as a superior alternative to slavery, that the moral legitimacy of slavery lost its status as a certainty. It is only under these changed circumstances that the

---

[72] Nigel Pleasants, 'Moral Argument Is Not Enough: The Persistence of Slavery and the Emergence of Abolition,' *Philosophical Topics* 38, no. 1 (2011): p. 144.

[73] Ibid., pp. 141 ff.

criticism of slavery could become 'widespread, organized, serious, and respectable'.[74]

The example of the abolition of slavery shows how it might be possible to abolish harmful institutionalised practices that characterise human societies today, such as the practice of animal exploitation mentioned in Chapter 5. Although the abolition of for instance factory farming still seems to be a long way off, it is at least possible that an alternative to this practice will continue to take shape, gradually gaining widespread recognition as plausible and superior. Once more and more people come to see that factory farming is by no means necessary in order to feed the world's population, criticism of this practice may become more widely respected and effective. A similar argument can be made in relation to the new forms of slavery that have replaced the old ones (see 5.4.3).

As argued above, moral progress is partly driven by cases of genuine moral disagreement (7.2.4). For instance, conflicting views of what is fair or just drive discussions about how to create a just society. Disagreement concerning the respective importance of individual rights and communal values could fuel a discussion that leads to societal arrangements in which the realisation of human rights contributes to the flourishing of the community.

Human nature and the functions of morality impose constraints on the changes that are possible. However, the reference to human nature can easily be abused, as the long history of oppression of women in most societies shows. We moreover have to admit that we are still in the process of investigating human nature, and that all references to it are tentative. Nevertheless, we know enough about our species to rule out the possibility that some moral certainties could ever lose their status. Creatures for which it was not certain that killing is wrong would be fundamentally different from us.

Let me summarise my response to the conservatism objection: the practice-based view allows for moral critique, change and progress. Moral certainties provide the axes around which moral criticism turns. If successful, moral training results in agents who are able to reflect critically on what they have learned and the contexts in which they have learned it. Changes in our moral world view are affected by factual

---

[74] Ibid., p. 153. There are of course alternative explanations for the abolition of slavery, but I shall not go into this debate here. I am presenting the explanation provided by Pleasants as one that I find plausible and that captures the idea that something that is morally certain can lose this status.

192 On Moral Certainty, Justification and Practice

changes in the environment of moral practices, such as technological development, and by corresponding changes in the beliefs that hold moral certainties in place. One of the driving forces behind moral progress is genuine moral disagreement.

7.4 Conclusion

In this chapter, I have addressed two interrelated objections to the practice-based view: the objections of relativism and conservatism. I have rejected the first objection on the grounds that: (a) moral practices transcend cultural boundaries, (b) there is intercultural moral agreement and (c) the possible diversity of moral codes is limited by human nature, physical circumstances and the functions of morality. Since we have good reasons to believe that today's anthropologists are right in emphasising the common elements in different moral practices, my account of moral competence as relative to the process and context in which it is acquired does not imply that justified intercultural critique is impossible. Not even the moral language-game of the Nazis differed radically from our own.

I have defended my account against the second objection by arguing that it allows for moral critique, change and progress. Moral training enables us to reflect critically on the moral views prevalent in our society. Moral change and progress are brought about by a combination of factual changes in the surroundings of moral practices, reasoning and genuine moral disagreement. Finally, I have emphasised that while moral practices and some of their certainties can change over time, some certainties will not lose their status due to constraints imposed by human nature.

8
Conclusion

At the beginning of this book, I mentioned the example of the moral debate about targeted killing and the use of military drones. The reader was asked to conduct a thought experiment and imagine that a participant in the debate questioned whether it was wrong to kill innocent civilians, and whether killing was wrong as such. In Chapter 5, further examples of questions of this kind were discussed. According to the practice-based view, not asking certain questions – and not attempting to answer them if they are asked by others – is a sign of moral competence. Moral debates like the one about targeted killing are urgent and it is an open question whether agreement on this matter can be reached, although this must not conceal the fact that there could no longer be any moral dispute if morally competent agents did not agree on some fundamental moral questions. The existence of moral disagreement thus assures underlying agreement on moral issues, which in turn provides us with a reason to be optimistic about the possibility of resolving moral disputes and changing existing practices for the better.

When I started writing this book, I conceived of it as an experiment in approaching philosophical accounts of the justification of moral beliefs and theories from a viewpoint which could be called 'Wittgensteinian'. The alternative account arising out of that perspective seemed to be located somewhere between foundationalist positions and coherence theories of moral justification, thus occupying a similar position to moral epistemological contextualism. When developing this account, which initially focused on moral propositions, I moved away from formulations of general moral principles towards the capacities that a person needs to have in order to act, think and feel morally. Despite following Wittgenstein in emphasising the primacy of practice, I moved beyond him. My account of moral competence draws not merely on

Wittgenstein but also on Aristotelian virtue ethics, Ryle's conception of knowledge-how, models of moral expertise and learning, research in developmental psychology and studies concerning the role of emotions in moral judgement.

As was pointed out in the introduction, I do not wish to ascribe to Wittgenstein any of the claims I make about moral practices, although it seems to me that he would probably have accepted at least some of them. My aim was to discover whether his reflections on certainty regarding the empirical world can help us to gain a better understanding of the conditions under which demanding justification for a moral belief is pointless. Moreover, I sought to explore several possible implications of Wittgenstein's later philosophy for how we should conceive of morality.

To conclude, let me sum up the main arguments of this book. Departing from a number of traditional philosophical views, it has been argued that we should conceive of morality as a set of overlapping practices and of moral knowledge first and foremost as the competence to participate in these practices. Philosophers sometimes ignore the role played by the justification of moral judgements in moral practices. As contextualists have emphasised, justification functions as a response to doubt based on reasons. The infinite regress of justification is an illusion based on the false assumption that every belief requires *per se* justification. By pointing to examples from everyday practice, it has been argued that moral justification is required when an action, institution, practice or judgement is morally objectionable, and that one of the main aims of the practice of moral justification is to reach agreement. However, some moral philosophers try to provide justification where no reasonable doubt is possible. In addition, they fail to see that the practice of justifying moral beliefs belongs to our more sophisticated practices, which presuppose bedrock practices. Justification is therefore not constitutive of moral practices in general.

Drawing an analogy between certainty regarding the empirical world and moral certainty, it has been argued through example that also in the moral domain there are cases in which reasons for doubting a particular belief are lacking. These beliefs function as 'axes' within moral reasoning. Disputes about targeted killing, for instance, turn around the certainty that killing is wrong. The wrongness of paradigmatic cases of killing, stealing, lying and so on is certain for morally competent agents. It is as certain as the existence of our hands or the fact that the earth has existed since long before we were born. Just like certainty regarding the empirical world, moral certainty is manifested in the way we act. Its objects are not amenable to propositional formulation.

As agents who possess moral competence, we have mastered numerous overlapping moral practices, such as the practice of promising and the practice of helping someone. Moral competence is similar to certain practical skills, in particular regarding the way in which it is acquired. We become morally competent through moral training, that is we learn how to act, feel and think morally through practice. Our sophisticated moral language-games of justification and evaluation are grounded in acting in different ways: they rest on primitive responses such as reactions to another person's suffering; they presuppose moral competence the acquisition of which starts, amongst others, with certain natural reactions of teachers and learners; and they presuppose moral action that does not require conscious thought.

This position implies that any attempt to justify morality as a whole is pointless. So too is any attempt to induce through argument a person who lacks moral competence to adopt a moral standpoint. Where capacities need to be developed, arguments are not sufficient. I rejected the conception of an amoralist who is fully morally competent on the grounds that we would not ascribe moral competence to a person whose actions and judgements revealed no concern whatsoever for the interests and feelings of others.

In Chapter 2, two ways of conceiving of the relationship between different moral codes were presented: different moral codes may be taken to reveal family resemblances and to share certain features by virtue of which we classify them as moral. It was mentioned that it might appear prima facie more convincing to take the concept of a moral practice or language-game, in the sense of moral code, as a family resemblance concept. However, as was argued in Chapter 7, there are moral universals, that is certain beliefs and forms of acting that are shared by all moral practices. Although the extent to which the moral practices of different societies differ is an empirical question, we can reasonably assume that, since they are constrained by human nature, the physical living conditions of human beings and the functions of morality, these practices do not differ radically. It was emphasised that we would for instance be unable to conceive of a viable society whose members followed a rule that required killing as many people as possible. Therefore, we have good reasons to assume that there is a basis of intercultural agreement that makes an intercultural practice of making moral judgements possible.

It follows that the practice-based view, which conceives of moral rightness and wrongness as being relative to moral practices, is not a form of cultural relativism. It ties the possibility of moral critique to the existence of standards of critique that are internal to moral practices. If we wish to criticise elements of a practice followed by people far away from us who claim to be playing a completely different game, we can look for the moral beliefs these people share with us, and for participants of the respective practice who agree with our objections.

The fact that I place a great deal of emphasis on the claim that there is more moral agreement than many people think should not be taken to mean that the existing moral disagreement can be disregarded. Far from wanting to discourage philosophers from dealing with the subjects of moral disagreement, I intend to make them aware of the fact that these are precisely the issues that deserve our particular attention. As I have sought to show, philosophers who spend much time and energy trying to answer questions such as 'What makes wrongful acts of killing wrong?' are engaging in a hopeless and – what is worse – pointless enterprise. As moral philosophers, we have to recognise when we have reached bedrock, and our spade is turned. Instead of looking for reasons in support of moral beliefs that morally competent agents do not call into question, we should direct our attention to those cases where the moral permissibility as well as the moral prohibition of a practice can be supported by reasons. By pointing out cases in which the demand for justification is pointless, I do not wish to deny that justification plays an important role in moral practices.

This study has left a number of questions unanswered. Should we conceive of moral certainty as being 'grammatical' in the broad sense of the term? How exactly do we exercise moral judgement? What are the criteria for distinguishing between cases involving moral incompetence and cases involving evil? I hope to have shown that moral philosophers can profit from engaging with Wittgenstein's later works, and that the practice-based view of morality opens up promising avenues for future research.

Bibliography

Ambrose, Alice, (ed.) *Wittgenstein's Lectures: Cambridge 1932–1935*. Oxford: Prometheus Books, 1979.

Annas, Julia. *Intelligent Virtue*. Oxford and New York: Oxford University Press, 2011.

Ariely, Dan. *The (Honest) Truth About Dishonesty: How We Lie to Everyone – Especially Ourselves*. New York: HarperCollins Publishers, 2012.

Aristotle. *The Nicomachean Ethics*. Translated by David Ross. Oxford and New York: Oxford University Press, 1998.

——. *Posterior Analytics*. Translated by Jonathan Barnes. Edited by J.L. Ackrill, Clarendon Aristotle Series. Oxford: Clarendon Press, 1975.

Armstrong, David Malet, Charles Burton Martin and Ullin T. Place. *Dispositions: A Debate*. London: Routledge, 1996.

Arrington, Robert L. "A Wittgensteinian Approach to Ethical Intuitionism." In *Ethical Intuitionism: Re-evaluations*, edited by Philip Stratton-Lake, 271–289. Oxford: Clarendon Press, 2002.

Audi, Robert. *The Good in the Right. A Theory of Intuition and Intrinsic Value*. Princeton, NJ: Princeton University Press, 2003.

Ayer, A. J. *Language, Truth and Logic*. Harmondsworth: Penguin, [1936] 1971.

Baker, G. P. and P. M. S. Hacker. *Wittgenstein: Rules, Grammar and Necessity*. 2nd, extensively revised (ed.) Chichester, U.K. and Malden, MA: Wiley-Blackwell, 2009.

——. *Wittgenstein: Understanding and Meaning*. 2nd extensively revised edition. II vols. Vol. I. Oxford: Blackwell, 2005.

Bales, Kevin. *Disposable People: New Slavery in the Global Economy*. 2nd edition. Berkeley: University of California Press, 2012.

Bambrough, Renford. *Moral Scepticism and Moral Knowledge*. London and Henley: Routledge and Kegan Paul, 1979.

Barnes, Christopher M., John Schaubroeck, Megan Huth and Sonia Ghumman. "Lack of Sleep and Unethical Conduct." *Organizational Behavior and Human Decision Processes* 115, no. 2 (2011): 169–180.

Barton, Roy Franklin. "Ifugao Law." *American Archaeology and Ethnology* 15, no. 1 (1919): 1–186.

Baumeister, Roy F., Mark Muraven and Dianne M. Tice. "Ego Depletion: A Resource Model of Volition, Self-Regulation, and Controlled Processing." *Social Cognition* 18 (2000): 130–150.

Bayertz, Kurt. *Warum überhaupt moralisch sein?* München: C. H. Beck, 2004.

Blackburn, Simon. "Reply: Rule-Following and Moral Realism." In *Wittgenstein: To Follow a Rule*, edited by Steven H. Holtzman and Christopher M. Leich, 163–187. London et al.: Routledge & Kegan Paul, 1981.

Blair, J. et al. "Neuro-Cognitive Systems Involved in Morality." *Philosophical Explorations* 9, no. 1 (2006): 13–27.

Blair, R. J. R. "A Cognitive Developmental Approach to Morality: Investigating the Psychopath." *Cognition* 57 (1995): 1–29.

——. "Moral Judgment and Psychopathy." *Emotion Review* 3 (2011): 296–98.

Boenink, Marianne, Tsjalling Swierstra and Dirk Sternerding. "Anticipating the Interaction between Technology and Morality: A Scenario Study of Experimenting with Humans in Bionanotechnology." *Studies in Ethics, Law, and Technology* 4, no. 2 (2010): 1–38.

BonJour, Laurence. *The Structure of Empirical Knowledge*. Cambridge, Mass. and London: Harvard University Press, 1985.

Brice, Robert Greenleaf. "Mistakes and Mental Disturbances: Pleasants, Wittgenstein, and Basic Moral Certainty." *Philosophia* 41 (2013): 477–487.

Brink, David Owen. *Moral Realism and the Foundations of Ethics*. New York: Cambridge University Press, 1989.

Cavell, Stanley. *The Claim of Reason: Wittgenstein, Skepticism, Morality and Tragedy*. Oxford: Oxford University Press, 1979.

Clark, Andy. "Word and Action: Reconciling Rules and Know-How in Moral Cognition." In *Moral Epistemology Naturalized*, edited by Richmond Campbell and Bruce Hunter, 267–289. Calgary, Alberta, Canada: University of Calgary Press, 2000.

Conte, A. G. "Regel." In *Historisches Wörterbuch der Philosophie*, edited by Joachim Ritter and Karlfried Gründer, 427–450. Basel: Schwabe, 1992.

Conway, G.D. *Wittgenstein on Foundations*: Humanity Books, 1989.

Crary, Alice. "Wittgenstein and Ethics: A Discussion with Reference to *On Certainty*." In *Readings of Wittgenstein's* On Certainty, edited by Danièle Moyal-Sharrock and W. Brenner, 275–301. Basingstoke: Palgrave Macmillan, 2005.

Dancy, Jonathan. *Ethics without Principles*. Oxford: Oxford University Press, 2004.

Darwin, Charles. *The Descent of Man and Selection in Relation to Sex*. New York: Modern Library, 1871.

——. *The Origin of Species*. London: John Murray, 1859.

de Waal, Frans. "Morally Evolved: Primate Social Instincts, Human Morality, and the Rise and Fall of 'Veneer Theory'." In *Primates and Philosophers. How Morality Evolved*, edited by Stephen Macedo and Josiah Ober, 1–58 Princeton and Oxford: Princeton University Press, 2006.

DePaul, Michael R. *Balance and Refinement. Beyond Coherence Methods of Moral Inquiry*. London and New York: Routledge, 1993.

Diagnostic and Statistical Manual of Mental Disorders. Third edition. Washington, D.C.: American Psychiatric Association, 1980.

Diamond, Cora. "Ethics, Imagination and the Method of Wittgenstein's *Tractatus*." In *The New Wittgenstein*, edited by A. Crary and R. Read, 149–173. London: Routledge, 2000.

——. "Wittgenstein, Mathematics, and Ethics: Resisting the Attractions of Realism." In *The Cambridge Companion to Wittgenstein*, edited by Hans Sluga and David G. Stern, 226–260. Cambridge and New York: Cambridge University Press, 1996.

Dilman, Ilham. "Universals: Bambrough on Wittgenstein." *Proceedings of the Aristotelian Society, New Series* 79 (1978–1979): 35–58.

Dreyfus, Hubert L. and Stuart E. Dreyfus. "Towards a Phenomenology of Ethical Expertise." *Human Studies* 14, no. 4 (1991): 229–250.

Dummett, Michael. "Wittgenstein's Philosophy of Mathematics." *The Philosophical Review* 68, no. 3 (1959): 324–348.

Engel, Pascal. "Propositions, Sentences and Statements." In *Routledge Encyclopedia of Philosophy*, edited by Edward Craig, 787–788. London and New York: Routledge, 1998.

Ertz, Timo-Peter. *Regel und Witz. Wittgensteinsche Perspektiven auf Mathematik, Sprache und Moral*. Berlin and New York: de Gruyter, 2008.

Feldman, Fred. *Confrontations with the Reaper. A Philosophical Study of the Nature and Value of Death*. Oxford: Oxford University Press, 1992.

Fitzpatrick, William. "Morality and Evolutionary Biology." In *The Stanford Encyclopedia of Philosophy*, edited by Edward N. Zalta, Fall 2014 Edition, <http://plato.stanford.edu/archives/fall2014/entries/morality-biology/>.

Foot, Philippa. *Natural Goodness*. Oxford 2001.

Freuchen, Peter. *Book of the Eskimos*. London: Arthur Barker Limited, 1962.

Garfield, Jay. "Particularity and Principle: The Structure of Moral Knowledge." In *Moral Particularism*, edited by Brad Hooker and Margaret Little, 178–204. Oxford: Oxford University Press, 2000.

Gauthier, David. *Morals by Agreement*. Oxford and New York: Clarendon Press and Oxford University Press, 1986.

Gennip, Kim van. *"Wittgenstein's On Certainty in the Making: Studies into Its Historical and Philosophical Background."* PhD dissertation, Rijksuniversiteit Groningen, 2008.

Goodman, Russell B. "Wittgenstein and Ethics." *Metaphilosophy* 13, no. 2 (1982): 138–148.

Greene, J.D. "Emotion and Cognition in Moral Judgment. Evidence from Neuroimaging." In *Neurobiology of Human Values*, edited by J. P. et al. Changeux. Berlin: Springer-Verlag, 2005.

Greene, J.D. and J. Haidt. "How (and Where) Does Moral Judgment Work?" *Trends in Cognitive Sciences* 6 (2002): 517–523.

Grundherr, Michael von. *Moral Aus Interesse: Metaethik Der Vertragstheorie*. Berlin and New York: de Gruyter, 2007.

Hacker, P. M. S. *Insight and Illusion: Themes in the Philosophy of Wittgenstein*. Revised edition. Oxford: Clarendon Press, 1986.

Haidt, Jonathan. "The Emotional Dog and Its Rational Tail: A Social Intuitionist Approach to Moral Judgment." *Psychological Review* 108 (2001): 814–834.

Hamilton, William D. "The Genetical Evolution of Social Behaviour" I and II, *Journal of Theoretical Biology* 7 (1964): 1–52.

Hanfling, Oswald. "Learning About Right and Wrong: Ethics and Language." *Philosophy* 78, no. 303 (2003): 25–41.

Hanna, Patricia and Bernard Harrison. *Word & World. Practice and the Foundations of Language*. Cambridge et al.: Cambridge University Press, 2004.

Harman, Gilbert. "Three Trends in Moral and Political Philosophy." *The Journal of Value Inquiry* 37 (2003): 415–425.

Hayden, Patrick. *The Philosophy of Human Rights*. St. Paul, MN: Paragon House, 2001.

Hermann, Julia. "Die Praxis als Quelle moralischer Normativität." In *Moral und Sanktion. Eine Kontroverse über die Autorität moralischer Normen*, edited by Eva Buddeberg and Achim Vesper. Frankfurt and New York: Campus, 2012.

——. "Learning to Be Moral." In *What Makes Us Moral: On the Capacities and Conditions for Being Moral*, edited by Bert Musschenga and Anton van Harskamp, 207–223. Dordrecht et al.: Springer, 2013.

——. "Man as a Moral Animal: Moral Language-Games, Certainty, and the Emotions." In *Language, Ethics and Animal Life: Wittgenstein and Beyond*, edited by Michael Burley, Niklas Forsberg and Nora Hämäläinen, 111–123. New York: Bloomsbury (formerly Continuum Publishing), 2012.

Hills, Alison. "Moral Testimony and Moral Epistemology." *Ethics* 120, no. 1 (2009): 94–127.

Hoebel, E. Adamson. *The Law of Primitive Man*. New York: Harvard University Press, 1968.

Hoffman, M. L. *Empathy and Moral Development. Implications for Caring and Justice*. Cambridge: Cambridge University Press, 2000.

Huang, Yong. "Religious Beliefs after Foundationalism: Wittgenstein between Nielsen and Phillips." *Religious Studies: An International Journal for the Philosophy of Religion* 31, no. 2 (1995): 251–267.

Huemer, Michael. *Ethical Intuitionism*. Basingstoke: Palgrave Macmillan, 2005.

Hume, David. *A Treatise of Human Nature*. Edited by L. A. Selby-Bigge. 2nd revised ed. by P. H. Nidditch. Oxford: Clarendon Press, 1978.

Iczkovits, Yaniv. *Wittgenstein's Ethical Thought*. Basingstoke: Palgrave Macmillan, 2012.

Johnston, Paul. *Wittgenstein and Moral Philosophy*. London: Routledge and Kegan Paul, 1989.

Joyce, Richard. *The Evolution of Morality*. Cambridge, MA and London, England: The MIT Press, 2006.

Kahneman, Robert. *Thinking, Fast and Slow*. New York: Farrar, Straus and Giroux, 2011.

Kant, Immanuel. *Critique of Pure Reason*. Translated by Norman Kemp Smith. Second revised edition. Basingstoke and New York: Palgrave Macmillan, 2007.

——. *Grundlegung zur Metaphysik der Sitten*. Vol. IV, Akademie-Ausgabe (Aa)1785.

Keller, Monika. "Moralentwicklung und moralische Sozialisation." In *Moralentwicklung von Kindern und Jugendlichen*, edited by Detlef Horster, 17–49. Wiesbaden: VS Verlag für Sozialwissenschaften, 2007.

Kelly, Thomas. "Evidence." In *Stanford Encyclopedia of Philosophy*, edited by Edward N. Zalta, Fall 2014 Edition, <http://plato.stanford.edu/archives/fall2014/entries/evidence/>.

Kemmerling, Andreas. "Bedeutung und der Zweck der Sprache." In *Von Wittgenstein Lernen*, edited by Wilhelm Vossenkuhl, 99–120. Berlin: Akademie Verlag, 1992.

——. "Gilbert Ryle: Können und Wissen." In *Grundprobleme der großen Philosophen – Philosophie der Gegenwart*, edited by Josef Speck, 126–166. Göttingen: Vandenhoeck & Ruprecht, 1975.

——. "Regel und Geltung im Lichte der Analyse Wittgensteins." *Rechtstheorie* 6 (1975): 104–131.

Kliemann, D. et al. "The Influence of Prior Record on Moral Judgment." *Neuropsychologia* 46, no. 12 (2008): 2949–2957.

Kober, Michael. *Gewißheit als Norm. Wittgensteins erkenntnistheoretische Untersuchungen in* Über Gewißheit. Berlin and New York: de Gruyter, 1993.

——. "On Epistemic and Moral Certainty: A Wittgensteinian Approach." *International Journal of Philosophical Studies* 5, no. 3 (1997): 365–381.

Kohlberg, Laurence. *Essays on Moral Development*. San Francisco: Harper & Row, 1981.

Krebs, Andreas. *Worauf man sich verlässt*. Würzburg: Königshausen & Neumann, 2007.

Kripke, Saul. *Wittgenstein on Rules and Private Language*. Oxford: Blackwell, 1982.

Larmore, Charles. *The Autonomy of Morality*. Cambridge and New York: Cambridge University Press, 2008.

——. *The Morals of Modernity*. Cambridge and New York: Cambridge University Press, 1996.

——. *Patterns of Moral Complexity*. Cambridge et al.: Cambridge University Press, 1987.

Levenbook, Barbara Baum. "Harming Someone after His Death." *Ethics* 94 (1984): 407–419.

Lichtenberg, Judith. "Moral Certainty." *Philosophy* 69, no. 268 (1994): 181–204.

Lovibond, Sabina. "Ethical Upbringing: From Connivance to Cognition." In *Essays for David Wiggins: Identity, Truth, and Value*, edited by Sabina Lovibond, 76–94. Oxford, UK and Cambridge, Mass.: Blackwell, 1996.

Lukes, Steven. *Moral Relativism*. New York: Picador, 2008.

Mackie, John L. *Ethics: Inventing Right and Wrong*. London 1977.

Maibom, Heidi L., (ed.) *Empathy and Morality*. Oxford and New York: Oxford University Press, 2014.

Margalit, Avishai. "Was Wittgenstein Moon-Blind?" In *Wittgenstein. Eine Neubewertung/Towards a Re-Evaluation* [Akten des 14. internationalen Wittgenstein-Symposiums 1989], 208–216. Wien: Hölder-Pilcher-Tempsky, 1990.

Marquis, Don. "An Argument That Abortion Is Wrong." In *Ethics in Practice*, edited by Hugh LaFollette, 91–102. Oxford: Blackwell, 1997.

McCloskey, Henry J. *Meta-Ethics and Normative Ethics*. The Hague: Nijhoff, 1969.

McDowell, John Henry. "Are Moral Requirements Hypothetical Imperatives?" In *Reason, Value, and Reality*, 77–94. Cambridge, Mass.: Harvard University Press, 1998.

——. "Non-Cognitivism and Rule-Following." In *Wittgenstein: To Follow a Rule*, edited by Christopher M. Leich Steven H. Holtzman, 141–162. London et al.: Routledge & Kegan Paul, 1981.

——. "Virtue and Reason." In *Mind, Value, and Reality*, 50–94. Cambridge, Mass.: Harvard University Press, 1998.

McGinn, Marie. *Sense and Certainty. A Dissolution of Scepticism*. Oxford: Basil Blackwell, 1989.

Moore, G.E. "Certainty." In *Philosophical Papers*, edited by G.E. Moore, 226–251. London: Allen & Unwin, 1959.

——. "A Defence of Common Sense." In *Philosophical Papers*, edited by G.E. Moore, 32–59. London and New York: Allen and Unwin, 1959.

——. *Principia Ethica*. London: Cambridge University Press, 1903.

——. "Proof of an External World." In *Philosophical Papers*, edited by G.E. Moore, 127–150. London and New York: Allen and Unwin, 1959.

Morawetz, Thomas. *Wittgenstein & Knowledge: The Importance of* On Certainty. Hassocks, Sussex: Harvester Press, 1980.

Morton, Adam. *On Evil*. New York and Oxon: Routledge, 2004.

Moyal-Sharrock, Danièle. "Beyond Hacker's Wittgenstein: Discussion of HACKER, Peter (2012) "Wittgenstein of Grammar, Theses and Dogmatism" *Philosophical Investigations* 35:1, January 2012, 1–17." *Philosophical Investigations* 36, no. 4 (2013): 355–380.

——. "Coming to Language: Wittgenstein's Social 'Theory' of Language Acquisition." In *Language and World: Essays on the Philosophy of Wittgenstein*, edited by V. Munz, K. Puhl and J. Wang, 291–313. Frankfurt am Main: Ontos Verlag, 2010.

——. *The Third Wittgenstein: The Post-Investigation Works*. Aldershot, UK: Ashgate, 2004.

——. *Understanding Wittgenstein's* On Certainty. Basingstoke: Palgrave Macmillan, 2004.

——. "Words as Deeds: Wittgenstein's 'Spontaneous Utterances' and the Dissolution of the Explanatory Gap." *Philosophical Psychology* 13, no. 3 (2000): 355–372.

Mulhall, Stephen. "Ethics in the Light of Wittgenstein." *Philosophical Papers* 31, no. 3 (2002): 293–321.

Nagel, Thomas. "Concealment and Exposure." *Philosophy and Public Affairs* 27, no. 1 (1998): 3–30.

Nietzsche, Friedrich. *Ecce Homo*. Translated by Walter Kaufmann and R. J. Hollingdale. Edited by Walter Kaufmann. New York: Vintage, 1967.

——. *On the Genealogy of Morality*. Translated by M. Clark and A. Swensen. Indianapolis: Hackett, 1998.

——. "Thus Spoke Zarathustra." In *The Portable Nietzsche*, edited by Walter Kaufmann. New York: Viking, 1954.

O'Connor, Timothy. "Free Will." In *The Stanford Encyclopedia of Philosophy*, edited by Edward N. Zalta, Fall 2014 Edition, <http://plato.stanford.edu/archives/fall2014/entries/freewill/>.

Patrick, Christopher J. et al. "Emotion in the Criminal Psychopath. Startle Reflex Modulation." *Journal of Abnormal Psychology* 102 (1993): 82–92.

Pleasants, Nigel. "If Killing Isn't Wrong, Then Nothing Is: A Naturalistic Defence of Basic Moral Certainty." *Ethical Perspectives* 22, no. 1 (2015): 197–215.

——. "Moral Argument Is Not Enough: The Persistence of Slavery and the Emergence of Abolition." *Philosophical Topics* 38, no. 1 (2011): 139–160.

——. "Wittgenstein and Basic Moral Certainty." *Philosophia* 37 (2009): 669–679.

——. "Wittgenstein, Ethics and Basic Moral Certainty." *Inquiry* 51, no. 3 (2008): 241–267.

Pollock, John. *Contemporary Theories of Knowledge*. Towota, NJ: Rowman and Littlefield Publishers, 1986.

Preen, Kristin and Hauke R. Heekeren. "Moral Brains – Possibilities and Limits of the Neuroscience of Ethics." In *Empirically Informed Ethics: Morality between Facts and Norms*, edited by Markus Christen et al., 137–157. Berlin: Springer, 2013.

Prichard, Harold Arthur. *Moral Obligation. Essays and Lectures*. Oxford: Clarendon Press, 1949.

Prinz, Jesse J. "The Emotional Basis of Moral Judgments." *Philosophical Explorations* 9, no. 1 (2006): 29–43.

Rachels, James. "The Challenge of Cultural Relativism." In *Exploring Ethics: An Introductory Anthology*, edited by Steven M. Cahn. New York and Oxford: Oxford University Press, 2009.

Rawls, John. *A Theory of Justice*. Revised edition. Cambridge, Mass.: The Belknap Press of Harvard University Press, 1999.

Redfield, Robert. "The Universally Human and the Culturally Variable." In *Ethical Relativism*, edited by John Ladd, 129–143. Belmont, CA: Wadsworth Publishing Company, 1973.

Reid, Thomas. *Essays on the Active Powers of the Human Mind*. Cambridge, MA: MIT Press, 1969 [1788].

Roeser, Sabine. *Moral Emotions and Intuitions*. Basingstoke: Palgrave Macmillan, 2011.

Rosefeldt, Tobias. "Is Knowing-how Simply a Case of Knowing-that?" *Philosophical Investigations* 27, no. 4 (2004): 370–379.

Ross, David. *The Right and the Good*. Oxford: Oxford University Press, 1930.

Rummens, Stefan. "On the Possibility of a Wittgensteinian Account of Moral Certainty." *The Philosophical Forum* 44, no. 2 (2013): 125–147.

Ruse, Michael. *Taking Darwin Seriously: A Naturalistic Approach to Philosophy*. Oxford: Basil Blackwell, 1986.

Russell, Bertrand. "The Limits of Empiricism." *Proceedings of the Aristotelian Society* 36 (1937): 131–150.

Rustin, Michael. "Innate Morality: A Psychoanalytic Approach to Moral Education." In *Teaching Right and Wrong: Moral Education in the Balance*, edited by Richard Smith and Paul Standish, 75–91. Staffordshire: Trentham Books, 1997.

Ryle, Gilbert. "Can Virtue Be Taught?" In *Education and the Development of Reason*, edited by R.F. Dearden, P.H. Hirst and R.S. Peters, 323–332. London and Boston: Routledge and Kegan Paul, 1972.

——. *The Concept of Mind*. Harmondsworth: Penguin Books, 1963.

——. "On Forgetting the Difference between Right and Wrong." In *Essays in Moral Philosophy*, edited by A. I. Melden, 147–159. Seattle: University of Washington Press, 1958.

Safranski, Rüdiger. *Nietzsche. Biographie Seines Denkens*. München and Wien: Carl Hanser Verlag, 2000.

Sauer, Hanno. "Educated Intuitions. Automaticity and Rationality in Moral Judgement." *Philosophical Explorations* 15, no. 3 (2012): 255–275.

Sayre-McCord, Geoffrey. "Coherentist Epistemology and Moral Theory." In *Moral Knowledge? New Readings in Moral Epistemology*, edited by Walter Sinnott-Armstrong and Mark Timmons, 137–189. New York and Oxford: Oxford University Press, 1996.

Scanlon, Thomas M. *What We Owe to Each Other*. Cambridge, Mass. and London: The Belknap Press of Harvard University Press, 1998.

Searle, John R. *Speech Acts: An Essay in the Philosophy of Language*. London: Cambridge University Press, 1969.

Sen, Amartya. "Development: Which Way Now?" *Economic Journal* 93, no. 372 (1983): 745–762.

——. "Human Rights and Asian Values." *The Sixteenth Morgenthau Memorial Lecture on Ethics and Foreign Policy*, Carnegie Council on Ethics and Foreign Affairs, available at http://www.carnegiecouncil.org/publications/archive/morgenthau/254.html (1997): accessed on 29 October 2014.

——. *Resources, Values and Development*. Cambridge, MA: Harvard University Press, 1997.

Shafer-Landau, Russ. *Moral Realism: A Defense*. Oxford: Oxford University Press, 2003.

Shiner, R. "Foundationalism, Coherentism and Activism." *Philosophical Investigations* 3 (1980): 33–38.

Sidgwick, Henry. *The Methods of Ethics*. London and New York: Macmillan, 1901 [1874].

Singer, Peter. "Famine, Affluence, and Morality." *Philosophy and Public Affairs* 1, no. 3 (1972): 229–243.

Sinnott-Armstrong, Walter. "Moral Skepticism." In *The Stanford Encyclopedia of Philosophy*, edited by Edward N. Zalta, Fall 2011 Edition, <http://plato.stanford.edu/archives/fall2011/entries/skepticism-moral/>.

Slote, Michael. *Moral Sentimentalism*. Oxford and New York: Oxford University Press, 2010.

Snowdon, Paul. "Knowing How and Knowing That: A Distinction Reconsidered." *Proceedings of the Aristotelian Society* New Series, 104 (2004): 1–29.

Stanley, Jason and Timothy Williamson. "Knowing How." *The Journal of Philosophy* 98, no. 8 (2001): 411–44.

Stemmer, Peter. *Handeln zugunsten anderer. Eine moralphilosophische Untersuchung*. Berlin and New York: de Gruyter, 2000.

Stichter, Matt. "Ethical Expertise: The Skill Model of Virtue." *Ethical Theory and Moral Practice* 10, no. 2 (2007): 183–194.

——. "Virtues, Skills, and Right Action." *Ethical Theory and Moral Practice* 14, no. 1 (2011): 73–86.

Stone, Valerie. "The Moral Dimensions of Human Social Intelligence. Domain-Specific and Domain-General Mechanisms." *Philosophical Explorations* 9, no. 1 (2006): 55–68.

Stout, Jeffrey. "On Having a Morality in Common." In *Prospects for a Common Morality*, edited by Gene Outka and John P. Reeder Jr, 215–232 Princeton, N.J: Princeton University Press, 1993.

Stratton-Lake, Philip, (ed.) Ethical Intuitionism: Re-evaluations. Oxford: Clarendon Press, 2002.

Street, Sharon. "A Darwinian Dilemma for Realist Theories of Value." *Philosophical Studies* 127 (2006): 109–166.

Stroll, Avrum. *Moore and Wittgenstein on Certainty*. New York and Oxford: Oxford University Press, 1994.

Stroud, Barry. "Concepts of Colour and Limits of Understanding." In *Wittgenstein on Colour*, edited by Frederik A. Gierlinger and Stefan Riegelnik, 109–121. Berlin and Boston: de Gruyter, 2014.

——. "Wittgenstein and Logical Necessity." *The Philosophical Review* 74, no. 4 (1965): 504–518.

Sumner, Leonard Wayne. "A Matter of Life and Death." *Noûs* 10 (1976): 145–171.

Swierstra, Tsjalling and Jozef Keulartz. "Obesity in 2020: Three Scenarios on Techno-Social-Ethical Co-Evolution." In *Genomics, Obesity and the Struggle over Responsibilities*, edited by Michiel Korthals, 97–112. Dordrecht: Springer Academic Publishers, 2011.

Tanney, Julia. "Gilbert Ryle." In *The Stanford Encyclopedia of Philosophy*, edited by Edward N. Zalta, Winter 2009 Edition, <http://plato.stanford.edu/archives/win2009/entries/ryle/>.

Thomas, Alan. *Value and Context: The Nature of Moral and Political Knowledge*. Oxford: Clarendon Press, 2006.

Timmons, Mark. *Morality without Foundations: A Defense of Ethical Contextualism*. New York: Oxford University Press, 1999.

Tully, James. "Wittgenstein and Political Philosophy. Understanding Practices of Critical Reflection." In *The Grammar of Politics. Wittgenstein and Political*

Philosophy, edited by Cressida J. Heyes, 17–42. Ithaca, NY: Cornell University Press, 2003.

Wallace, R. Jay. *Responsibility and the Moral Sentiments*. Cambridge, Mass. and London: Harvard University Press, 1994.

Watson, Gary, (ed.) *Free Will*. 2nd ed., Oxford Readings in Philosophy. Oxford and New York: Oxford University Press, 2003.

——. "Responsibility and the Limits of Evil: Variations on a Strawsonian Theme." In *Agency and Answerability. Selected Essays*, edited by Gary Watson, 219–259. Oxford: Clarendon Press, 2004.

Wellman, Carl. *Challenge and Respons: Justification in Ethics*. London and Amsterdam: Southern Illinois University Press, 1971.

Wiedemann, Uwe. "Auswege Aus Agrippas Trilemma." http://www.pyrrhon.de/cohere/agrippa.htm.

Willaschek, Marcus. "Moralisches Urteil und begründeter Zweifel. Eine kontextualistische Konzeption moralischer Rechtfertigung." In *Argument und Analyse. Ausgewählte Sektionsvorträge des 4. internationalen Kongresses der Gesellschaft für analytische Philosophie*, edited by Andreas Beckermann und Christian Nimtz, 630–641: http://gap-im-netz.de/gap4Konf/Proceedings4/Proc.htm, 2002.

Williams, Bernard. *Ethics and the Limits of Philosophy*. London: Fontana Press/Collins, 1985.

Williams, Meredith. *Wittgenstein, Mind and Meaning*. London: Routledge, 1999.

Williams, Michael. "Wittgenstein, Truth and Certainty." In *Wittgenstein's Lasting Significance*, edited by Max Kölbel and Bernhard Weiss, 247–281. London and New York: Routledge, 2004.

Winch, Peter. "Judgment: Propositions and Practices." *Philosophical Investigations* 21 (1998): 189–202.

Wittgenstein, Ludwig. *The Blue and Brown Books. Preliminary Studies for the 'Philosophical Investigations'*. Oxford: Basil Blackwell, 1958.

——. "Cause and Effect: Intuitive Awareness." In *Philosophical Occasions 1912–1951*, edited by James C. Klagge and Alfred Nordmann, 370–426. Indianapolis and Cambridge: Hackett Publishing Company, 1993.

——. *Last Writings on the Philosophy of Psychology*. Translated by C. G. Luckhardt and Maximilian A. E. Aue. Edited by G. H. von Wright and Heikki Nyman. II vols. Vol. II. Oxford and Cambridge, Mass.: Blackwell, 1992.

——. "A Lecture on Ethics." In *Ludwig Wittgenstein: Philosophical Occasions (1912–1951)* Edited by J. Klaage and A. Nordman, 115–155. Indianapolis: Hackett, 1993.

——. *On Certainty*. Translated by Denis Paul and G.E.M. Anscombe. Edited by G.E.M. Anscombe and G.H. von Wright. New York: Harper & Row, 1972.

——. *Philosophical Investigations*. Translated by G.E.M. Anscombe. Third edition. Oxford: Basil Blackwell, 1968.

——. *Remarks on Colour*. Translated by Linda L. McAlister and Margarete Schättle. Edited by G.E.M. Anscombe. Oxford: Basil Blackwell, 1978.

——. *Remarks on the Foundations of Mathematics*. Translated by G.E.M. Anscombe. Edited by G.H. von Wright et al. Third, revised and reset edition. Oxford: Basil Blackwell, 1978.

——. *Remarks on the Philosophy of Psychology*. Translated by G.E.M. Anscombe. Edited by G.E.M. Anscombe and G.H. von Wright. II vols. Vol. I. Oxford: Basil Blackwell, 1980.

——. *Remarks on the Philosophy of Psychology*. Translated by C. G. Luckhardt and M. A. E. Aue. Edited by G.H. von Wright and Heikki Nyman. II vols. Vol. II. Oxford: Basil Blackwell, 1980.

——. *Tractatus Logico-Philosophicus*. Translated by D.F. Pears and B.F. McGuiness. Revised edition. London and New York: Routledge & Kegan Paul, 1974.

——. *Zettel*. Translated by G.E.M. Anscombe and G. H. von Wright. Edited by G.E.M. Anscombe and Georg Henrik von Wright. Second edition. Oxford: Blackwell, 1981.

Young, Liane and R. Saxe. "An FMRI Investigation of Spontaneous Mental State Inference for Moral Judgement." *Journal of Cognitive Neuroscience* 21, no. 7 (2009): 1396–1405.

——. "The Neural Basis of Belief Encoding and Integration in Moral Judgment." *NeuroImage* 40, no. 4 (2008): 1912–1920.

Young, Liane et al. "Damage to Ventromedial Prefrontal Cortex Impairs Judgment of Harmful Intent." *Neuron* 65, no. 6 (2010): 845–851.

——. "Neural Evidence for 'Intuitive Prosecution': The Use of Mental State Information for Negative Moral Verdicts." *Social Neuroscience* 6, no. 3 (2011): 302–315.

——. "The Neural Basis of the Interaction between Theory of Mind and Moral Judgment." *Proceedings of the National Academy of Sciences of the United States of America* 104, no. 20 (2007): 8235–8240.

Young, Robert. "What Is So Wrong with Killing People?" *Philosophy* 54 (1979): 515–528.

Index

abilities, *see also* capacities
ability to do otherwise, 101–03
abortion, 70–73, 79, 109–10
acting
  'at the bottom of the language-
    game', 3, 4, 58–66, 93, 96–97,
    111–13, 135, 155–56, 179
  unreflective/without conscious
    thought, 58, 119, 124–25, 142
actions
  moral, 94, 152
  pre-linguistic, 61
  primitive, 60–62, 112, 118, 152
agent
  morally competent, 90, 91, 93, 96,
    97, 99, 122–26, 129, 132, 142,
    147, 156, 161
  virtuous, 132
agreement
  human, 150
  in opinions, 71
  in/over judgements, 37, 62–66, 69,
    85, 149
  in/over moral judgements, 63, 69,
    70–74, 156, 177
  intercultural moral, 168, 171–75,
    184, 192
  intra-cultural moral, 171
  moral, 116, 171–75, 192
amoralist, 156, 160–62, 166, *see also*
  scepticism, moral sceptic
analogy
  axis-analogy, 117
  chess-analogy, *see* chess, chess-
    analogy
  between moral certainty and
    certainty regarding the empirical
    world, 86–94, 112–16, 183, 194
  between virtues and practical skills,
    18, 120–21, 127, 129, 132, 133–34,
    135, 138, 141, 165, 185, 195
  game-analogy, 20, 30–37
animals, *see also* certainty, animal

drilling of, 137
exploitation of, 110
non-human, 14, 65, 112
social, 155–56
Annas, Julia, 129, 132, 138, 141–42,
  154, 186
anthropology, 175, 180, 192
anti-social personality disorder, *see*
  psychopath
arbitrariness, 36, 116, 152, 176, 177
Aristotle, 15–16, 134–35, 154, 190
  Aristotelian logic, 10, 15
  Aristotelian virtue ethics, 125, 134,
    135, 190, 194
Arrington, Robert, 107, 108, 109, 159
attitudes
  evaluative, 38
  moral, 105, 115, 118
  propositional, 3
automatism
  automatic actions, 59, 62, 137, *see*
    also reflex
  automatic responses, 30
axes
  axis-metaphor, 56, 63, 66, 93
  axis- versus hinge-metaphor, 56
  judgements that function as axes
  within our moral reasoning, 92, 93,
    102, 109, 186, 188, 190–91, 194

background
  beliefs, 71, 79
  cultural, 123, 168–71
  inherited, 49
Baker, G. P. and Hacker, P. M. S., 148,
  150, 176
Bambrough, Renford, 86–94, 104
bedrock
  beliefs, 55
  certainty, 64
  doubts at, 44
  judgements, 64
  practices, 64, 109, 111, 117, 151, 165

207

Printed and bound by CPI Group (UK) Ltd, Croydon, CR0 4YY